# Ethnicity, Health and Health Care

Sociology of Health and Illness Monograph Series

Edited by Hannah Bradby
Department of Sociology
University of Warwick
Coventry
CV4 7AL
UK

Current titles:

# Ethnicity, Health and Health Care
## Understanding Diversity, Tackling Disadvantage

Edited by

Waqar I. U. Ahmad and Hannah Bradby

**Blackwell**
Publishing

First published as Volume 29, Number 6 of *Sociology of Health & Illness*

BLACKWELL PUBLISHING
350 Main Street, Malden, MA 02148-5020, USA
9600 Garsington Road, Oxford OX4 2DQ, UK

First published 2008 by Blackwell Publishing Ltd

2   2008

*Library of Congress Cataloging-in-Publication Data*

Ethnicity, health, and health care : understanding diversity, tackling disadvantage/edited by
Waqar Ahmad and Hannah Bradby.
    p.; cm. — (Sociology of health and illness monograph series)
Includes bibliographical references and index.
ISBN 978-1-4051-6898-4 (pbk. : alk. paper) 1. Minorities—Medical care. 2. Discrimination
in medical care. I. Ahmad, W. I. U. (Wagar Ihsan-Ullah), 1957– II. Bradby, Hannah,
1966– III. Series.
[DNLM: 1. Delivery of Health Care—Great Britain. 2. Delivery of Health Care—United
States. 3. Cultural Competency—Great Britain. 4. Cultural Competency—United States.
5. Ethnic Groups—Great Britain. 6. Ethnic Groups—United States. 7. Minority Health—Great
Britain. 8. Minority Health—United States. W 84 AA1 E82 2008]

RA563.M56E852 2008
362.1089—dc22

                                                                2007051240

A catalogue record for this title is available from the British Library.

Set in 10pt Times NR Monotype
by Graphicraft Limited, Hong Kong
Printed and bound in Singapore
by C.O.S. Printers Pte Ltd

The publisher's policy is to use permanent paper from mills that operate a sustainable
forestry policy, and which has been manufactured from pulp processed using acid-free
and elementary chlorine-free practices. Furthermore, the publisher ensures that the text paper
and cover board used have met acceptable environmental accreditation standards.

For further information on
Blackwell Publishing, visit our website at
www.blackwellpublishing.com

# Contents

# List of Contributors

**Waqar I. U. Ahmad**
Social Policy Research Centre
Middlesex University
London, UK

**Naureen Ahmad**
Research Unit in Health,
Behaviour and Change
The University of Edinburgh
Medical School
Edinburgh, UK

**Peter Riley Bahr**
Department of Sociology
Wayne State University
Detroit, MI, USA

**Hannah Bradby**
Department of Sociology
University of Warwick
Coventry, UK

**Alice Chapman**
Institute for Health Research
Lancaster University
Lancaster, UK

**Punita Chowbey**
School of Nursing and Midwifery
University of Sheffield
Sheffield, UK

**Trisha Greenhalgh**
Department of Primary
Care and Population Sciences
University College London
London, UK

**Nina Hallowell**
Public Health Science
University of Edinburgh
Edinburgh, UK

**Kaveri Harriss**
Centre for Population Studies
London School of Hygiene and
Tropical Medicine
London, UK

**Margaret Holloway**
Department of Social Work
University of Hull
Hull, UK

**James Jackson**
Institute for Social Research
University of Michigan
Ann Arbor, MI, USA

**Saffron Karlsen**
Department of Epidemiology and
Public Health
University College London
London, UK

**Julia Lawton**
Research Unit in Health,
Behaviour and Change
The University of Edinburgh Medical
School
Edinburgh, UK

**Sara Mallinson**
Institute for Health Research
Lancaster University
Lancaster, UK

**James Nazroo**
Sociology, School of Social Sciences
University of Manchester
Manchester, UK

**Sheila Payne**
Institute for Health Research
Lancaster University
Lancaster, UK

**Elizabeth Peel**
School of Life and Health
Sciences
Aston University
Birmingham, UK

**Lucinda Platt**
Institute for Social and Economic
Research
University of Essex
Colchester, UK

**Jennie Popay**
Institute for Health Research
Lancaster University
Lancaster, UK

**Nadia Robb**
Department of Primary Care and
Population Sciences
University College London
London, UK

**Sarah Salway**
Centre for Health and Social Care
Research
Sheffield Hallam University
Sheffield, UK

**Jane Seymour**
School of Nursing
University of Nottingham
Nottingham, UK

**Myriam Torres**
Institute for Social Research
University of Michigan
Ann Arbor, MI, USA

**Christopher Voisey**
Department of Primary Care and
Population Sciences
University College London
London, UK

# 1

# Locating ethnicity and health: exploring concepts and contexts

# Waqar I. U. Ahmad and Hannah Bradby

## Introduction

Sociologists of health and illness explore the role of social, cultural and economic divisions in the experience of health and illness, with class, age, gender, sexuality, impairment and, increasingly, race, culture and ethnicity being crucial dimensions of analysis. Divisions of various orders are a given feature of industrial societies and the arrival of migrants, travellers or scholars from outside provides further dimensions to understand and manage. In the British Isles, and particularly England, with a longstanding, stable Anglo-Saxon population, and a national character imbued with a colonial past, minority ethnic identity has particular meaning. The post-World War II mass migration was met, in Britain, with ambivalence and hostility coupled, simultaneously, with assumptions that the white privileged position would persist and yet immigrants would assimilate to the British way of life.

This chapter is not aimed at providing an overview of literature and debates on ethnicity and health. Such overviews are available elsewhere (Smaje 1995, Davey Smith *et al.* 2000b). Our aim is to locate ethnicity and health in an appropriate context by considering how conceptual and policy apparatus has developed over recent decades. We therefore start with a discussion of how 'race' and 'ethnicity' have been conceptualised, articulated and employed historically and across cultures. The management of ethnic diversity is a key policy concern for most industrialised countries. We discuss the key trends and developments in the history of ethnicity and health in Britain. This leads to a discussion of how sociologists of health have responded to an increasingly ethnically diverse Britain, with an interest in both the positive developments and the areas that have been neglected. Finally, we introduce the papers selected for this Monograph which make distinctive contributions to the literature by extending some of the debates introduced in this opening chapter.

## Locating ethnicity, culture and 'race'

Like 'community', 'ethnicity' is an over-employed term, sometimes used with such imprecision that it risks losing its analytical value. Isajiw (1974) identified over 70 elements in defining ethnicity in US and Canadian literature between 1945 and 1971, of which ancestry, culture, language, 'race' and religion were most prominent. Others emphasise 'ethnicity' as an identification articulated through negotiating boundary and social processes, requiring both self-affirmation but also others' acceptance of such claims. Ethnicity is thus a dynamic concept, characterised by its relationship to forms of heritage (national, linguistic, cultural), notions of belonging and external recognition of such claims, but also by its malleability, flexibility and situationality. Contemporary notions of 'ethnicity' conceptualise it as a marker of identity, a vehicle for community mobilisation and a possible indicator of disadvantage, discrimination or privilege. How notions of ethnic identity play in time and space may vary. For example, in Pakistan, ethnic relations take on a regional and linguistic flavour – inter-ethnic conflicts in the country continue to be termed 'lissani' (language) conflicts. Canada gives French- and English-speaking people secure status as 'founding peoples', with French and English defined as 'official' languages. Indigenous 'First Nationals', enjoy a variety of legal protections, and yet remain economically and socially marginal in Canadian society. Similarly, in the US and Australia, being indigenous to a land equates with a socioeconomic status even worse than many of the recently arrived minorities. In most countries ethnic minority status, often deriving from having migrated from elsewhere, goes hand in hand with social, economic and health disadvantage.

Ethnic identity can be powerfully related to access to resources such that the formation, maintenance and transformation of ethnic relations is crucial to wellbeing. The transformation of inter-ethnic group relations sometimes occurs through extreme violence: the slaughter of Tutsies by Hutus in Rwanda; of Bosnian Muslims by their neighbours; the apparently un-ending war between Tamil Tigers and the Sinhalese dominated government in Sri Lanka, to give a few recent examples. Referring to conflicts in East Asia, Mackerras (2003) argues that ethnic conflict may have replaced ideological conflict since the end of the cold war. While he may be overstating the case, it is clear that ethnic identity cannot be ignored in any meaningful contemporary analysis of relations between groups as well as between nations.

Historically, the pseudoscientific notion of 'race', supported by both science and Christianity, created hierarchies of people and justified slavery, bonded labour and colonialism. Science and the Church decreed such oppression to be in the best interests of the colonised and the enslaved. Colonising and enslaving people has been justified both as a means of civilising slaves and of saving their souls. The contention that slavery and colonisation benefit the slaves and colonised has also been used to oppose the abolition of slavery in the American South and to prevent colonised countries from gaining the right to self-rule. This is illustrated by the following paraphrasing of the fears expressed by the white elite about the abolition of slavery in the United States:

> Enlarged freedom, too often ending in licence, excessive use of stimulants, excitement of emotions, already unduly developed [could lead to insanity. The black people] are removed from much of the mental excitement to which the free population . . . is necessarily exposed in the daily routine of life, not to mention the liability of the latter to the influence of the agitating novelties of religion, the intensity of political discussion . . . They were taught from infancy obedience and self control . . . The cause of insanity and other diseases with them now, from which they were exempted in slavery, is the removal of all healthful restraints that formerly surrounded them (Littlewood and Lipsedge 1989: 37–8).

Medicine was a strong ally in giving racist systems of thought a scientific gloss. Entirely rational actions, such as running away from a slave master or disrupting the slave system, were medicalised with the invention of new diagnoses, respectively *drapetomania* (an 'irrational' desire of slaves to run away from their masters), and *Dysaethesia Aethiopica* (or rascality) (Littlewood and Lipsedge 1989). While freedom from slavery was opposed in the American South, on the grounds of threats to the mental wellbeing of the enslaved, decolonisation too was deemed dangerous to the natives. In Egypt, for example, Lord Cromer opposed independence on the basis that Egyptian society possessed insufficient democratic maturity and was guilty of the poor treatment of women. Simultaneously, and with no sense of irony, he stopped an indigenous Egyptian movement for women's education as disruptive and counterproductive and, in Britain, staunchly opposed the Suffragette movement (Ahmed 1992).

While hierarchical, immutable categories of 'race' are no longer explicitly used to differentiate between groups, many features of racial thinking have permeated concepts of ethnicity and culture. Culture is often referred to as if it possessed primordial, innate and immutable features which manifest as properties of specific ethnic groups. However, the desire to attribute particular characteristics to other groups, and to denigrate those characteristics is not unique to Western societies. Growing up in rural Pakistan, WA 'knew' that the service castes such as 'mirasis' were inappropriately jovial, assured to be a sign of mental immaturity, the 'jolahas' were inherently cowardly and could not be trusted in times of danger, and the 'musallies' were dull, fit only for menial labour. The 'mirasis' were story-tellers and musicians and the 'jolahas' were weavers. Both groups were often better educated than the 'zamindars' (land-lord farmers) and skilled in their occupations. But this did nothing to challenge their institutionalised oppression at the hands of the dominant 'zamindars' to whom they provided a variety of routine and life-cycle-related services in exchange for land for their houses, fodder for their animals and a share of the harvest.

Culture as a presumed primordial feature allows the same justification of unique and immutable nature of particular groups that 'race' allowed previously. 'Ethnicity' and 'culture' take on 'social meanings and importance when physical and cultural traits are paired with social attributes, such as intellectual, moral or behavioural characteristics' (Li 1999: 7). Barker, in an influential book, argued that cultural or 'new' racism offered justification for hostility towards 'others' by locating such hostility in our 'nature' and downplaying the role of politics and economy:

> Nations, on this view, are not built out of politics, or economics, but of human nature. It is our biology, our instinct, to defend our way of life, traditions and customs against outsiders, not because they are inferior, but because they are part of different cultures (1981: 23).

Li (1999) notes that:

> This line of reasoning puts disadvantaged groups in an even more disadvantaged position since their culture becomes the source of their misfortunes. Thus, the economic problems of First Nations [indigenous Canadians] is often seen as caused by Native people's own ineptitudes and cultural inadequacies (1999: 4).

Using culture and ethnicity as an explanation of inequality between groups distorts perceptions of how ethnic relations, and the related inequities of power are produced. Defined by those in power, the disadvantage of minority ethnic groups too often continues to be seen as 'caused' by their diseased genetic and dysfunctional cultural inheritance. Notions of biology and culture mingle in a messy but complementary mortar, cementing inferiority of some, while conveniently absolving powerful groups and states from responsibility. Such thinking has seriously influenced definitions of health and care needs of minority ethnic groups in Britain, and elsewhere.

## Ethnic diversity and its management in Britain

The presence of 'blacks' and 'coloureds' in the UK is not new. Given Britain's central involvement in the slave trade, its role as a major colonial power, and the size, reach and labour needs of its navy, this is not surprising. There were such sizeable numbers of non-White people in Britain in the 16$^{th}$ century as to worry Queen Elizabeth I that they were consuming welfare rightfully belonging to her loyal and deserving (White) subjects. She ordered a mass expulsion of such people from her land. These themes of whiteness being linked to belonging, citizenship and entitlement to welfare relief have remained common features in relation to minority ethnic life in Britain ever since: access to health and other services remains intrinsically linked to claims of citizenship, with health and social care professionals increasingly required by the state to act as a second (often reluctant) line of immigration control. Britain's ports had settlements of non-white sailors and merchants before, and since, the 16$^{th}$ century, while high society has long included the odd 'coloured' nabob. In the early 20$^{th}$ century British Universities and Inns of Court had the elite from the colonies being trained as the transitional or buffer classes between the natives and the white master class, and increasing numbers of both workers and students were arriving from the colonies as the century progressed. It is perhaps ironic that the death of British imperialism in South Asia was plotted by some of these visitors, with the chief architects of Indian and Pakistani independence – Iqbal, Gandhi, Nehru and Jinnah – all students or legal pupils in London, Oxford or Cambridge in the early 1900s.

Mass migration of people from the ex-colonies, however, is a relatively recent phenomenon. The need to rebuild Britain following World War II, the demands of an expanding economy, and the development of the welfare state required labour on a scale that could not be provided locally. The arrival of the Empire Windrush in 1946 from the Caribbean, to Tilbury in Essex, carrying some 500 men and women migrants, remains the iconic symbol of the start of mass colonial immigration to Britain. Migration, with its heyday in the 1960s, followed relatively predictable patterns, dictated by the needs of local and regional industries and driven by networks and patronage more than by direct recruitment in the ex-colonies. This period of economic expansion meant that in spite of blatant racist discrimination – in employment, health, housing and other services – new arrivals could secure initial employment and move jobs easily.

The needs of the local economy and patronage of fellow villagers or family explained the patterns of settlement of different minority ethnic groups more than other factors. Caribbeans settled in large numbers in London and were employed on public transport and in hospitals. Their settlement patterns demonstrate the importance of identities associated with particular islands, with Jamaicans, St Lucians and so on settling in small enclaves alongside friends and kinfolk of the same island. Indians too arrived in large numbers in the 1960s. A diverse community, their settlement patterns were more scattered than Caribbeans in terms of residential location and the industries in which they gained employment. The so-called 'East African Asians' entered Britain in the 1970s. Predominantly a business community, and British passport holders, they sought resettlement in Britain following expulsions from Uganda, Kenya and Tanzania. Pakistanis, a more homogenous group dominated by those with backgrounds as small-scale land-owning farmers, were recruited to provide semi-skilled labour in the steel industry in the Midlands and the textile industry in the northern belt running between Manchester in the west, through the Pennine towns, to Bradford and Leeds in the east. The Chinese arrived in various phases, opting predominantly to settle into family-run restaurant and take-away businesses, and remain highly dispersed with 'Chinatowns' in London and Manchester acting as cultural and community hubs. Bangladeshis arrived after the other major groups in the late 1970s when employment opportunities and immigration opportunities were increasingly restricted. This had an impact on their ability to accumulate capital and to be joined by their families. Family formation and unification followed in the next couple of decades and for many, remains an unfinished business.

This story of migration to and settlement in Britain in the second half of the 20<sup>th</sup> century has shown that the fortunes of certain communities have been inextricably tied to certain industries and regions – decline in these industries has had a disproportionate impact on some minorities, while having little or no effect on others. For example, the heavy concentration of migrants from Pakistan in the textile industry and the relative homogeneity of their skills meant that large numbers suffered from the rapid decline in the regional textile industry. Communities with greater internal diversity, which settled in a number of different regions and industries, such as migrants from India, were better able to respond to changes in the fortunes of particular industries. Equally, cities and regions with diverse industrial bases fared better in both cushioning partial industrial decline and in reinventing themselves through growth in new industries. Settlement patterns have had an impact on the availability of cultural resources and support networks, for instance social and cultural isolation is a key issue for the highly dispersed Chinese community, whereas Bangladeshis in East London, Indians in Leicester or Pakistanis in Bradford do not face this problem. However, the advantages of areas where minorities are highly concentrated have to be considered alongside the disadvantages.

At the time of the 2001 Census, ethnic minorities constituted 7.9 per cent of Britain's population (or 4.6 million people). They are concentrated in the major urban areas, with 45 per cent in London alone. Their age profile is younger compared to the White population and 50 per cent of Britain's people of Indian, Pakistani, Bangladeshi, Black Caribbean and Black African origin are now British born. While there is greater diversity within minority populations than between them, overall (with some exceptions), minority ethnic groups do worse than their White fellow citizens in health, employment, earnings, education and housing.

Ethnic concentration has received attention by academics, policy makers and politicians. The British state has benefited from the emerging ethnic enclaves in Britain from the 1960s onwards in that concentration in particular neighbourhoods enabled the establishment of voluntary-sector provision of welfare services within and for these minority communities (Rex 1991). Concentration has allowed the development of community networks, economic activity, community resources, reaffirmation of positive self-identity and resources for its maintenance. Migrants and minorities (re)create structures and institutions which allow the maintenance and reproduction of cherished cultural and religious values. Religious and community institutions as well as established systems of mutual support took rapid root in these communities in British towns and cities. Werbner (1990) notes the importance of family and community networks in the establishment and success of minority ethnic businesses. Such concentration potentially acts as a buffer against prejudice and racism, provides role models, accords status to individuals for skills or knowledge not acknowledged outside the community, offers social and moral support, and provides resources for the recreation of community. But all this happens at a price, including in terms of health.

Ethnic strife and street disturbances in the 1980s and more recently in 2001, brought attention to the 'problem' of such concentration, referred to negatively as 'segregation'. The Chairman of the Commission for Racial Equality, the official watchdog in this field, in a much hyped, but ill-informed speech warned the nation that Britain was 'sleepwalking to segregation' – he painted a picture of US style segregated ghettos and no-go areas (Philips 2005). The picture of 'parallel' universes, un-integrated young minority ethnic people and of a cultural rift between generations that he painted also emerges in a plethora of official reports into the 2001 street disturbances. The evidence suggests, however, a different, more complex picture in which deprivation and oppression as well as contestations over identity and territory play a significant role. Amin (2002) identifies four main reasons for street fighting and disturbances: the increasing activity by the far right and often violent, British National Party in areas of Pakistani and Bangladeshi concentration; prolonged heavy-handed policing targeted against Asian youth, combined with little if any protection against racist activity; inflammatory media reporting of Asian-led crime and violence; and young Asians' anger over political marginalisation and paternalism of their leaders. Amin notes that by the 1990s, the new generation of British-born-and-bred young South Asians in the northern towns, was unwilling to accept the second-class status endured by their elders. The street violence by South Asian young people was thus a claim to Britishness and their way of defending their streets from racists, almost exclusively from outside of their areas.

The exceptionally punitive sentencing meted out to the South Asian young people involved in, what they regarded as, the defence of their streets from racist British National Party and racist police, confirmed for many that the police and the judiciary were there to control their communities without offering them protection.

While a high concentration of minority ethnic communities in specific areas may have been over-played as a cause of street disturbances, or as a harbinger of an ethnically segregated Britain, it merits attention for other reasons. The areas where disturbances have occurred suffer multiple deprivation: over two-thirds of minority ethnic people in Britain live in the 88 most deprived local authority districts, compared to 40 per cent of the general population (NRU 2004). The problems that afflict these districts therefore have a disproportionate effect on minority ethnic groups. Around one third of all British children live in poverty – defined as having family income below 60 per cent of the national average – compared to 74 per cent of Pakistani and Bangladeshi children and 63 per cent of Black Caribbean children. Such blatant and significant inequalities matter. Housing, public amenities, health and welfare services, employment opportunities and, perhaps most importantly, aspirations and expectations may all be poor in these areas. Primary care services, especially dental health provision, in such areas are extremely poor and since primary care acts as a conduit to secondary care, this neglect diminishes prospects for appropriate and timely secondary care.

Furthermore, if, as is sometimes the case, White parents living in deprived areas are more successful in placing their children in better-performing and predominantly White schools outside the area, the local schools can become almost exclusively non-White. This process represents a severe reduction of the opportunity for routine, everyday, mundane, and yet vital, inter-ethnic dialogue, and permits apathy or even hostility to develop between sections of communities whose interests and problems are often the same (Amin 2002). Social solidarity may therefore be damaged alongside the life chances of both the majority and the minority communities. We discuss the culture of 'special provision' and 'anti-racist' approaches below.

## Ethnicity, health and care

Early interest in minority ethnic health came from public health and tropical medicine specialists with an initial focus on protecting the British population from diseases which could be imported by immigrants. This was followed by an interest in the exotic and peculiar, and above all that which was 'different' from the British 'norm'. The focus on diseases and conditions peculiar to minorities was unfortunate in that it had the effect of ignoring both the health issues that concerned the communities themselves and the diseases which afflicted the largest numbers of people in these communities. Instead, and not sur-prisingly, the focus reflected the prevalent racial and cultural stereotypes and fears, from deficient parenting in relation to child health, restrictive cultures and their impact on nutritional deficiency among South Asians, low pain thresholds and proneness to addiction to pain killers among African Caribbean sickle cell sufferers, to dangerous and irresponsible behaviour on the part of Muslim consanguineous parents 'causing havoc' of death and disability among their off-spring.

The focus on deficient minority culture turns conditions without any necessary connection to a given culture into 'ethnic' conditions, with assumed racial or cultural features. Conditions thus become racialised, with ethnic or cultural features over-emphasised to the extent that the commonly understood aetiological or prognostic factors are ignored and new solutions invented, aimed at changing the presumed deficient cultures of the communities concerned. The victims are thus blamed for their own ills, as illustrated in the following two examples. First, vitamin D deficiency in children was endemic in the poor British population of the mid-20th century. Pictures of bow-legged children adorned basic clinical medicine text books of the period. Eradication owed much to better outdoor facilities for children and, in particular, the fortification of margarine with vitamin D and the universal free availability of milk in schools. When rickets appeared in South Asians in the 1970s, after it had largely disappeared in the majority population, it was re-cast as an exotic disease (Donovan 1984). Now termed 'Asian rickets', its cause was located in deficient South Asian diets and codes of gender and dress. It was also assumed that South Asian skins were too pigmented to convert northern hemisphere sunlight into vitamin D and that modest clothing further hampered the process. It was suggested that 'the long-term answer to Asian rickets probably lies in health education and a change towards the Western diet and lifestyle' (Goel *et al.* 1981: 405). Remarkably, for some considerable time, the solution that worked for the white population – fortification of a staple diet with vitamin D – was considered inappropriate on the pretext that such fortification of South Asian staple diets (ghee or chapatti flour) may lead to vitamin D toxicity. Why toxicity was not an issue in the case of fortification of margarine was never discussed.

Secondly, a more recent fascination in Britain has concerned consanguinity, the practice of marriage between blood relatives. Marriage between first cousins has been quite acceptable in Britain, and among the well-known cases of cousin marriages was Charles Darwin's marriage to Emma Wedgwood, with whom he had 10 children. Cousin marriage is a common and favoured pattern of family formation in Britain among South Asian Muslims and remains normal in many parts of the world. In current day Britain, first cousin marriage has become highly stigmatised, even bordering on incest, such that the true prevalence among the ethnic majority is likely to be underestimated. The presumed ill effects of consanguineous marriage among South Asians have been indicated as 'explaining' a variety of ills, from bleeding disorders, to heightened rates of physical impairment and deafness. For certain recessively inherited genetic conditions such as thalassaemia, marriages within a family group with a particular genotype will undoubtedly increase the chance of the two partners having the condition or being carriers, and will increase the statistical probability of passing on the genes and/or the condition to offspring. In relation to South Asian, especially Pakistani, parents, there is a marked tendency on the part of health professionals to blame consanguinity for a child's ills, irrespective of the known mechanisms of causation and often without clinicians confirming whether or not parents are in fact blood relatives. South Asian parents of thalassaemic children were regularly told that the child's condition had been 'caused' by parental consanguinity and yet in several cases, parents were not in a consanguineous marriage and were puzzled by this information (Ahmad *et al.* 2000). Some parents did not make the link between consanguinity 'causing' thalassaemia and the genetic transmission of the condition, so the attribution of cause did not inform further reproductive decisions. Clinicians' emphasis on consanguinity causing various conditions was based on a moral belief about the evil of consanguinity, rather than an appraisal of the available evidence (Ahmad *et al.* 2000). This is illustrated by the very different approach to the explanation of the transmission of sickle cell disorder, like thalassaemia a recessively inherited condition with the same mode of transmission. The parents of children with sickle cell disorder, mostly of African Caribbean origin, were given historical explanations about the sickle cell gene being endemic in Western Africa, or were simply told about the transmission of recessive disorders. For many African Caribbeans, these explanation underlined and affirmed their heritage and identity, whereas explanations of thalassaemia focusing on consanguinity offered to South Asians undermined their cultural values and induced self-blame (Ahmad *et al.* 2000). Clinicians' anxieties around consanguinity, this time in relation to heightened rates of deafness among children, were exemplified in the following quote, which followed a tirade against arranged marriages as a practice alien to British culture, and the need to protect young British Asian women from such oppression:

> And it's that one factor [arranged marriage between consanguines] which is causing this awful dilemma of deafness. Whether it's responsible for some of the other factors that we have, mainly multiple congenital abnormalities we see in this group of children I cannot comment on that . . . But it seems to me a dire tragedy that this isn't being rectified . . . I think that it's a shame when a culture can't see that something they're doing which is near and dear to their wishes is causing such havoc among their children (Ahmad *et al.* 2000: 39–40).

Healthcare practitioners, while well meaning, were revisiting the arguments which previous generations of colonists, policy makers and practitioners had employed to convince themselves that the ills of the 'other' were located in the other's own diseased genes or pathological culture, and that they, as enlightened Westerners, were in a privileged position to define what is in the best interests of these children and communities. The communities are, as before, being maligned and denied both respect for their values and their citizenship rights. Even worse, their legitimate health needs are undermined by a racist discourse, employed by powerful health services gatekeepers such that undue attention is focused on inappropriate issues, which distracts from the factors underlying significant inequities in health. The difficulty of avoiding a culture-blaming effect when considering the connection between minority culture and its relationship with specific health outcomes is described in Rocheron's (1988) analysis of the high profile 'Asian Mother and Baby Campaign'.

Much of the literature on ethnicity and health in Britain is not social scientific, but medical and epidemiological. In exploring population and environmental characteristics, epidemiology has a strong interest in comparative studies and the notion of relative risk. Comparisons of minority ethnic communities with the majority community 'norm' in terms of morbidity, mortality or health-related behaviour, including use of services, have been a common form of research which tends to find excess morbidity, mortality, or deleterious health behaviour among the minority in question. Two problems arise from this approach. First, the impression is given that minority ethnic health should only be explored as a comparative problem, rather than as a significant or interesting phenomenon in its own right. Secondly, the focus tends to be on those conditions where minority ethnic groups have a raised incidence or prevalence of a condition, irrespective of whether this in itself has significance for the minority or the majority population. For example, while tuberculosis rates remain higher among some minority ethnic groups compared with the white population, this is of limited significance as the overall prevalence rates are relatively low, and improved treatment has reduced mortality from tuberculosis. In contrast, cancers which account for around one sixth of all deaths among minority ethnic groups are neglected as the relative prevalence rates for minorities are lower than in the white population. This emphasis on 'relative risk', and thus 'treatment' of heightened risk, has parallels with the culture of 'special initiatives' in health and welfare services.

The culture of special initiatives in the National Health Service was located in the crude multiculturalism of the 1970s, which stripped minority cultures of their complexity, contingency and dynamism and presented them as static, homogenous artefacts, whereby all members of a 'culture' were assumed to share common features. Cultural guidebooks mushroomed in state services, educating service providers about the peculiarities of 'ethnic' cultures. Racism and discrimination did not fit well with this formulation of ethnic minority 'special' needs. If the difference between the majority and minority cultures could be identified, state provision should address this 'difference' either through its own special initiatives or by cultivating the minority ethnic voluntary sector. Rex (1991) notes that the British state keenly supported the development of minority ethnic voluntary organisations soon after the start of the large-scale migration in the 1960s and 1970s. Such organisations were regarded as efficient, cheap and often popular means of meeting the 'additionality', located in cultural or linguistic difference, and which could not be met by the state or established voluntary sectors. The definition of minority ethnic needs in terms of 'cultural difference' gave important impetus to both separate provision (supported through earmarked streams of state funding) and statutory-sector-funded 'special initiatives', to support transition to assimilation into British society. Such 'special projects' had two advantages for the statutory sector. By locating minorities' needs in their own presumed cultural deviance the statutory sector could absolve itself of any responsibility to change. Secondly, the provision of separate services was a considerably cheaper and a higher profile option: the authority could be seen to be taking action at little cost and with little disruption to mainstream services.

The policy and academic backlash against 'multiculturalism' as an academic discourse and a formal policy framework was located in a critique which argued that multiculturalism neglected the fundamental causes of disadvantage, which were located in the deeply ingrained 'racism' within British society. The central tenet of this argument was that the colonial history and ideology of White superiority are deeply embedded in British institutions and popular culture and disadvantage the 'racialised' (that is seen predominantly in terms of their 'racial' difference) ex-colonial subjects. Fundamental to this critique was the notion of 'institutional racism', which describes the routine expectations, processes and practices of institutions which disadvantage the racialised groups irrespective of individual functionaries being racist. The movement was supported by a new form of academic literature (Hall 1978, CCCS 1982, Sivanandan 1982) and a strong policy current. The latter included the Greater London Council, led by Ken Livingston (the current Mayor of London), the Central Council for Education and Training in Social Work and several local authorities who spent time and effort in articulating and implementing anti-racist policies, often in the face of abuse from tabloid press for being 'anti-White' and of criticism from White staff and users. The policy mood was one of creating sometimes uncomfortable 'alliances of the dispossessed' and articulating inclusive notions of solidarity which privileged colour over culture or religion. The term 'black' symbolised this alliance of the 'racialised'. In 'anti-racism', tackling racism was only possible collectively and any recognition of diversity by religion or culture was to fragment and disempower the movement and fall into the 'culturalist' trap. The policy movement lasted into the 1980s when, under increasing opprobrium and resistance from an overtly hostile, Conservative-led central state and challenges from within the alliance, including over the importance of religion, it came to a faltering end. However, there remains an acceptance (albeit contested) of racism and racial disadvantage as key and enduring features of British life which is supported by significant new legislation in the form of the *Race Relations (Amendment) Act* (2001) which places a duty of care on public services to ensure racial equality in their organisations.

## The sociology of ethnicity and health

Sociologists of health arrived on this scene relatively late compared to other branches of British sociology. By the 1970s, 'race relations' had developed into a significant field in British sociology, with major works already published by John Rex, Robert Moore (Rex and Moore 1969), Charles Husband (Hartman and Husband, 1974) and Michael Banton (1977). The first generation of 'race relations' doctoral graduates, such as Anwar (1979) and Saifullah Khan (1979), both of whom studied under Sheila Allen at Bradford University, were publishing their works in the 1970s. The importance of 'race relations' as a field of study was reflected in published outputs from the Universities of Aston, Bradford, Birmingham, Bristol and later Warwick, and the development of Masters and Undergraduate courses at these and other Universities. By the 1980s a powerful critique of dominant academic and policy approaches to 'race relations' was emerging from the influential Centre for Contemporary Cultural Studies, Birmingham University, under Stuart Hall (CCCS 1982, Hall 1982), the Institute of Race Relations, under A. Sivanandan (Sivanandan 1982), and others.

Meanwhile sociologists of health and illness continued to ignore ethnicity and 'race'. Two important interventions in the mid-1980s were papers by Jenny Donovan (1984) and Maggie Pearson (1986), both highlighting problems with extant literature on ethnicity and health and the importance of locating minority ethnic health and care needs in the context of socioeconomic disadvantage, racial discrimination, racialisation and minority status. The field developed slowly, however, tempting one of the authors (Ahmad 1992) to publish a provocation in the medical sociology group's newsletter, entitled 'Is medical sociology an ostrich?', arguing that both the discipline and its mouthpieces, including this journal, had shunned their responsibility to reflect in their work the ethnic and religious diversity in modern Britain.

Recent years, however, have seen an increase in sociological work focusing on minority ethnic health. A number of areas of improvement can be highlighted. First, learning from developments in the sociologies of ethnicity, migration, identity, nationalism and citizenship, researchers have contributed to literature on nomenclature, and operationalising definitions such as ethnicity, ethnic classifications, 'race' and racism. Aspinall (1997) has published interesting work on ethnic classifications in the 2001 Census, and the use of 'ethnicity' as a variable in health research. Bradby (1995, 2003) has explored the complexities and contradictions of conceptualising ethnicity and racism. Nazroo (1997), Smaje (1995, 1996) and others have introduced sophistication to debates around ethnic health inequalities. Ahmad (1999) has highlighted the complex and contingent nature of culture and the importance of context in the choice of identity definitions to be employed in research and practice. Bhopal (*e.g.* 1997) has argued for a more considered approach to research in this area within epidemiology.

Secondly, a number of significant studies have explored ethnic differentials in morbidity, mortality and access to health services. Davey Smith *et al.* (2000a), based on an extensive qualitative study, explored challenges involved in developing appropriate measures of socio-economic position. Nazroo (1997, 1998) was among the first to have a significant focus on the interplay between ethnicity and socioeconomic position, using data from the Policy Studies Institute's Fourth National Survey which included a nationally representative sample of the numerically significant minority ethnic groups. This work demonstrated that to a significant extent, ethnic inequalities were reduced or eradicated once differences in socioeconomic conditions were taken into account. Nazroo also argued that given the difficulties of applying simple measures of socioeconomic position across cultures (a point developed in depth by Davey Smith et al. 2000a), composite measures of socioeconomic status might be preferable. The effect of the experience of racism on ill health, independent of class has been demonstrated by Karlsen and Nazroo (2002) and the potential impact of impoverished neighbourhood environment on minority ethnic health (Karlsen et al. 2002) has been underlined. While these and other colleagues have introduced a critical edge to explorations of ethnicity and health, Smaje, in a well argued book (1995) and paper (1996), has warned against reducing ethnic inequalities in health and illness to socio-economic factor differentials alone. These are significant (albeit belated) developments in the sociology of health and the literature on ethnicity and health.

Thirdly, while the sociology of health has a proud tradition of studying the 'meaning' of health and illness, through careful qualitative studies of illness experience, especially of chronic illness (Bury 1991, Herzlich 1973, Williams 1993, Blaxter 2004), such literature has been lacking in relation to minority ethnic groups. The work of a group of researchers working with Ahmad and Atkin (Ahmad 2000, Ahmad et al. 2000, Atkin and Ahmad 2000a 2000b, Ahmad et al. 2002) has made an important contribution in this field. Focusing on young people growing up with chronic conditions and physical impairments (deafness, haemoglobinopathies, impairments) they explore how notions of identity are developed, maintained and policed; how the interface between users and providers is negotiated; and how professionals understand and manage ethnic difference. In another strand of their work (Katbamna et al. 2004), they explore the negotiation of caring responsibilities within communities, including the strategies that people living and dying with cancer employ to retain a sense of positive selfhood when identity is threatened by deteriorating, often leaky, bodies (Chattoo and Ahmad 2003). This volume shows that other sociologists are now making valued contributions to the experience of chronic illness and disability in minority ethnic groups.

Fourthly, the complexity of analysis is increasing in the study of ethnicity and health. Both qualitative (e.g. Bush et al. 1998) and quantitative (e.g. Nazroo 1997) analysis has compared different minority groups against one another and with the majority. The inclusion of various minorities in a comparison hinders simplistic essentialising of the effect of minority cultures, and consequent culture-blaming tendencies. Furthermore, it can facilitate consideration of the complexity of how minority and majority cultures influence one another. Inter-ethnic comparisons that consider gender, as well as class as explanatory variables for health outcomes are a welcome development (Cooper 2002).

While we have witnessed improvements in both the level of sophistication and the extent of work published in this field in recent years, there remain several gaps. Much of the focus on research is on South Asians while several smaller groups remain under-researched. For example, among the established minority ethnic groups, there is a paucity of literature on Somalis and other Africans, those from the Middle East, Eastern Europeans and Latin Americans. Equally, there is little health research on refugees and asylum seekers. As previously, it seems that sociology of health is waiting for other branches of sociology and social policy to take the lead, before joining in.

Furthermore, while in Britain we become ever more sophisticated at defining, documenting and monitoring racism and disadvantage, we seem to be no better at tackling such disadvantage. Recent evidence (Palmer and Kenway 2007) demonstrates that the gap in poverty between sections of the minority ethnic communities and the general population has not reduced for decades.

Finally, there is a greater acceptance in Britain that religion is an increasingly important variable in addressing ethnic relations. Research in the sociology of health and illness remains relatively poor in this area. However, while we must recognise the importance of religion, both in terms of its importance as a marker of identity and its links to ethnic relations, to socio-economic position and oppression, we must not allow it to become the new 'master identity', but rather keep it in play with other dimensions of identity and structural position (Bradby 2007).

## Introduction to the chapters in this volume

This volume offers a survey of current research in the field of the sociology of ethnicity, racism, health and illness in Britain and the US. The study of ethnicity and health is perhaps more clearly developed as a sub-field of medical sociology in Britain than elsewhere in Europe. British research has developed out of Marxist traditions of studying labour relations and an interest in whether the reserve army of labour drawn from the former colonies would develop a class consciousness. While Britain's obsession with class is not replicated in the US, 'race' has long been a highly significant social and economic division and therefore an important public health variable. The terms 'race' and ethnicity are used in the UK and the US, and yet they refer to somewhat different constellations of the various dimensions that the terms encompass (as discussed earlier). The search for a universally applicable code of terms is not feasible or appropriate in research which seeks to delineate the particularities as well as the generalisations of experience and outcome. The adoption of regularised terminology (even if it could be agreed) does not address the underlying historical and contemporary contrasts between the US and Britain which make simplistic comparison meaningless.

James Nazroo and colleagues' chapter in this volume shows that the discontinuities in social and economic conditions of minorities do not render comparisons across the Atlantic impossible. The secondary analysis of data-sets from England and the US has allowed some conclusions to be drawn about the conditions which make migrants more and less likely to thrive in their new settings. Black, Caribbean and White Americans are compared with Caribbean and White English on self-assessed general health, and the poorer health of English Caribbeans compared with their US counterparts suggests that the historical and economic context of a group's migration experience is an important consideration. Riley Bahr in his paper in this volume pursues the issue of health inequalities by ethnic group in seeking 'to explain the residual racial gap in health remaining after adjustment for socioeconomic status and correlates of socioeconomic status'. Using detailed survey material on nutritional behaviours among Blacks and Whites in California, and the accumulated evidence of the links between nutrition and health outcomes, Riley Bahr suggests that at least some of the residual gap can be explained by Blacks having less healthy nutritional behaviours compared with Whites. The relationship between 'nutritional healthfulness' and 'race', independent of socioeconomic status, is linked to residential segregation and the lack of availability of healthier foods in poorer neighbourhoods where Blacks tend to live.

The welcome attention being paid to common and chronic conditions among minority ethnic groups is illustrated in this volume by research on diabetes and depression. The well-researched nature of these conditions in the general population ensures that commonalities as well as divergence in their expression, experience and treatment among minorities can be explored. The longstanding discussion of the 'somatisation' of psychological conditions among minority groups in the Anglophone world has, at its crudest, implied that some cultures conceptualise bodily but not psychological suffering and therefore can only express distress in somatic terms. Mallinson and Popay's research based on White and South Asian adults' accounts of depression presents a more nuanced picture, with some variation in the metaphors used to express emotional distress between the groups, but in the context of considerable overlap in the types of narrative and symbolism employed. Similarly, in Seymour and colleagues' research with White and Chinese elders on their expectations of end-of-life care, there were many common themes reflecting people's concern for their families in the British urban environment, and the divergence, while of interest, was again subtle. Lawton and colleagues consider how people explain the genesis of their type 2 diabetes mellitus and, again, find similarity in White and South Asian accounts. They consider the effect that the researcher's cultural context has in shaping analysis and charge us with paying attention to the expectations that we bring to the research encounter.

Another welcome move, which takes institutional forms of discrimination seriously, is the interest in organisational features of health and welfare services which may disadvantage particular ethnic groups. The British NHS has formally acknowledged that interpretation should be available to ensure that services are delivered in an appropriate language; how this can be achieved equitably and economically has not yet been established. Greenhalgh and colleagues present their findings on how General Practices in London meet the language needs of their patients, viewing the interpreted consultation as an organisational routine and suggesting that variation in how this routine operates can be related to the type of General Practice. Salway and colleagues' secondary analysis of the Labour Force Survey focuses on variation across ethnic groups in claiming Disability Living Allowance. Here too similarities between groups were highlighted in terms of disincentives to claim the allowance, along with some differences between ethnic groups. However, the solution to the low uptake of the allowance by some groups is seen to lie in improving the information flow from the welfare agencies, rather than in rectifying the 'deficiencies' of minority culture.

## Acknowledgements

Carol Capper ensured order during the process of commissioning and reviewing material for this monograph. Karl Atkin was generous and exceptionally prompt in providing comments on an earlier draft of this article. To both, our heartfelt thanks. We owe a great debt of gratitude to numerous referees who commented on successive drafts of the chapters in this volume.

## References

Ahmad, W.I.U. (1992) Is medical sociology an ostrich? reflections on 'race' and the sociology of health, *Medical Sociology News*, 17, 2, 16–21.

Ahmad, W.I.U. (1999) Ethnicity and statistics: better than nothing or worse than nothing? In Dorling, D. and Simpson, S. (eds) *Statistics in Society*. London: Edward Arnold.

Ahmad, W.I.U. (ed.) (2000) *Ethnicity, Disability and Chronic Illness*. Buckingham: Open University Press.

Ahmad, W.I.U., Atkin, K. and Chamba, R. (2000) 'Causing havoc to their children': parental and professional perspectives on consanguinity and childhood disability. In Ahmad, W.I.U. (ed.) *Ethnicity, Disability and Chronic Illness*. Buckingham: Open University Press, 28–44.

Ahmad, W.I.U., Atkin, K. and Jones, L. (2002) Being deaf and being other things: young Asian people negotiating identities, *Social Science and Medicine*, 55, 10, 1757–69.

Ahmed, L. (1992) *Women and Gender in Islam*. New Haven, CT and London: Yale University Press.

Amin, A. (2002) Ethnicity and the multicultural city: living with diversity, *Environment and Planning*, 34, 959–80.

Anwar, M. (1979) *The Myth of Return*. London: Heinemann.

Aspinall, P.J. (1997) The conceptual basis of ethnic group terminology and classification, *Social Science and Medicine*, 45, 5, 689–98.

Atkin, K. and Ahmad, W.I.U. (2000a) Pumping iron: compliance with chelation therapy among young people who have thalassaemia major, *Sociology of Health and Illness*, 22, 4, 500–24.

Atkin, K. and Ahmad, W.I.U. (2000b) Family caregiving and chronic illness: how parents cope with a child with a sickle cell disorder or thalassaemia, *Health and Social Care in the Community*, 8, 1, 57–69.

Barker, M. (1981) *The New Racism*. London: Junction Books.

Banton, M. (1977) *The Idea of Race*. London: Tavistock.

Bhopal, R.S. (1997) Is health into ethnicity and health, racist, unsound or important science? *British Medical Journal*, 314, 1751–6.

Blaxter, M. (2004) Life narrative, health and identity. In Kelleher, D. and Leavey, G. (eds) *Identity and Health*. London: Routledge.

Bradby, H. (1995) Ethnicity: not a black and white issue, *Sociology of Health and Illness*, 17, 3, 405–17.

Bradby, H. (2003) Describing ethnicity in health research, *Ethnicity and Health*, 8, 1, 5–13.

Bradby, H. (2007) Watch out for the Aunties! Young British Asians' accounts of identity and substance use, *Sociology of Health and Illness*, 29, 5, 656–72.

Bury, M. (1991) The sociology of chronic illness, *Sociology of Health and Illness*, 13, 4, 451–65.

Bush, H., Williams, R., Bradby, H., Anderson, A. and Lean, M. (1998) Family hospitality and ethnic tradition among South Asian, Italian and general population women in the West of Scotland, *Sociology of Health and Illness*, 20, 3, 351–80.

Centre for Contemporary Cultural Studies (1982) *The Empire Strikes Back*. London: Heinemann.

Chattoo, S. and Ahmad, W.I.U. (2003) The meaning of cancer: illness, biography and identity. In Kelleher, D. and Leavey, G. (eds) *Identity and Health*. London: Routledge.

Cooper, H. (2002) Investigating socio-economic explanations for gender and ethnic inequalities in health, *Social Science and Medicine*, 54, 5, 693–706.

Davey Smith, G., Charsley K., Lambert H., Paul S., Fenton, S. and Ahmad, W.I.U. (2000a) Ethnicity, health and the meaning of socio economic position. In Graham, H. (ed.) *Understanding Health Inequalities*. Buckingham: Open University Press.

Davey Smith, G., Chaturvedi, N., Harding, S., Nazroo, J. and Williams, R. (2000b) Ethnic inequalities in health: a review of UK epidemiological literature, *Critical Public Health*, 10, 4, 375–408.

Donovan, J. (1984) Ethnicity and race: a research review, *Social Science and Medicine*, 19, 7, 663–70.

Goel, K.M., Campbell, S., Logan, R.W., Sweet, E.M., Atttenburrow, A. and Arneil, G.C. (1981) Reduced prevalence of rickets in Asian children in Glasgow, *Lancet*, 2, 405–06.

Hall, S. (1978) *Policing the Crisis: Mugging, the State, and Law and Order*. Basingstoke: Macmillan.

Hartman, P. and Husband, C. (1974) *Racism and the Media*. New Jersey: Rowman and Littlefield.

Herzlich, C. (1973) *Health and Illness*, London: Academic Press.

Isajiw, W. (1974) Definitions of ethnicity, *Ethnicity*, 1, 11–24.

Karlsen, S. and Nazroo, J. (2002) Relation between racial discrimination, social class and health among ethnic minority groups. *American Journal of Public Health*, 92, 4, 624–31.

Karlsen, S., Nazroo, J. and Stephenson, R. (2002) Ethnicity, environment and health: putting health inequalities in their place, *Social Science and Medicine*, 55, 9, 1647–61.

Katbamna S., Ahmad, W.I.U., Bhakta, P., Baker, R. and Parker, G. (2004) Do they look after their own? Informal support for South Asian carers, *Health and Social Care in the Community*, 12, 5, 398–406.

Li, P.S. (1999) Race and ethnicity. In Li, P.S. (ed.) *Race and Ethnic Relations in Canada*. Toronto: Oxford University Press.

Littlewood, R. and Lipsedge, M. (1989) *Aliens and Alienists. Ethnic Minorities and Psychiatry*. London: Unwin Hyman.

Mackerras, C. (2003) *Ethnicity in Asia*. London: Routledge.

Nazroo, J. (1997) *The Health of Britain's Ethnic Minorities: Findings of a National Survey*. London: Policy Studies Institute.

Nazroo, J. (1998) Genetic, cultural and socioeconomic vulnerability? Explaining ethnic inequalities in health, *Sociology of Health and Illness*, 20, 5, 710–30.

Neighbourhood Renewal Unit (2004) *Race Equality and Neighbourhood Renewal*. London: Office of the Deputy Prime Minister.

Palmer, G. and Kenway, P. (2007) *Poverty among ethnic groups: how and why does it differ?* York: Joseph Rowntree Foundation (available to download from www.jrf.org.uk).

Pearson, M. (1986) The politics of ethnic minority health studies. In Rathwell, T. and Phillips, D. (eds) *Health, Race and Ethnicity*. London: Croom Helm.

Philips, T. (2005) After 7/7: Sleepwalking to segretation. (Speech by the then Chair of the Commission for Racial Equality) http://www.cre.gov.uk/Default.aspx.LocID-0hgnew07s.RefLocID-0hg00900c002. Lang-EN.htm (accessed 26 May 2007).

Rex, J. (1991) *Ethnic Identity and Ethnic Mobilisation in Britain*. Warwick: Centre for Research in Ethnic Relations.

Rex, J. and Moore, R. (1969) *Race, Community and Conflict*. Oxford: Oxford University Press (for the Institute of Race Relations).

Rocheron, Y. (1988) The Asian Mother and Baby Campaign: the construction of ethnic minority health needs, *Critical Social Policy*, 22, 4–23.

Saifullah Khan, V. (1979) *Minority Families in Britain*. Basingstoke: Macmillan.

Sivanandan, A. (1982) *A Different Hunger: Writings on Black Resistance*. London: Pluto Press.

Smaje, C. (1995) *Health, Race and Ethnicity: Making Sense of the Evidence*. London: Kings Fund.

Smaje, C. (1996) The ethnic patterning of health: new directions for theory and research, *Sociology of Health and Illness*, 18, 2, 139–71.

Werbner, P. (1990) *The Migration Process: Capital, Gifts and Offerings among British Pakistanis*. Oxford: Berg.

Williams, G. (1993) The genesis of chronic illness: narrative reconstructions, *Sociology of Health and Illness*, 6, 2, 175–200.

# 2

## The Black diaspora and health inequalities in the US and England: does where you go and how you get there make a difference?

## James Nazroo, James Jackson, Saffron Karlsen and Myriam Torres

### Introduction

Differences in health across ethnic groups, in terms of both morbidity and mortality, are a dominant feature of developed countries and of great significance to population health. They have been repeatedly documented in England (Marmot *et al.* 1984, Harding and Maxwell 1997, Nazroo 2001, Bhopal *et al.* 1999, Erens *et al.* 2001), the US (Department of Health and Human Services 1985, Rogers 1992, Davey Smith *et al.* 1998, Pamuk *et al.* 1998, Williams 2001), Canada (Sheth *et al.* 1999, Wu *et al.* 2003, Wu and Schimmele 2005), Latin America (Pan American Health Organization 2001), South Africa (Sidiropoulos *et al.* 1997), Australia (McLennan and Madden 1999) and elsewhere (Polednak 1989).

The patterning of these inequalities is complex; nevertheless a consistent finding is the poorer health profile of Black Americans in the US and Black Caribbean people in England across a range of outcomes, most notably hypertension, diabetes and mental illness, as well as broad measures of general health.[1] Given these inequalities, much research activity has focused on a comparison of Black and white populations within these two locations, with the aim of understanding the factors that underlie the greater risk of disease and poor health among Black populations. Here the findings are contested, with some emphasising the genetic underpinning of such inequalities (Wild and McKeigue 1997) and others arguing that ethnic inequalities in health are predominantly determined by social and economic inequalities (Nazroo 1998, 2003). Regardless of the contribution of genetic factors, it is clear that there is a socioeconomic patterning of the health of Black populations, with higher rates of disease and poorer health related to both poorer economic positions and exposure to racial harassment and discrimination (Krieger *et al.* 1993, Williams *et al.* 1994, Davey Smith *et al.* 1998, Williams 1999, Nazroo 1998, Krieger 2000, Nazroo 2001, Karlsen and Nazroo 2002, Harris *et al.* 2006a and 2006b). And once such factors are adjusted for in statistical models, differences in health between Black and white populations diminish (Davey Smith *et al.* 1998, Nazroo 1998 and 2003, Harris *et al.* 2006a). The implication is that socioeconomic factors at least interact (in both a causal and statistical sense) with genetic (and other) influences and, therefore, a greater understanding of socioeconomic inequalities and their origins will both increase our understanding of causal processes and point to opportunities for the development of public-health policy.

Nevertheless, the majority of existing research has, not surprisingly, focused on proximal influences and pathways, including a mix of social, psychological, biological and genetic factors – such as current socioeconomic position, experiences of racism and discrimination, social networks, insulin resistance and metabolic syndrome. Less attention has been paid to the more distal processes that have led to the contemporary social and economic location of ethnic minority groups and the related ethnic patterning of health outcomes. There is no certainty that the disadvantages of ethnic groups are fixed across countries, generations, or across different 'Black identities' (Agyemang *et al.* 2005). Indeed, while there are many similarities between the health, social, economic and demographic profiles of Black Americans in the US and Caribbean people in England, there are also marked differences in the history of these groups. While Black Americans have been resident in the US since they arrived as slaves, Caribbean people arrived in England after World War II as labour migrants. This migration happened in the face of considerable hostility from some of the English population, but at a time when the civil rights movement was emerging in the US, with a consequent opening up of opportunities for Black Americans. There is, however, evidence to suggest that the civil rights movement most affected those who subsequently migrated into the US, rather than those who were already there (Butcher 1994, Model 1995). Indeed, the socioeconomic profile of Caribbean people who migrated to the US appears better than that of Black Americans (Foner 2005, Jackson and Antonucci 2006). And a series of US studies that have explored race inequalities in birth outcomes by country of birth have generally found that Black women born overseas have more favourable outcomes than those born in the US (Cabral *et al.* 1990, Pallotto *et al.* 2000, Acevado-Garcia *et al.* 2005, Howard *et al.* 2006, but see Fuentes-Afflick *et al.* 1998 for an exception to this).

This points to the need to move beyond the treatment of ethnicity as an unproblematic variable in health analysis, where 'Caribbean', or even 'Black', labels are seen as representing global uniform categories whose meaning can be assumed and for whom findings can be generalised from one context or group to another (Cabral *et al.* 1990, Bhopal 2004, Howard *et al.* 2006). Central to an understanding of socioeconomic inequalities and how they relate to the ethnic patterning of health is approaching ethnicity as a social identity, recognising the variable nature of such identities across contexts and generations, and the factors that underpin such variability (Hall 1992). To what extent does being 'Black' have different meanings in different locations, for different Black groups, and for different generations? How does this configure social (ethnic/race) relations? And what implications does this have for health inequalities? One way forward is to consider how the pattern and context of migration has influenced the social and economic circumstances of populations post-migration and, consequently, health inequalities.

Investigating these issues in one country context – which has typically been the case, especially with large population-based surveys – limits variability across social, economic and historical contexts, making it difficult to identify the factors that lead to positive and negative outcomes for migrants. For example, the migration from the Caribbean to England happened in a circumscribed period and was driven by particular economic and political factors, leaving little variation in the characteristics of the migration population, the circumstances into which they migrated, and their post-migration experiences. Data on similar populations who have migrated in, and to, very different circumstances provide the opportunity to conduct the kinds of comparative analyses that will facilitate greater understanding of how the variable patterns and contexts of migration drive ethnic inequalities in health. Although distal in the causal pathway, these factors remain relevant to contemporary migrant and post-migration populations.

We aim to advance this agenda by examining the patterning of ethnic inequalities in health between five ethnic groups in the US and England – Black American, Caribbean American, white American, Caribbean English and white English – and the social and economic factors that might underlie any differences in health that are observed. We hypothesise that differences between the three Black groups in their migration histories and consequent social and economic positions will lead to differences in the health inequalities they experience.

**Methods**

*Survey design*

The analysis uses survey data from three sources, each with a probability sample design. US data are from the National Survey of American Life (NSAL), which was conducted in 2001–3. Full details of the study have been reported elsewhere (Jackson *et al.* 2004, Jackson and Antonucci 2006, Heeringa *et al.* 2006). In brief, it is based upon an integrated national household probability sample of 3,570 Black American adults and 810 co-resident adolescents (aged 13–17) (response rate 71%), 1,621 Caribbean adults and 360 co-resident adolescents (response rate 78%) and 891 non-Hispanic white adults (response rate 70%). Respondents were allocated into the Black American and Caribbean American categories if they self-identified as 'Black', with the Caribbean category further defined using questions on country of ancestry. Migrants identifying as Black but not from the Caribbean were excluded from the sample for this analysis (most of these were born in Africa). The Black American and white samples were selected from geographical segments in proportion to the Black American population distribution; the Caribbean sample was selected from the Black American segments and from additional metropolitan segments with more than 10 per cent Caribbean people. This makes NSAL the first national sample of people of different race and ethnic groups who live in the same contexts and geographical areas as Black Americans. This does however mean that the white sample is representative only of white people who live in areas where the density of the black population is 10 per cent or greater. Interviews were conducted by ethnically matched interviewers using a standardised face-to-face computerised interview.

English data were drawn from the Health Survey for England (HSE) 1998 and 1999, and a follow-up study on mental illness (EMPIRIC – Ethnic Minority Psychiatric Illness Rates in the Community). These studies are described in detail elsewhere (Erens and Primatesta 1999, Erens *et al.* 2001, Sproston and Nazroo 2002). In brief, the HSE is a series of surveys about the health of people in England that has been conducted annually since 1991. The HSE sampling procedures are similar to those for NSAL and are designed to select probability samples of both individuals and households, with respondents recruited from a sample of addresses selected from within a stratified sample of postcode sectors using the Postcode Address File. Black Caribbean respondents were drawn from the 1999 HSE (Erens *et al.* 2001), which was boosted to contain greater proportions of people from ethnic minority groups. The white English group was drawn from the 1998 HSE (Erens and Primatesta 1999), because a full interview was not administered to white informants at the 1999 HSE. For the 1999 HSE, sampling points were identified using information from the 1991 Census, which allowed postcode sectors to be stratified and selected on the basis of their ethnic composition. Areas with low concentrations of ethnic minority people were also identified and included. Screening for non-white ethnic minority respondents in areas with few ethnic minority residents was carried out using the validated focused enumeration technique (Smith and Prior 1997, Brown and Richie, 1981). Respondents were identified as suitable for inclusion and allocated to an ethnic group on the basis of their responses to a question on their ethnic family origins, a categorisation that correlates highly with self-identified ethnicity (Nazroo 2001), with those identifying Caribbean origins included in the analyses presented here. Overall, the 1998 and 1999 HSEs yielded a sample of 14,538 white English respondents (response rate 70%) and 1,217 Caribbean respondents (response rate estimated at 55%).

EMPIRIC (Sproston and Nazroo 2002) was a follow-up survey of those aged 16 to 74 in the 1998 (a subsample only) and 1999 HSE samples, collecting additional information on mental health, ethnic identity and experiences and perceptions of racism and discrimination. This resulted in a sample of 753 white English respondents (response rate 71%) and 647 Caribbean respondents (response rate 68%) for analyses involving racism variables.

For this paper we have altered the labelling of ethnic groups from those used in the original surveys, to clearly distinguish national origin. The labels we use are: Black American, Caribbean American, white American, white English, Caribbean English. In addition, because of differences in the ages covered in the different surveys, only those aged 18 to 74 are included in the analyses we present.

*Measures and equivalence of data items*
Although the US and English data collections were designed independently, similar topics were covered in their questionnaires, giving the potential for a joint analysis of their data. The following describes the measures that were used in the analyses presented in this paper, after which we discuss issues relating to the non-equivalence of data items in the surveys.

General (self-assessed) health was established using different measures in the different surveys. In NSAL, respondents were asked: 'How would you rate your overall physical health at the present time? Would you say it is excellent, very good, good, fair or poor?'. In the HSE respondents were asked 'How is your health in general? Would you say it was very good, good, fair, bad or very bad?' And the HSE respondents included in EMPIRIC were asked: 'In general, would you say your health is excellent, very good, good, fair or poor?' For this analysis, NSAL respondents are coded according to whether they had responded 'excellent', 'very good' or 'good', as opposed to those responding 'fair' or 'poor'. Respondents to the HSE were grouped according to whether they had responded 'excellent' or 'good', as opposed to those responding 'fair', 'bad' or 'very bad'. The comparability of these questions is explored at the end of this section of the paper.

Both NSAL and the HSE included questions on diagnosed conditions and, in their list of conditions, both included: heart disease, hypertension, diabetes and stroke. For all but heart disease the questions were almost identical. For heart disease, NSAL asked one question asking about 'heart trouble', while the HSE had several questions covering: angina, heart attack, heart murmur, irregular heart rhythm and other heart trouble.

Household income was collected in categories using a showcard on both sites. It was equivalised using the McClements scoring system, which takes account of the number of people in the household (McClements 1977). A score was allocated to each household member, and these were added together to produce an overall McClements score. The head (or first adult) of the household was given a score of 0.61, the spouse/partner of the head was given a score of 0.39. Other second adults were given a score of 0.46, third adults, 0.42 and subsequent adults, 0.36. Dependent children aged below two were given a score of 0.09, those aged between two and four, 0.18, those between five and seven, 0.21, those between eight and ten, 0.23, those between 11 and 12, 0.25, those between 13 and 15, 0.27 and those aged 16 or over were given a score of 0.36. For these analyses it was assumed that the respondent was the head of household and that adulthood begins at 18 years. Equivalised income was derived as the annual household income divided by the McClements score, which was then attributed to all members of the household. Rather than attempting directly to equate US and English incomes, the equivalised income was categorised into US and English population specific quintiles. About 13 per cent of respondents did not report their income (ranging from 8.6 per cent in the white American group to 15.5 per cent in the Black American group), so these respondents have been included as an additional category for the income variable.

Employment status was coded 'employed or in fulltime education', 'unemployed', 'unemployed due to long term sickness', 'looking after the home' and 'retired'.

Differences in education systems between England and the US made it necessary to remove some of the detail contained in the country-specific education measures to create comparable scales. NSAL respondents were asked how many years of education they had completed and were then asked if they had obtained a high school graduation certificate, a college degree or certificate and if they had had any other form of schooling. HSE respondents were simply asked about any qualifications gained. For these analyses, educational level was categorised according to the highest qualification gained: those with less than a high-school certificate or A-level; those with A-levels or an American high-school graduation certificate; those with higher educational qualifications, such as college or university degrees; and those with other types of qualifications.

Experience of racist victimisation covered three dimensions in both sites: being verbally insulted, threatened or harassed; being treated unfairly at work; or being refused employment. In NSAL, the questions explored whether the respondent experienced verbal insults or name calling and/or was threatened or harassed 'in your day-to-day life almost everyday, at least once a week, a few times a month, a few times a year or less than once a year?'. These variables were combined into one measure of whether the respondent had experienced either form of insult more frequently than 'less than once a year' and with the respondent attributing this to his/her ancestry, race or skin colour in response to a follow-up question. This coding was to allow comparability with the British data, which asked respondents 'In the last twelve months, has anyone insulted you for reasons to do with your ethnicity? By insulted I mean verbally abused, threatened or been a nuisance to you.'.

To determine experience of discrimination in employment, respondents to NSAL were told: 'In the following questions we are interested in the way other people have treated you or your beliefs about how other people have treated you. Can you tell me if any of the following have ever happened to you? Have you ever been unfairly denied a promotion?'. And: 'For unfair reasons, have you ever not been hired for a job?'. Again only those cases where the respondent attributed the behaviour to his/her ancestry, race or skin colour were included. In EMPIRIC, respondents were asked: 'Have you yourself ever been treated unfairly at work with regard to promotion or a move to a better position for reasons which you think were to do with race, colour or your religious or ethnic background? (I don't mean when applying for a new job.)'. And: 'Have you ever been refused a job for reasons which you think were to do with your race, colour or your religious or ethnic background?'.

As this description of the questions used shows, there were some differences between the NSAL and HSE surveys in the approach to measurement and in the wording of particular items, even if there was equivalence between data items at a conceptual level. This is particularly striking for our main outcome measure, general health, where the wording of the question and the outcome categories differs. Fortunately, the EMPIRIC survey included a version of the general health question that was very close to the NSAL version, allowing a direct comparison between the different versions of the questions. Analysis of data from the HSE/EMPIRIC respondents who were asked both versions of the question showed that in response to the HSE question 23 per cent of the white English and 32 per cent of the Caribbean English samples described their health as fair, bad or very bad (rather than very good or good), compared with 21 per cent and 31 per cent respectively describing their health as fair or poor (rather than excellent, very good or good) in response to the EMPIRIC question. This suggests that the problems with differences in wording for this item did not greatly affect the findings.

Other issues relating to the equivalence of data items that are worth highlighting at this point include: heart disease being covered by several specific questions in the HSE, and one broad question in NSAL, which is likely to lead to the inclusion of more cases in the HSE data; the use of country specific quintiles for household income; the merging of quite different classifications for education level, reflecting differences in the education systems; and the collection of similar categories of exposure to racism and discrimination, but using quite different questioning techniques.

Finally, the subjective nature of the general health measure might mean that it does not map onto similar health constructs in the differing national and cultural contexts in which we use it, either at the level of underlying health concept or in terms of thresholds behind response options (so the threshold between, for example, 'fair' and 'good' might vary); and that the self-reports of diagnosed disease might vary across nations, because of institutional variations in opportunities for diagnosis. In both cases, the implication would be that we cannot use these measures to draw comparisons across the countries and groups (including within countries) that we study. We return to these important issues when we consider possible limitations in the discussion section of the paper.

*Statistical methods*

Analyses of the data involve both crosstabulations and multivariate analyses using logistic regression. For crosstabulations we compute means (for age) and distributions. For the multivariate analyses we build stepwise logistic regression models to examine the contribution of explanatory factors to ethnic differences in our dichotomised general health outcome. First, models are adjusted for age and gender, then explanatory variables are included in a series of steps, so that their impact on the odds ratios associated with ethnicity can be shown. Respondents who are missing on variables included in one or more steps in the model are excluded from the whole model, with the exception of those missing only on the income variable (who, as we describe above, have been included as an additional category).

The complex survey designs for NSAL, HSE and EMPIRIC meant that the samples had to be weighted to correct for the unequal probabilities of selection for different classes of respondents. In addition, weights were applied to adjust for the non-response to the NSAL and EMPIRIC surveys. For EMPIRIC, these non-response weights were obtained using regression modelling based on HSE data (available for both respondents and non-respondents to the follow-up) (Sproston and Nazroo 2002). For NSAL, post-stratification weights were applied, adjusting the weighted distribution of the sample to conform to the known distribution of the population for age, region, and gender within each ethnic group (Heeringa *et al.* 2004 and 2006). In addition all standard errors and confidence intervals were corrected for auto-correlation within the stratified and clustered sample design. These analyses were conducted using the survey commands within Stata.

**Results**

Table 1 shows the characteristics of the sample stratified by ethnicity. The English ethnic groups are on average older than their US counterparts. On the whole, respondents, particularly in the Caribbean English group, are more likely to be female, although this is not the case for the Caribbean American group. The income distributions show marked ethnic differences, with the white groups better off than others in both the US and England (though the advantage is greater in the US with 27 per cent in the top income quintile compared with 23 per cent of white English respondents). The Caribbean American group

Table 1  *Social and economic factors by ethnicity*

| | Per cents (except for age) | | | | |
|---|---|---|---|---|---|
| | Black American | Caribbean American | White American | White English | Caribbean English |
| Mean age (years) | 41.0 | 39.0 | 42.7 | 44.8 | 42.6 |
| *Gender* | | | | | |
| Male | 44 | 51 | 47 | 46 | 41 |
| Female | 56 | 49 | 53 | 54 | 59 |
| *Equivalised income* | | | | | |
| Bottom quintile | 27 | 20 | 13 | 15 | 31 |
| Second quintile | 23 | 19 | 17 | 18 | 21 |
| Middle quintile | 20 | 22 | 20 | 21 | 15 |
| Fourth quintile | 17 | 17 | 24 | 23 | 16 |
| Highest quintile | 13 | 22 | 27 | 23 | 17 |
| *Employment status* | | | | | |
| Employed or student | 66 | 76 | 72 | 66 | 61 |
| Unemployed | 15 | 13 | 8 | 3 | 6 |
| Long-term sick | 8 | 4 | 4 | 5 | 6 |
| Looking after the home | 3 | 2 | 7 | 11 | 14 |
| Retired | 9 | 5 | 10 | 15 | 14 |
| *Education level* | | | | | |
| Below A-level/high school | 16 | 13 | 8 | 29 | 28 |
| A-level/high school | 58 | 52 | 53 | 42 | 41 |
| Post degree/high school | 21 | 30 | 36 | 25 | 27 |
| Other | 4 | 6 | 2 | 4 | 4 |
| *Experiences of racism/discrimination* | | | | | |
| Insulted in last 12 months | 16 | 15 | 2 | 5 | 14 |
| Refused a job | 15 | 18 | 3 | 2 | 30 |
| Treated unfairly at work or denied promotion | 13 | 10 | 2 | 2 | 24 |
| *Unweighted base for main analyses* | *3,354* | *1,568* | *826* | *13,089* | *1,175* |
| *Unweighted base for racism analyses* | *3,316* | *1,553* | *822* | *751* | *646* |

has an income profile that is very similar to that of the white English group and that is markedly better than that of the Caribbean English and Black American groups. These groups have only 17 per cent and 13 per cent in the top income quintile respectively, in comparison with 22 per cent for the Caribbean American group. Not surprisingly, the employment measure shows a similar ethnic pattern to the income measure, with the Caribbean English and Black American groups disadvantaged compared with their white counterparts. But the Caribbean American group have a higher proportion in the employment/ student category than white Americans, and a higher proportion in the unemployed category, both, perhaps, because of the smaller proportion in the retired category. The measure of education level shows fewer ethnic differences, with the two Caribbean groups having a similar profile to their white counterparts. The Black American group, however, has a

Table 2 *Health outcomes by ethnicity*

|  | Black American | Caribbean American | White American | White English | Caribbean English |
|---|---|---|---|---|---|
| *Fair or bad/poor health* | | | | | |
| Per cent | 20 | 17 | 17 | 24 | 33 |
| Age/gender standardised | 1.28 | 1.07 | 1 | 1.40 | 2.43 |
| odds ratio (95% C.I)* | (0.97–1.68) | (0.74–1.55) | | (1.08–1.81) | (1.82–3.26) |
| *Any cardiovascular disease or diabetes* | | | | | |
| Per cent | 37 | 31 | 31 | 26 | 38 |
| Age/gender standardised | 1.46 | 1.24 | 1 | 0.96 | 1.37 |
| odds ratio (95% C.I)* | (1.18–1.80) | (0.95–1.63) | | (0.80–1.16) | (1.10–1.71) |
| *Diagnosed diabetes* | | | | | |
| Per cent | 11 | 8 | 7 | 3 | 9 |
| Age/gender standardised | 1.80 | 1.37 | 1 | 0.30 | 1.17 |
| odds ratio (95% C.I)* | (1.40–2.31) | (0.89–2.11) | | (0.24–0.38) | (0.85–1.62) |
| *Diagnosed heart disease* | | | | | |
| Per cent | 7 | 8 | 9 | 14 | 10 |
| Age/gender standardised | 0.86 | 0.95 | 1 | 1.45 | 1.14 |
| odds ratio (95% C.I)* | (0.48–1.53) | (0.39–2.34) | | (0.83–2.54) | (0.62–2.10) |
| *Diagnosed hypertension* | | | | | |
| Per cent | 33 | 27 | 24 | 23 | 30 |
| Age/gender standardised | 1.77 | 1.48 | 1 | 0.86 | 1.37 |
| odds ratio (95% C.I)* | (1.39–2.27) | (1.10–1.99) | | (0.68–1.08) | (1.06–1.78) |
| *Diagnosed stroke* | | | | | |
| Per cent | 2.8 | 2.5 | 2.7 | 1.6 | 1.5 |
| Age/gender standardised | 1.25 | 1.19 | 1 | 0.51 | 0.52 |
| odds ratio (95% C.I)* | (0.72–2.17) | (0.43–3.35) | | (0.32–0.84) | (0.27–1.05) |
| *Unweighted base* | *3418* | *1568* | *826* | *13089* | *1175* |

*White American is the reference category

poorer profile than the other two US ethnic groups, with only 21 per cent in the post-high school qualifications group compared with 30 per cent of Caribbean Americans and 36 per cent of white Americans. Interestingly, the differences between the US and English groups are also large.

All three measures of racism and discrimination show, not surprisingly, low levels for the two white groups. For the measure of racial insult, rates are very similar across the three Black groups, with around 15 per cent of respondents reporting such an experience within the last year. Being refused a job is experienced at a similar level by the Black American (15%) and Caribbean American (18%) groups, but by around 30 per cent of the Caribbean English group. Likewise, being treated unfairly at work or denied promotion is reported at a higher rate by the Caribbean English group than the Caribbean American and Black American groups.

Table 2 shows differences in reported fair or bad/poor health and reports of diagnosis of a range of cardiovascular diseases by ethnic group. As well as showing the prevalence of

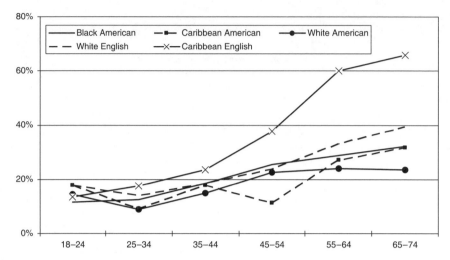

Figure 1  *Self-reported fair or bad/poor health by ethnicity and age*

these conditions (in percentages), the table also shows age and gender adjusted odds ratios (with 95% confidence intervals), to address differences in age profiles across the various groups. For these analyses the white American group is used as the reference category. For reported fair or bad/poor health differences are large, both between the US and English groups and when comparing ethnic groups within countries. Notably, the difference between the white and Caribbean English groups is much larger than that between the white and Caribbean American groups, and the Black American group seems to have poorer health than the Caribbean (and white) American group. The pattern of findings is similar for any diagnosed condition, although the English groups do not always have higher rates than their US counterparts. Indeed for all of the diagnosed conditions, differences between the US and English groups are smaller (hypertension and any diagnosed condition), or reversed (diabetes and stroke). Diagnosed diabetes shows a similar pattern to that seen for any diagnosed condition and, apart from the US-England difference, reported fair or bad/poor health. Differences between groups within a country are small for heart disease. All three Black groups have higher rates of hypertension than the white groups, with the Black American group having particularly high rates. And for all groups differences are small for stroke.

Figure 1 shows the prevalence of reporting fair or bad/poor health by ethnicity and age. There are relatively small differences until age 35. From that age onwards the Caribbean English group has an increasingly greater prevalence than the other groups, with the white English and Black American groups also showing higher rates than the white American group from the age of 55 onwards. The Caribbean American group appear to have the lowest rates at ages 45–54, but then their rates rise to a similar level to other groups.

One possible explanation for the apparent differences between the Caribbean American and Caribbean English groups, shown in Tables 1 and 2 and Figure 1, is that they are a consequence of differences in patterns of migration from the Caribbean to these two locations. Differences in the timing of migration are explored in Table 3, which shows that the Caribbean American group were more likely than the Caribbean English group to be aged 12 or older when they migrated and less likely to be born in their country of residence.[2] It also shows that of those who migrated, around 80 per cent of the English Caribbean group

Table 3 *Age of and year of migration for Caribbean respondents*

|  | Column per cents | |
|---|---|---|
|  | Caribbean American | Caribbean English |
| *Age on migration* | | |
| Born in the US/England | 41 | 50 |
| Aged 11 or younger | 11 | 9 |
| Aged 12 or older | 48 | 40 |
| *Year of migration (migrants only)* | | |
| Before 1960 | 3 | 27 |
| 1960s | 12 | 51 |
| 1970s | 21 | 11 |
| 1980s | 33 | 4 |
| 1990s onwards | 31 | 8 |

Table 4 *Social and economic factors by age on migration for Caribbean respondents*

|  | Cell per cents (except for age) | | | |
|---|---|---|---|---|
|  | Caribbean American | | Caribbean English | |
|  | Born in US or migrated <12 | Migrated aged 12 or older | Born in England or migrated <12 | Migrated aged 12 or older |
| Mean age (years) | 34.7 | 43.7 | 33.1 | 56.7 |
| Highest quintile of income | 28 | 15 | 22 | 9 |
| Not employed or student (excluding retired) | 23 | 16 | 25 | 39 |
| Educated post degree/high school | 33 | 27 | 33 | 16 |
| Experiences of racism/discrimination | | | | |
| Insulted in last 12 months | 19 | 11 | 16 | 11 |
| Refused a job | 22 | 14 | 33 | 24 |
| Treated unfairly at work or denied promotion | 12 | 9 | 22 | 28 |

had migrated before the 1970s, while over 80 per cent of the American Caribbean group migrated from the 1970s onwards.

Table 4 explores differences in the profiles of 'migrant' and 'second-generation' Caribbean people in the two locations. (The second generation is defined as either those who were born in the US or England, or who migrated before the age of 12. The latter group were included because their numbers were too small to analyse separately (see Table 3) and, as most of their education had occurred in the host country, conceptually they fitted better in this group. Including them in the first generation group made little difference to the findings.) It shows that in both locations the second generation are better off in terms of income and education, although for employment the second generation are disadvantaged

Table 5 *Self-reported fair or bad/poor health by income, racist verbal abuse in the last 12 months and ethnicity*

| | Cell per cents | | | | |
|---|---|---|---|---|---|
| | Black American | Caribbean American | White American | White English | Caribbean English |
| *Equivalised income* | | | | | |
| Bottom quintile | 32 | 19 | 35 | 39 | 40 |
| Second quintile | 23 | 25 | 27 | 35 | 47 |
| Middle quintile | 11 | 16 | 13 | 23 | 31 |
| Fourth quintile | 11 | 13 | 14 | 16 | 20 |
| Highest quintile | 9 | 5 | 11 | 13 | 13 |
| Income not reported | 24 | 22 | 9 | 25 | 38 |
| *Verbally abused* | | | | | |
| Yes | 26 | 32 | n/a | [23][1] | 39 |
| No | 19 | 14 | 17 | 22 | 31 |

[1]Base is only 35 respondents experiencing racist verbal abuse.

in the US and advantaged in England. Indeed, the second generation compare quite favourably to the figures shown for their white counterparts in Table 1, with, for example, a similar proportion in the top income quintile. It also shows that the second generation are more likely to report experiences of racism and discrimination in all but one case (unfair treatment at work for Caribbean English people).

Beyond migration, the main factors considered here that may explain ethnic differences in health are those relating to economic and social inequalities, including experiences of racism and discrimination. Table 5 shows the relationship between general health and income and experiencing verbal abuse. It shows that for each of the ethnic groups there is a strong relationship with income, with the prevalence of self-reported fair or bad/poor health decreasing steadily with increasing income, and with those not reporting their level of income generally having a high prevalence of fair or bad/poor health (the white American group being the exception to this). Similarly, those who reported experiencing racist verbal abuse in the last 12 months had higher rates of fair or bad/poor health, with the exception of the white groups (who had a low prevalence of exposure; so estimates are either based on small numbers – for the white English group – or cannot be calculated – for the white American group).

Table 6 reports the multivariate (logistic regression) modelling of the relationship between general health and ethnicity, showing the odds of the various ethnic groups compared with the white American group to report their health as fair or bad/poor; it also shows how these odds change as additional explanatory factors are entered into the model. At the first step, with only age and gender included in the model, the Caribbean American group has an odds ratio of close to 1 for fair or bad/poor health, the odds for the Black American group are higher (though note that the confidence intervals cross 1), the white English group has a significantly higher odds of 1.4, and the odds for the Caribbean English group are close to 2.5. The second step of the model includes measures of income and education level and, after this adjustment, only the Caribbean English group have odds of fair or bad/poor health that are significantly different from those of the white American

Table 6 *Ethnic differences in self-reported fair or bad/poor health: effect of economic factors and migration*

| | Odds ratios with 95 confidence intervals | | | | |
| --- | --- | --- | --- | --- | --- |
| | Black American | Caribbean American | White American | White English | Caribbean English |
| **Model adjusted for** | | | | | |
| Age and gender | 1.28 (0.97–1.68) | 1.07 (0.74–1.55) | 1 | 1.40 (1.09–1.81) | 2.43 (1.82–3.26) |
| + Income quintile, education level | 0.95 (0.75–1.20) | 0.90 (0.64–1.27) | 1 | 1.14 (0.92–1.41) | 1.75 (1.34–2.28) |
| + Migrant and year of migration | 0.95 (0.75–1.20) | 0.91 (0.59–1.42) | 1 | 1.14 (0.92–1.41) | 1.33 (0.97–1.82) |

Table 7 *Ethnic differences in self-reported fair or bad/poor health: effect of racism*

| | Odds ratios with 95 confidence intervals | | | | |
| --- | --- | --- | --- | --- | --- |
| | Black American | Caribbean American | White American | White English | Caribbean English |
| **Model adjusted for** | | | | | |
| Age and gender | 1.27 (0.96–1.67) | 1.08 (0.73–1.58) | 1 | 1.36 (0.99–1.85) | 2.43 (1.76–3.36) |
| + Racial verbal abuse only | 1.16 (0.88–1.54) | 0.99 (0.68–1.45) | 1 | 1.33 (0.97–1.82) | 2.25 (1.62–3.11) |
| + Income quintile, education level, migrant and year of migration only | 0.90 (0.69–1.18) | 0.97 (0.58–1.62) | 1 | 1.11 (0.82–1.51) | 1.36 (0.88–2.11) |
| All of the above | 0.84 (0.64–1.09) | 0.86 (0.52–1.42) | 1 | 1.10 (0.81–1.49) | 1.27 (0.83–1.96) |

group (at 1.75); the odds for the white English and Black American groups drop to close to 1. The final step includes migrant status and year of migration in the model, resulting in an additional reduction in the odds for the Caribbean English group, bringing them down to a non-significant level (at 1.33).

We also included the measure of experiencing racist verbal abuse in a model using the NSAL and EMPIRIC samples, which is reported in Table 7. Although racial verbal abuse was strongly related to risk of reporting fair or bad/poor health (with statistically significant odds of 1.87 in a gender- and age-adjusted model and 1.74 in a model including all other explanatory variables – data not shown in the table) including this measure in the model made only a small difference to the ethnic differences in risk of fair or bad/poor health. So the odds for all three of the Black groups dropped when this variable was included in the model, but for the Black American and Caribbean English groups they dropped to a much greater extent when the economic measures and the measure of migration status and period of migration were included in the model.

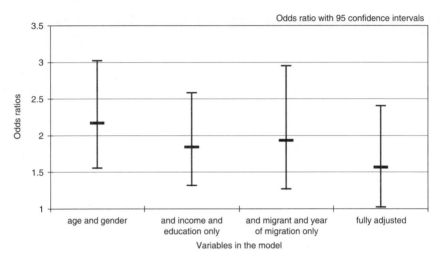

Figure 2  *Fair bad/poor health, Caribbean English compared with American Caribbean*

Our final model compares the two Caribbean groups directly and is reported in Figure 2. The first bar shows the age- and gender-adjusted odds and 95 per cent confidence intervals for the Caribbean English compared with the Caribbean American group to report fair or poor/bad health. As expected from Table 6, the odds are significantly different (at 2.17). Adjustment for income and education reduces the odds somewhat (to 1.84), while adjustment for migrant status and year of migration (without adjustment for income and education), leads to a slight reduction in odds (1.93). Finally, adjustment for all of income, education, migrant status and year of migration brings the odds down to 1.57, although this is still statistically significant (95% confidence intervals 1.02–2.40).

## Discussion

This paper has used independent, but similarly designed, surveys in England and the US to compare the health of five ethnic groups – Black American; Caribbean American; white American; white English; and Caribbean English – with the intention of exploring how the context of migration and post-migration circumstances might influence health inequalities between Black and white groups. Our main health measure, self-assessed general health, revealed a stark contrast between the situations in England and the US. The Caribbean English group have worse health than the white English group, while in the US the Caribbean American group has a very similar health profile to the white American group. In addition, there were marked differences in health between the groups in the US compared with those in England, with those in the US having better health than their English equivalents. Finally, the Black American group had worse health than the white American group, although this difference was not statistically significant. Although there were differences for the reports of diagnosed conditions, as would be expected for specific diseases and different healthcare systems, findings for these were broadly the same as for self-assessed general health.

This pattern of findings for health was also found for markers of economic inequality, including income, employment and education. On the whole, the white groups were better off than the Black groups in both countries, but while the Caribbean English profile matched that of the Black American profile (with the exception of level of education), the Caribbean American group was better off than their Black American and Caribbean English counterparts (with a profile close to that of the white American group). An exploration of migration effects revealed that the Caribbean American group were more likely than the Caribbean English group to be first generation, and to have migrated more recently. Generation was shown to be strongly related to social and economic inequalities, with the 'second' generation in both countries on the whole better off for economic markers, but more likely to report exposure to racism and discrimination.

Not surprisingly, markers of economic and social inequality – income and exposure to racial verbal abuse in the last 12 months – were strongly correlated with health for each ethnic group. And multivariate analyses showed that differences in self-reported health between the white American and the other ethnic groups diminished greatly and became non-significant when adjustments were made for economic inequalities and period of migration/generation effects. Although exposure to racial verbal abuse was strongly and negatively related to health, it did not make a large contribution to the observed ethnic inequalities in health, perhaps because of its relatively low prevalence (14–16% across the three Black groups). Finally, in multivariate analysis comparing the two Caribbean groups, the English disadvantage reduced from an odds ratio for fair/bad or poor health of 2.18 to (a still significant) 1.57 on adjustment for socioeconomic and migration effects.

The most striking finding – the differences in health between the two Caribbean groups and how this appears to be driven by economic and migration factors – indicates once again the need to take social context seriously when considering ethnic inequalities in health. When placed alongside the differences between the Caribbean American and Black American groups, we are encouraged to place our understanding of social context within a historical frame of reference. Not only should we avoid essentialising ethnic differences in health in terms of 'innate' characteristics, we must also avoid an essentialist approach to ethnic inequalities in economic and social position. Ethnic inequalities should not be considered as somehow a product of processes internal to ethnic minority groups, but as generated by wider social (ethnic) relations that have developed differently in different (historical) contexts, which will change over time. So, rather than focusing on the psychological and biological mechanisms that link a pre-existing social inequality to health inequalities, we suggest a focus on the social and economic mechanisms that produce ethnic inequalities and how these, and their outcomes, have varied. In the context of this paper, we can ask how social and economic forces have led to the relative advantage of one Black group (Caribbean American) in comparison with one in the same location (Black American), and one that migrated from the same geographical region to a different location (Caribbean English).

In answering such questions, comparative studies of migrant and post-migrant populations can provide important evidence. Although migration issues have long been identified in work on ethnic inequalities in health, the focus has very much remained on issues of health selection (the possibility that individuals are selected into a migrant group on the basis of health, or factors that relate to health, such as education) and the stresses and strains that surround the migration process (Marmot et al. 1984). We would propose that when considering ethnic inequalities in health, migration needs to be considered in more fundamental ways, such as:

- the social and economic forces that drive migration;
- selection of the population into migrant and non-migrant groups;
- the social and economic contexts into which migrants arrive;

- how these contexts develop over time and across generations, in part as a consequence of the actions of migrant populations.

It is easy to observe how these are different for the three Black groups studied here. Oliver and Shapiro (1995) demonstrate how the social and economic disadvantage of Black American people is the outcome of a long history of institutional racism and discrimination that has its roots in slavery and has produced the levels of disadvantage that are currently observed. Similarly, while the post-war migration of Caribbean people into Britain was driven by a shortage of labour, this process and the socioeconomic disadvantage faced by ethnic minority migrants in England was, and continues to be, structured by racism that has its roots in colonial history (Gilroy 1987, Miles 1982). The migration from the Caribbean to the US happened later than that to England, into a different race relations context, and at a time when, perhaps, migrants were able to take advantage of the civil rights movement in a way that the pre-existing Black population (and the population in England) was not (Butcher 1994, Model 1995, Jackson and Antonucci 2006).

Such observations show that social and economic circumstances will vary, in quite specific ways, across these three groups and across time, and allow us to develop hypotheses on how this may have led to the relative advantage of the Caribbean American group. Additional data would be required to test likely hypotheses, but central to this must be an exploration of how the significance, or meaning, of a 'Black' social identity has varied across groups and over time and place. And it might well vary from first to second and third generations. For example, the contemporary social and economic experiences of a migrant and non-migrant generation might be quite different, with the non-migrant generation more likely to do well economically (Nazroo 2004, Platt 2005) – perhaps as a consequence of different childhood experiences and consequent trajectories (Jackson and Antonucci 2006) – and to have less traditional ethnic identities (Nazroo and Karlsen 2003). In addition, the arrival of a new migrant group into an existing race relations context may well lead to a shift in the nature of that context.

Given the exploratory and opportunistic nature of the analysis conducted here – using two data sets that were not designed to be combined – there are inevitably some important limitations with the analysis we have presented, but also some strengths. The most important limitations concern issues of measurement and the equivalence of data items in the US and English surveys. Although there was remarkable equivalence in terms of the coverage of concepts and at the level of particular data items, there was limited semantic equivalence. As shown in the methods section of the paper, many of the questions had different wording in the US and English studies. We were able to explore this in relation to the measure of health that was used, and this exploration indicated that semantic non-equivalence did not produce a serious threat to the validity of our analysis. But we were unable to do this for the other measures used.

Equally important is the possibility that the different cultural frames of England and the US influence responses to questions, such that apparently similar, or indeed identical, questions may not have had identical meanings to respondents in the two locations. While this is relevant to all our measures, most significant, as we pointed out in the measures section of the paper, is the possibility that our health measures do not map onto similar constructs in the US and England. An examination of differences between the US and English findings shown in Table 2 lends support to this possibility, as do the findings of Banks and colleagues (2006a, 2006b), who show that the US population has better health than the UK when assessed using a general health measure, but worse health for a range of cardiovascular diseases and biomarkers.[3] For this paper, two points are worth making.

First, in terms of relative comparisons of the situation *within* countries we show important differences between the three Black groups we study. The position of Caribbean people compared with white people in the US (where they report similar levels of health) is remarkably different from that in England (where Caribbean people report worse health than their white counterparts). The crucial issue here is not the absolute differences between countries, but the difference in the relative position of the two Caribbean groups within their countries, which, by definition, will not be influenced by differences in context between nations. Second, if the issue is one of differences in reporting thresholds between white and Caribbean people in the two countries, our analysis allows for a direct comparison between Caribbean groups that also shows better health for Caribbean people in the US compared with those in the UK. In addition, Caribbean people in the US are not only better off in terms of this self-report of health, they are also better off in terms of more objective markers of socioeconomic position (such as income), lending support to the conclusions drawn in relation to health. And the health differences we show are largely explained by our models, something we would not expect if the differences were simply a consequence of reporting bias.

Another important limitation is that the white American group was only representative of those who live in areas where the density of the Black population is greater than 10 per cent. How this influences the findings reported here is not certain, but comparisons with other data sources suggest that the profile of the white American group in NSAL matches that of white Americans generally. A final limitation is that our range of explanatory variables did not include all that might help us understand differences in the US-English context, such as neighbourhood effects, and differences in migration effects, such as early life exposures. Despite these limitations, however, we have been able to use surveys with probability samples, very similar conceptual orientations, and with similar coverage, to carry out a novel comparison.

## Conclusions

This paper illustrates marked differences between three Black populations in two locations (Caribbean English, Caribbean American and Black American), both in comparison with each other and with their white counterparts. The differences between these groups illustrate the significance of social and historical context when considering not only health inequalities, but also social and economic inequalities. The multivariate analyses reveal the overriding significance of economic effects for the ethnic inequalities in health that we observe. With these data we cannot identify how far the economic differences between the two Caribbean populations are driven by differential selection into migrant groups, perhaps on the basis of human capital, or by differences in available opportunities in the destination countries, or by a specific period effect, such as the opportunity provided by the civil rights movement in the US. This is an important area on which to focus future inquiry, if we are concerned with the distal origins of ethnic inequalities in health and the development of upstream policies to address them.

## Acknowledgements

The data collection for the Health Survey for England and EMPIRIC was funded by the Department of Health, England. The National Survey of American Life (NSAL) was funded by the National

Institute of Mental Health (U01-MH57716) with supplemental support from the National Institutes of Health Office of Behavioural and Social Science Research; National Institute on Aging (5R01 AG02020282) supplemented by the National Institute on Drug Abuse and the University of Michigan. Preparation of this article was also aided by grants from the National Institute of Mental Health (1T01 MH58565, 1T32 MH67555, and 5TMH16806). We appreciate the assistance provided in all aspects of the NSAL study by the Program for Research on Black Americans faculty and research staff. We are grateful to anonymous reviewers for their suggestions on an earlier version of this manuscript, which led to improvements to the paper.

## Notes

1 In England there are two important exceptions to this. The first is low rates of detected coronary heart disease among Caribbean people. The second is the lower all-cause mortality rates for those born in the Caribbean, as estimated using death certificate data. It is worth noting that English death certificate data do have some limitations, most notably, because country of birth rather than ethnicity is collected on death certificates, they only cover those born in the Caribbean, and they do not cover the non-trivial number who return to the Caribbean (Office for National Statistics 2006), who remain in the denominator, but not in the numerator.
2 Of those Caribbean Americans classified as born in the US, eight were born in Puerto Rico, five in the Virgin Islands, two in St Thomas and one in St. Croix. We keep them in the 'Born in US' group, because for our later analyses we do not know when they actually migrated into 'mainland' US. Eight of the 16 report that they grew up in the US.
3 It is, of course, worth noting that health is a broader concept than cardiovascular disease, or, indeed, mortality. The broader domain of health and wellbeing, captured in part by a measure of general health, is relevant to an investigation such as this, concerned as it is with inequalities, rather than the aetiology of specific diseases.

## References

Acevado-Garcia, D., Soobader, M.J. and Berkman, L.F. (2005) The differential effect of foreign-born status on low birth weight by race/ethnicity and education, *Pediatrics*, 115, e20–30.
Agyemang, C., Bhopal, R. and Bruijnzeels, M. (2005) Negro, Black, Black African, African Caribbean, African American or what? Labelling African origin populations in the health arena in the 21st century, *Journal of Epidemiology and Community Health*, 59, 2, 1014–18.
Banks, J., Marmot, M., Oldfield, Z. and Smith, J.P. (2006a) Disease and disadvantage in the United States and in England, *Journal of the American Medical Association*, 295, 17, 2037–45.
Banks, J., Marmot, M., Oldfield, Z. and Smith, J.P. (2006b) The SES Health Gradient on both sides of the Atlantic. In Wise, D. (ed.) *Developments in the Economics of Aging*. Chicago: Chicago University Press. Available at: http://www.nber.org/books/boulders05/index.html
Bhopal, R. (2004) Glossary of terms relating to ethnicity and race: for reflection and debate, *Journal of Epidemiology and Community Health*, 58, 441–5.
Bhopal, R., Unwin, N., White, M., Yallop, J., Walker, L., Alberti, K.G., Harland, J., Patel, S., Ahmad, N., Turner, C., Watson, B., Kaur, D., Kulkarni, A., Laker, M. and Tavridou, A. (1999) Heterogeneity of coronary heart disease risk factors in Indian, Pakistani, Bangladeshi, and European origin populations: cross sectional study, *British Medical Journal*, 319, 215–20.
Brown, C. and Ritchie, J. (1981) *Focussed Enumeration: the Development of a Method for Sampling Ethnic Minority Groups*. London: Policy Studies Institute/SCPR.
Butcher, K.F. (1994) Black immigrants in the United States: a comparison with native blacks and other immigrants, *Industrial and Labor Relations Review*, 47, 2, 265–84.
Cabral, H., Fried, L.E., Levenson, S., Amaro, H. and Zuckerman, B. (1990) Foreign-born and US-born

black women: differences in health behaviours and birth outcomes, *American Journal of Public Health*, 80, 1, 70–2.

Davey Smith, G., Neaton, J.D., Wentworth, D., Stamler, R. and Stamler, J. (1998) Mortality differences between black and white men in the USA: contribution of income and other risk factors among men screened for the MRFIT, *The Lancet*, 351, 934–9.

Department of Health and Human Services (1985) *Report of the Secretary on Black and Minority Health*. Washington, D.C.: U.S. Department of Health.

Erens, B. and Primatesta, P. (1999) *Health Survey for England 1998: Cardiovascular Disease*. London: The Stationery Office.

Erens, B., Primatesta, P. and Prior, G. (2001) *Health Survey for England 1999: The Health of Minority Ethnic Groups*. London: The Stationery Office.

Foner, N. (2005) *In a New Land: a Comparative View of Immigratiuon*. New York: New York University.

Fuentes-Afflick, E., Hessol, N.A. and Perez-Stable, E.J. (1998) Maternal birthplace, ethnicity, and low birth weight in California, *Archives of Pediatric and Adolescent Medicine*, 152, 11, 1105–12.

Gilroy, P. (1987) *There Ain't No Black in the Union Jack: the Cultural Politics of Race and Nation*. London: Hutchinson.

Hall, S. (1992) The question of cultural identity. In Hall, S., Held, D. and McGrew, T. (eds) *Modernity and its Futures*. Cambridge: Polity Press.

Harding, S. and Maxwell, R. (1997) Differences in the mortality of migrants. In Drever, F. and Whitehead, M. (eds) *Health Inequalities: Decennial Supplement Series DS no. 15*. London: The Stationery Office.

Harris, R., Tobias, M., Jeffreys, M., Waldegrave, K., Karlsen, S. and Nazroo, J. (2006a) Racism and health: the relationship between experience of racial discrimination and health in New Zealand, *Social Science and Medicine*, 63, 6, 1428–41.

Harris, R., Tobias, M., Jeffreys, M., Waldegrave, K., Karlsen, S. and Nazroo, J. (2006b) Māori health and inequalities in New Zealand: the impact of racism and deprivation, *The Lancet*, 367, 2005–09.

Heeringa, S.G., Wagner, J., Torres, M., Duan, N., Adams, T. and Berglund, P. (2004) Sample designs and sampling methods for the collaborative psychiatric epidemiology studies (CPES), *International Journal of Methods in Psychiatric Research*, 13, 221–40.

Heeringa, S.G., Torres, M., Sweetman, J. and Baser, R. (2006) *Sample Design, Weighting and Variance Estimation for the 2001–2003 National Survey of American Life (NSAL) Adult Sample, Technical Report*. Michigan: Survey Research Center of the Institute for Social Research at the University of Michigan.

Howard, D.L., Marshall, S.S., Kaufman, J.S. and Savatz, D.A. (2006) Variations in low birth weight and preterm delivery among blacks in relation to ancestry and nativity: New York City, 1998–2002, *Pediatrics*, 118, 5, e1399–405.

Jackson, J.S. and Antonucci, T.C. (2006) Physical and mental health consequences of aging-in-place and aging-out-of-place among black Caribbean immigrants, *Research in Human Development*, 2, 4, 229–44.

Jackson, J.S., Torres, M., Caldwell, C.H., Neighbors, H.W., Nesse, R.M., Taylor, R.J., Trierweiler, S.J. and Williams, D.R. (2004) The National Survey of American Life: a study of racial, ethnic and cultural influences on mental disorders and mental health, *International Journal of Methods in Psychiatric Research*, 13, 4, 196–207.

Karlsen, S. and Nazroo, J.Y. (2002) The relationship between racial discrimination, social class and health among ethnic minority groups, *American Journal of Public Health*, 92, 4, 624–31.

Krieger, N. (2000) Discrimination and health. In Berkman, L. and Kawachi, I. (eds) *Social Epidemiology*. Oxford: Oxford University Press.

Krieger, N., Rowley, D.L., Herman, A.A., Avery, B. and Philips, M.T. (1993) Racism, sexism, and social class: implications for studies of health, disease, and well-being, *American Journal of Preventive Medicine*, 9, Supplement, 82–122.

Marmot, M.G., Adelstein, A.M., Bulusu, L. and OPCS (1984) *Immigrant Mortality in England and Wales 1970–78: Causes of Death by Country of Birth*. London: HMSO.

McClements, L. (1977) Equivalence scales for children, *Journal of Public Economics*, 8, 191–210.

McLennan, W. and Madden, R. (1999) *The Health and Welfare of Australia's Aboriginal and Torres Strait Islander Peoples*. Commonwealth of Australia: Australian Bureau of Statistics.

Miles, R. (1982) *Racism and Migrant Labour*. London: Routledge and Kegan Paul.

Model, S. (1995) West Indian prosperity: fact or fiction? *Social Problems*, 42, 4, 535–53.

Nazroo, J.Y. (1998) Genetic, cultural or socio-economic vulnerability? Explaining ethnic inequalities in health, *Sociology of Health and Illness*, 20, 5, 710–30.

Nazroo, J.Y. (2001) *Ethnicity, Class and Health*. London: Policy Studies Institute.

Nazroo, J. (2003) The structuring of ethnic inequalities in health: economic position, racial discrimination and racism, *American Journal of Public Health*, 93, 2, 277–84.

Nazroo, J. (2004) Ethnic disparities in aging health: what can we learn from the United Kingdom? In Anderson, N., Bulatao, R. and Cohen, B. (eds) *Critical Perspectives on Racial and Ethnic Differentials in Health in Late Life*. Washington, D.C.: National Academies Press.

Nazroo, J.Y. and Karlsen, S. (2003) Patterns of identity among ethnic minority people: diversity and commonality, *Ethnic and Racial Studies*, 26, 5, 902–30.

Office for National Statistics (2006) *Migrants Entering or Leaving the United Kingdom and England and Wales, 2004*. London: Office for National Statistics.

Oliver, M.L. and Shapiro, T.M. (1995) *Black Wealth/White Wealth: a New Perspective on Racial Inequality*. New York: Routledge.

Pallotto, E.K., Collins, J.W. Jr. and David, R.J. (2000) Enigma of maternal race and infant birth weight: a population-based study of US-born Black and Caribbean-born Black women, *American Journal of Epidemiology*, 151, 11, 1080–5.

Pamuk, E., Makuc, D., Heck, K., Reuben, C. and Lochner, K. (1998) *Socioeconomic Status and Health Chartbook. Health, United States*. Hyattsville, Maryland: National Center for Health Statistics.

Pan American Health Organization (2001) *Equity in Health: from an Ethnic Perspective*. Washington D.C.: PAHO.

Platt, L. (2005) *Migration and Social Mobility: the Life Chances of Britain's Minority Ethnic Communities*. Bristol: Joseph Rowntree Foundation/Policy Press.

Polednak, A.P. (1989) *Racial and Ethnic Differences in Disease*. New York: Oxford University Press.

Rogers, R. (1992) Living and dying in the USA: sociodemographic determinants of death among blacks and whites, *Demography*, 29, 2, 287–303.

Sheth, T., Nair, C., Nargundkar, M., Anand, S. and Yusuf, S. (1999) Cardiovascular and cancer mortality among Canadians of European, south Asian and Chinese origin from 1979–93, *Canadian Medical Association Journal*, 161, 132–8.

Sidiropoulos, E., Jeffery, A., Mackay, S., Forgey, H., Chipps, C. and Corrigan, T. (1997) *South Africa Survey 1996/97*. Johannesburg: South African Institute of Race Relations.

Smith, P. and Prior, G. (1997) *The Fourth National Survey of Ethnic Minorities: Technical Report*. London: Social and Community Planning Research.

Sproston, K. and Nazroo, J. (eds) (2002) *Ethnic Minority Psychiatric Illness Rates in the Community (EMPIRIC)*. London: The Stationery Office.

Wild, S. and McKeigue, P. (1997) Cross sectional analysis of mortality by country of birth in England and Wales, *British Medical Journal*, 314, 705–10.

Williams, D.R. (1999) Race, SES, and health: the added effects of racism and discrimination, *Annals of the New York Academy of Sciences*, 896, 173–88.

Williams, D.R. (2001) Racial variations in adult health status: patterns, paradoxes and prospects. In Smelser, N.J., Wilson, W.J. and Mitchell, F. (eds) *America Becoming: Racial Trends and Their Consequences*. Washington DC: National Academy Press.

Williams, D.R., Lavizzo-Mourey, R. and Warren, R.C. (1994) The concept of race and health status in America, *Public Health Reports*, 109, 1, 26–41.

Wu, Z., Noh, S., Kaspar, V. and Schimmele, C. (2003) Race, Ethnicity and depression in Canadian society, *Journal of Health and Social Behaviour*, 44, 426–41.

Wu, Z. and Schimmele, C. (2005) Racial/ethnic variation in functional and self-reported health, *American Journal of Public Health*, 95, 710–16.

# 3

# Race and nutrition: an investigation of Black-White differences in health-related nutritional behaviours
# Peter Riley Bahr

## Introduction

Racial differences in the incidence and prevalence of chronic disease and premature morbidity are subjects of long-standing interest in the social sciences, and the differences between Blacks and Whites in this regard are striking, disturbing, and, by some accounts, widening (Byrd and Clayton 2002). For example, the life expectancy gap between White and Black males in the US *increased* in favour of Whites from 6.4 years to 6.9 years between 1983 and 1998, such that White males now have expected life spans 10.2 per cent greater than Blacks (Murphy 2000). Similarly, the life expectancy gap between White and Black females, while relatively stable over the 15-year period, continues to favour Whites by 5.2 years (7.0%).

To characterise this underlying mortality gap from a different perspective, Blacks and Whites differ substantially in estimates of survival rates to middle age. Only 73.3 per cent of Black males born in 1970 in the United States are expected to survive to age 50 compared with 87.6 per cent of White males in that birth cohort (Hayward *et al.* 2000). The gap between Blacks and Whites widens with age, as the expected 60-year survival rates drop to 57.5 per cent and 76.0 per cent, respectively (Hayward *et al.* 2000). Consistent with these statistics, the age-adjusted mortality rate for Blacks is 153 per cent of that of Whites (Murphy 2000).

Given the racial differences in life expectancy, survival rates, and overall mortality, it is not surprising to find that Blacks are disadvantaged relative to Whites, after age adjustment, on 12 of the 15 major causes of death in the US (Murphy 2000).[1] Among the top seven causes of death in 1998 (76.7% of all mortality) were five chronic diseases: heart disease, cancer, cerebrovascular disease (*e.g.* stroke), chronic obstructive pulmonary disease, and diabetes (the first, second, third, fourth, and seventh leading causes of death, respectively). Blacks were disadvantaged on all of these except chronic obstructive pulmonary disease. Blacks experienced a rate of mortality due to diabetes that was 240 per cent of the rate of Whites. Likewise, rates of mortality due to cerebrovascular disease, heart disease, and cancer were 178 per cent, 150 per cent, and 133 per cent of the rates of Whites. Taken together, these four chronic diseases constituted 61.2 per cent of all mortality in the US in 1998, and 56.8 per cent of *excess* deaths among Blacks.

In this paper, I test for differences between Blacks and Whites in nutritional behaviours with established associations to the development of heart disease, cancer, stroke, and diabetes. In addition to other variables, I control for socioeconomic status (SES) – the historically favoured explanation for racial disparities in health outcomes – in order to differentiate racial differences in nutritional behaviour from variation in nutritional behaviour associated with SES.[2] The purpose of these tests is to investigate whether empirical evidence supports the finding of Black-White disparities in health-related nutritional quality, independent of SES. Any such identified disparities would provide a rationale for the inclusion of nutritional quality in future data collection efforts and analyses addressing race and health. However, the data used here do not include measures of health, so the mediating role of nutrition in the race-health relationship cannot be ascertained, and this study must rely upon the existing body of literature supporting inverse associations between nutritional healthfulness and the development of chronic disease.

## Background

*Race and health*
There is a growing debate in the literature concerning whether race and the emphasis on different racial ethnic groups should continue to play a prominent role in health research. The argument against it is premised upon the facts that race is essentially an ideological construction, that race is not the basis upon which differential health outcomes can be explained, and that racial identification is not necessarily stable over time (Nazroo 1998, Smaje 1995). However, from an epidemiological perspective, race remains a significant predictor of health outcomes and, therefore, is arguably a matter worthy of continued empirical attention. This perspective is consistent with the historical inclination of socio-logical research concerning matters of race on a wide variety of substantive topics (*e.g.* Emerson *et al.* 2001, Hughes and Thomas 1998, Hunt *et al.* 2000). Moreover, Byrd and Clayton (2002: 564) argue against the reinforcement of 'the general perception in the scien-tific community that race and ethnicity research lacks rigor in conceptualization, terminol-ogy, and analysis', as it obscures the need to study, understand, and rectify continuing disparities in health outcomes among a health underclass defined, in part, along racial lines. Thus, it would be reasonable to conclude that, so long as multiple social inequalities intersect in categories of a variable labelled 'race', sociological inquiry into matters of race will remain important.

Nevertheless, race is a social construction, not a biological fact (Smaje 2000), and explanations for racial differences in health premised upon genetic dissimilarity for the most part have been dismissed (Hayward *et al.* 2000, Kong *et al.* 1994). In fact, fewer than one per cent of excess deaths among Blacks can be attributed to differential propensity for hereditary conditions (Leigh 1995). Thus, observed racial patterns of health outcomes are primarily consequences of social forces, rather than genetic history. As Smaje (2000: 114) explains, 'race in itself can never be invoked as a self-adequate explanation for patterns of health experience'. Nevertheless, as Schulz *et al.* (2000: 315) argue, '[r]ace, as a social construct, remains a powerful organizing feature of American social life, and racial categories both reflect and reinforce group differentials in power and access to social resources'. It follows that race is still a useful organising tool in efforts to understand and rectify inequity on many fronts, not the least of which is health (Gillum 2004).

*Socioeconomic status and the racial gap in health*
Historically, efforts to explain racial disparities in health in Western societies have focused on socioeconomic inequality and related correlates. In research dating back seventy years, Tibbits (1937) argued:

> [i]t is well known that the Negro population is less fortunately situated than the white in terms of income, education, opportunities for obtaining medical care, etc. Hence it seems relatively safe to assume that where there is variation in the degree of health among different economic and social groups of the white population and where Negroes show a higher rate of ill health than the whites, the explanation lies partly, at least, in the low-income status of the Negro (1937: 417–18).

Much of the subsequent research on the topic has adhered to this theory, attempting to explain observed racial differences in chronic disease and premature morbidity through mechanisms rooted in socioeconomic inequality. This theory invariably leads to the hypothesis that, once inequality and related variables are controlled, racial differences in the incidence and prevalence of chronic disease and premature morbidity will disappear. A number of recent studies have continued the longstanding investigation of this hypothesis (*e.g.* Lantz *et al.* 1998, Mutchler and Burr 1991, Potter 1991, Rogers 1992), and the findings of these studies support the argument that SES is an important explanatory variable in Black-White differences in a variety of health outcomes.

Much attention also has been given to the proximal causes of this health differential as distinct from the distal cause (*i.e.* socioeconomic inequality). The objective underlying this class of papers is the enumeration of the mechanisms connecting SES to health. Generally speaking, these proximal causes can be divided into two broad categories: (1) health risk behaviours that are correlated with SES, such as smoking, excessive alcohol consumption, and physical inactivity (*e.g.* Wickrama *et al.* 1999, Williams and Collins 1995), and (2) mechanisms arising directly from unequal distribution and access to resources, such as inadequate medical care, dangerous working conditions, and exposure to environmental toxins (*e.g.* Smith and Kington 1997a, Williams and Collins 1995). While this distinction is important, an extensive review of this topic is outside the scope of this paper.[3]

*The residual racial gap in health*
While research on the relationship between socioeconomic inequality and health has explained a substantial segment of the racial disparities in health outcomes, most research still documents an unexplained racial gap in health after adjustment for socioeconomic differences. For example, Rogers (1992) found that adjusting for income and a set of demographic variables narrowed the health gap between Blacks and Whites, but did not fully eliminate it. Christenson and Johnson (1995) found that the protective effect of education on mortality benefited Blacks less than Whites. Huie *et al.* (2003) found a residual Black disadvantage in mortality net of racial differences in educational attainment, income, net worth, and demographic variables. Mutchler and Burr (1991), adjusting for four indicators of SES as well as various demographic measures, found significant differences between older Blacks and Whites remaining on one of six self-reported health measures and an *increase* in the Black-White differential on another of the six measures. Ferraro and Farmer (1996) found significant disadvantages for Blacks relative to Whites in the incidence of serious illness, in the declination of self-assessed health over time, and in survival rates, despite numerous controls, including education, income, access to medical care, and prominent health risk behaviours. Ferraro *et al.* (1997) found greater erosion of self-assessed health and greater increases in the incidence of chronic illness and disability among Blacks compared with Whites, net of prior health conditions, SES, and other relevant controls. Schnittker (2004) found poorer self-assessed health and lower scores on an index of physical health among Blacks relative to Whites after controlling for education, income, and the income-health gradient as it varied by level of educational attainment. In a particularly comprehensive study, Hayward *et al.* (2000) found a significant Black-White health gap remaining on seven health outcomes after controlling for educational attainment, household income, wealth, availability of health insurance, numerous health risk behaviours, a number of psychosocial characteristics, and other variables.

While just a few of the recent analyses of racial differences in health are documented here, the findings of numerous similar studies agree that SES and its correlates can explain much, but not all, of the differences in health outcomes between Blacks and Whites (Crimmins *et al.* 2004, Livingston *et al.* 2004, Smith and Kington 1997a). Authors' conclusions often agree with the explanation offered by Williams and Collins (1995) in their review of the research addressing the White/Black health differential: 'within each level of SES, blacks generally have worse health than whites' (1995: 364). For example, Mutchler and

Burr (1991) note that, 'in terms of self-rated health and some associated health-related behaviours, older Blacks appear to have poorer health than Whites regardless of socioeconomic status' (1991: 353). Likewise, Ferraro and Farmer (1996) observe that, even after accounting for the SES differential between Blacks and Whites, 'there are important differences between the health status and health assessments of Black and White Americans' (1996: 37). Thus, prior research repeatedly demonstrates a stubborn racial gap in health outcomes that persists despite adjustment for socioeconomic inequality and related mechanisms.

Consequently, we must ask, what are the missing factors that will explain the residual racial differences in health outcomes? Socioeconomic status and related mechanisms have been controlled statistically, yet health differences between Whites and Blacks remain. Why?

*Explaining the unexplained racial gap in health*
One possible explanation for the residual racial gap in health lies in the nature of socioeconomic controls. Measures of SES can only approximate the complex and multifaceted construct, leaving open the possibility of unmeasured covariation between SES and health outcomes (Krieger 2000, Williams and Collins 1995). In other words, the inability of SES to explain fully the race-health relationship may be a methodological artifact (Kaufman *et al.* 1997). However, the persistence of the residual race-health relationship in numerous studies, using a variety of data, and despite increasingly comprehensive measures of SES, suggests at least the possibility of an excluded explanatory variable operating independently of SES.

Among the potential excluded explanatory variables, chronic stress caused by experiences of racial discrimination is receiving increased attention in the literature (*e.g.* Brondolo *et al.* 2003, Clark 2003, Clark and Adams 2004, Karlsen and Nazroo 2002, Krieger 2000, Krieger *et al.* 1993, Leigh 1995, Livingston 1994, Myers *et al.* 2004). This line of research argues that the excess of stressors experienced by Blacks as a result of both intergroup and intragroup racism contribute to a chronic elevated physiological stress response (Clark *et al.* 1999). This elevated stress response is associated with a range of health problems (Berkman and Kawachi 2000, Fremont and Bird 2000, Krieger 2000), including at least two chronic diseases for which Blacks are severely disadvantaged: coronary heart disease and diabetes (Livingston and Carter 2004).

Another potential explanatory variable that is sometimes mentioned, but which has received comparatively little empirical attention, is nutritional healthfulness. Interestingly, the health-related consequences of stress are intertwined closely with nutritional deficiencies. Prolonged stress tends to deplete physiological stores of, and increase physiological demand for, essential nutrients (Semmes 1996). In addition, healthy nutritional behaviours serve as a barrier against the damaging effects of prolonged stress, and poor nutrition itself can induce a physiological stress response (Semmes 1996). Lastly, chronic stress contributes to feelings of helplessness, hopelessness, and loss of control, which, in turn, are associated with a greater propensity for unhealthy lifestyle behaviours, such as poor nutritional choices (Kristenson *et al.* 2004). Thus, as they pertain to health outcomes, nutritional quality and stress are interrelated.

In addition to the interrelationship between nutrition and stress, nutritional quality has a well-established, strong, and *direct* relationship to health outcomes.[4] As Blocker (1994) observes, '[g]ood nutrition is crucial to the maintenance of health, and dietary factors contribute substantially to preventable chronic illness and premature death' (2004: 267). The relationships between nutrition and cardiovascular disease, cancer, stroke, and diabetes – the first, second, third, and seventh leading causes of death in the United States – are particularly strong (Blocker 1994). An estimated 30 per cent of all deaths due to cancer in the United States can be attributed to diet (Harvard School of Public Health 1996), and dietary and physical inactivity patterns collectively cause 14 per cent of all deaths in the United States, second only to tobacco as the leading cause of death (McGinnis and Foege 1993). In addition to cancer prevention, it is estimated that dietary changes could reduce the risk of heart attack and stroke by 20 per cent to 30 per cent and the risk of preventable diabetes by 50 per cent to 75 per cent (Foerster *et al.* 1999).

The specific dietary practices associated with reduced risk of chronic diseases have been demonstrated repeatedly and, due in part to expanding public health campaigns, are rapidly becoming topics of common knowledge (although not necessarily common practice). Weisburger (2000) details a number of nutritional factors associated with lowered risk of chronic disease, including: reduced consumption of dietary fat, increased consumption of cereal bran fibre (*e.g.* wholegrains), increased consumption of fruits and vegetables, reduced consumption of fried and broiled foods, and increased consumption of dairy products. The consumption of saturated fats is correlated positively with the incidence of cancer, while the consumption of fruits, vegetables, and fibre is associated negatively with the incidence of cancer (Bal *et al.* 2001, Colditz *et al.* 2000, Willett 1994). The incidence of diabetes has been connected to dietary fat consumption (Blair *et al.* 1996). Consumption of fruits, vegetables, and whole grains is associated with reduced risk of stroke (Joshipura *et al.* 1999, Liu *et al.* 2000a). The incidence of cardiovascular disease (the broader category of chronic disease within which belong strokes) varies negatively with fruit, vegetable, and dietary fibre consumption, and varies positively with fat consumption and dietary cholesterol (Blair *et al.* 1996, Foerster *et al.* 1999, Liu *et al.* 2000b, Stampfer *et al.* 2000, Willett 1994). Moreover, these findings of specific associations between particular nutritional behaviours and the incidence of chronic disease are buttressed by research linking reduced risk of several major chronic diseases to comprehensive patterns of healthful eating (Hu *et al.* 2000, McCullough *et al.* 2000a, 2000b, Willett 1994). Also of note, foods that are high in fat have an interesting dual role in the development of chronic disease in that, in addition to being associated with increased incidence of chronic disease, they also tend to supplant healthier nutritional choices that have protective effects (Kant 2000). In sum, there is general agreement between medical and health researchers that increased consumption of fruits, vegetables, grains, fibre-rich foods, beans, and dairy products, and decreased consumption of dietary fat, substantially reduce the risk of many of the most common chronic diseases, including cardiovascular disease, cancer, stroke, and diabetes (Eyre *et al.* 2004, Foerster *et al.* 1999, Willett 1994).

*Racial differences in nutritional behaviour*
The omission of nutritional behaviour from prior analyses of the race-health relationship introduces one of two assumptions. The analyses must assume either that nutritional healthfulness does not differ meaningfully between racial groups or, alternatively, that nutritional healthfulness, as one expression of the general class of personal health behaviours, is perfectly correlated with (accounted for by) measures of SES. In point of fact, when variation in nutritional quality is mentioned as a potential mediating variable underlying Black-White differences in health outcomes, it is most often attributed to disparities in SES (*e.g.* Siewe 1999, Wickrama *et al.* 1999) or, more specifically, to the high rate of poverty among Blacks (*e.g.* Blocker 1994, Kittler and Sucher 1989, Leigh 1995). In other words, nutritional quality is theorised to mediate the SES-health relationship, to the exclusion of any mediating role it may play in the residual race-health relationship existing independently of the SES-health relationship.

Given, however, that controlling for SES has not eliminated the Black-White health disparities, and given the well-established relationship between nutrition and health, it is reasonable to conclude that other causal channels linking race to nutritional quality are worthy of exploration. In support of this argument, there is limited evidence that suggests that health-related nutritional behaviours do vary between Blacks and Whites *independent of SES* (Airhihenbuwa *et al.* 1996, Lindquist *et al.* 2000, Popkin *et al.* 1996). But each of the several previous studies that address the race-nutrition relationship, independent of SES, evidence significant weaknesses. For example, the Popkin *et al.* (1996) study was weakened by an oversimplified operationalisation of SES as a trichotomous indicator and the absence of controls for important demographic variables. The Lindquist *et al.* (2000) study was limited to a small convenience sample of young children. The Airhihenbuwa *et al.* (1996) qualitative study relied upon respondents' own assessment of the effect of income on nutritional behaviour.

In addition to the limited empirical evidence, racial differences in health-related nutritional behaviours, independent of SES, would be expected for a number of reasons. Among these, Semmes (1996: 128) argues that nutritional deficiencies among Blacks are, in part, a result of 'maladaptive dietary practices rooted in slave culture', which is a perspective echoed in the interviews of Blacks conducted by Airhihenbuwa *et al.* (1996). Semmes (1996) argues that many present nutritional practices among Blacks are derived from 'slave culture', leading to an over-reliance on processed sugars and fatty meats and an underutilisation of fruits and vegetables. Kiple and King (1981) offer a contrasting, and much more detailed, assessment of Black nutrition under slavery, but the conclusion of significant nutritional deficiencies is the same. Other researchers have documented support for the influence of racial subcultures on dietary practices (*e.g.* Witt 1999) and, following from this, differences in nutritional quality (Kittler and Sucher 1989). In other words, cultural differences in preferred foods and cooking methods may contribute to differences in nutritional quality between Blacks and Whites, independent of SES. This causal explanation points to the importance of dietary patterns as components of social history and cultural memory, whereby knowledge and practice of nutritional behaviours are passed from generation to generation within families (Airhihenbuwa *et al.* 1996, Birch 1999).

One should note that, although this argument may be interpreted as 'blaming the victim', such an interpretation would be inaccurate. In particular, Semmes' (1996) use of the word 'maladaptive' appears, on the surface, to imply that Black slaves had some degree of choice in the nutritional content of their diets. Of course, this was not the case. Instead, this argument points to the opposite situation: a people group who, by enslavement, were deprived of their culture, including their food culture, and forced to adapt to a severe state of scarcity, dislocation, and dispossession.

Racial differences in nutritional quality also may be rooted in residential segregation, which is, itself, another expression of racial discrimination (Krieger 2000). Blacks are subjected to the highest rate of residential segregation of any minority group in the US (Steinmetz and Iceland 2003), and Blacks in the US are 144 per cent more likely to live in 'urban cores' than are Whites (McKinnon 2003). The overrepresentation of Blacks in urban cores holds even for affluent Blacks (Bullard 1994), indicating that poverty is not the only contributing factor to racial residential segregation (Emerson *et al.* 2001, Erbe 1975, Farley 1977, Farley and Frey 1994, Iceland and Wilkes 2006, Massey *et al.* 1987). In fact, the evidence suggests that improvements in SES among Blacks generally contribute little to rectifying rates of residential segregation (Hwang *et al.* 1985, Villemez 1980).

Urban neighbourhoods, poor neighbourhoods, and neighbourhoods in which the residents are predominantly Black are characterised disproportionately by the notable absence of major supermarkets and specialty food stores, requiring residents to rely on the similarly notable excess of small convenience stores, which generally have higher prices and limited nutritional options (Cheadle *et al.* 1991, Emmons 2000, Krebs-Smith and Kantor 2001, Leigh 1995, Macintyre and Ellaway 2000, Morland *et al.* 2002, Williams and Collins 2001). A similar problem, termed 'food deserts' to refer to urban environments that lack adequate nutritional infrastructure, has been identified in the UK (Wrigley 2002), and improvements in nutritional infrastructure have been found to be associated with improvements in dietary quality (Wrigley *et al.* 2002). Furthermore, the problem of limited nutritional infrastructure is exacerbated by the high rate of poverty among Blacks, which tends to limit transportation alternatives, placing access to supermarkets in suburban and predominantly White neighbourhoods out of reach (Krebs-Smith and Kantor 2001, Leigh 1995, Morland *et al.* 2002).

Interestingly, several recent studies have found that Black-White differences on certain health outcomes shrink substantially, or even to statistical insignificance, once variables that address overarching aspects of community context (*e.g.* neighbourhood affluence or poverty, neighbourhood population, residential stability, racial segregation) are controlled (*e.g.* Browning and Cagney 2003, Huie *et al.* 2002, Robert 1998, Robert and Lee 2002, Subramanian *et al.* 2005). While the mechanisms that mediate the relationship between community context and health outcomes are still unclear, and while these prior studies do not address nutritional infrastructure specifically, these findings represent an intriguing parallel to the literature that addresses racial segregation, nutritional infrastructure, and nutritional quality. In particular, the contextual variables found to be significant in prior studies would be expected (either intuitively or based on prior research) to be correlated with nutritional infrastructure. Thus, nutritional infrastructure may constitute a key mediating variable in the relationship between community context and racial health disparities.

Another potential explanation for racial differences in nutritional quality is disparities in the nutritional information provided to Blacks via race-targeted product advertising. Semmes (1996) notes that advertisers of alcohol and tobacco have a long history of targeting the Black segment of the market, which, as one would expect, is correlated with residential segregation (Williams and Collins 2001). Research has identified differences in nutritional advertising as well. For example, Pratt and Pratt (1996) found evidence of significant disparities in the healthfulness of nutritional product advertising in popular print media targeted at Blacks versus that targeted at Whites. Specifically, in a longitudinal content analysis, Pratt and Pratt found that one widely circulated magazine targeted at Whites (*Ladies' Home Journal*) carried significantly more nutritional advertising in support of dairy products, breads, cereals, vegetables, and fruits, than did two widely circulated magazines targeted at Blacks (*Ebony* and *Essence*). It follows that, to the extent that consumers depend upon nutritional advertising for making healthy nutritional choices, the gap in healthful nutritional information provided to Blacks may contribute to racial disparities in nutritional practice. In this regard, there is limited evidence that Blacks depend more heavily on advertising in making decisions about food choices than do Whites (Bock *et al.* 1998), potentially amplifying the effects of any differences in racially-targeted product advertising.

Finally, differences in the household compositions of Blacks and Whites may contribute to average differences in nutritional quality. Fully 58 per cent of all Black family households with children in the US are single-parent households, compared to 23 per cent of White family households with children (Fields 2004). While the effect of single-parent versus dual-parent living arrangements on adult nutritional quality is unknown, one might reason that single-parent living arrangements allow less time for grocery shopping and meal preparation, on average, than do dual-parent living arrangements. Thus, the excess of single-parent families among Blacks may contribute to a depression in average nutritional quality among Black adults.

## Hypothesis

In this analysis, I expect to find relatively fewer healthy nutritional behaviours among Blacks as compared with Whites, after adjustment for SES and other variables. In other words, I hypothesise that a relationship exists between race and nutritional quality that is independent of SES. Given the documented significance of nutritional quality in the development of the chronic diseases for which Blacks are disadvantaged relative to Whites, it follows that identifying significant racial differences in nutritional quality, independent of SES, would provide evidence that favours the potential utility of nutritional behaviour in future studies that seek to explain the residual racial gap in health. Any other finding would suggest that nutritional behaviour lacks explanatory utility in modeling racial disparities in health outcomes.

## The study

### Data and measures

*Data*

I use data collected by the California Department of Health Services (CDHS) in the California Dietary Practices Survey (CDPS) to test the hypothesis that Blacks differ significantly and negatively from Whites in terms of health-related nutritional behaviour, net of SES and other controls. The CDPS is a computer-assisted telephone interview of randomly selected California residents, employing a prescreened random digit dialing procedure. The sampling procedure draws upon a sampling frame that includes approximately 97 per cent of all households in California. The survey was administered in six biennial waves over 11 years (1989 through 1999) with samples varying in size from 1,000 to 1,703 (Foerster *et al.* 1999).

The CDPS collects data on a wide variety of health-related practices and beliefs. The centrepiece of the survey is a 24-hour dietary recall (Krebs-Smith and Kantor 2001), consisting of a comprehensive set of questions designed to elicit from the respondent all foods and beverages consumed during the previous 24 hours. The dietary data are then collapsed into a series of measures of key nutritional behaviours. In addition, a set of demographic measures is integrated into the survey.

*Dependent variable*

I selected the CDHS Healthy Eating Practices Index (HEPI) as the primary outcome measure for exploring racial differences in health-related nutritional behaviour (Foerster *et al.* 1999). The HEPI offers a global summary of important nutritional health behaviours and is consistent with previous findings of clusters of healthy and unhealthy nutritional behaviours (Hu *et al.* 1999). The HEPI is constructed by tallying points for key nutritional behaviours. In accordance with the earlier discussion, it addresses five dimensions of nutritional behaviour related to the incidence and prevalence of chronic disease and premature morbidity: fruit and vegetable consumption, consumption of dairy products, consumption of fibre/grains, consumption of beans, and consumption of fat. Specifically, a single point is added to a respondent's index score if he/she consumed at least one serving of fruit *and* at least one serving of vegetables (including fruit and vegetable juices) during the previous 24 hours. An additional point is added if a respondent's combined total number of servings of fruits, vegetables, and fruit/vegetable juices is at least five. A point is added if a respondent consumed any milk, yogurt, or cheese. An additional point is added for the consumption of any low fat milk, nonfat milk, or yogurt. Finally, a point each is added for the consumption of any wholegrain breads or corn tortillas, the consumption of high fibre cereals, and the consumption of any beans (Foerster *et al.* 1999).

The HEPI is weakened by three problems. First, the data upon which it is based are dichotomous rather than continuous, reducing actual variation in the measure. In analyses such as this one, however, the dichotomous nature of the variables composing the index tends to attenuate differences between groups, leading to underestimation, rather than overestimation, of coefficients. Likewise, the dichotomous nature of the variables tends to minimise bias associated with reporting error by ignoring small differences in respondent recall of number of servings consumed.

Secondly, the Healthy Eating Practice Index lacks specific focus on substantial sources of dietary fat, which, as noted earlier, play a dual role in the development of chronic disease. While the HEPI includes a single index point for the consumption of low fat and nonfat milk products, it does not address nutritional choices that would increase dramatically a respondent's total dietary fat. To treat this problem, the HEPI is modified here to include an additional point added to a respondent's score if he/she did *not* consume any deep-fried foods and fried snacks. To distinguish between the HEPI as defined by the California Department of Health Services and the modified HEPI employed here, I refer to the index used in this analysis as the Expanded Healthy Eating Practices Index (EHEPI).

Finally, it should be noted that the HEPI and EHEPI do not attempt to account for culturally specific eating behaviours, which may lead to racial bias in the measurement of nutritional healthfulness. However, empirical work on the topic of racially specific nutritional measurement (*e.g.* Schlundt *et al.* 2003) suggests that the HEPI and EHEPI have only two deficiencies in this regard. In particular, they do not account for added fats in cooking and seasoning vegetables, and they do not account for variation in the healthfulness of consumed meats (*e.g.* fish and poultry versus beef and pork) (Airhihenbuwa *et al.* 1996, Kumanyika and Adams-Campbell 1991, Schlundt *et al.* 2003).

Data were not collected for all components of the index in early sample years, so use of the index is confined to sample years 1993 through 1999, which are pooled for this analysis. Scores on the index range from a minimum of zero points, indicating very poor nutritional behaviours, to a maximum of eight points, indicating compliance with recommended healthy-eating practices. The mean EHEPI score in the pooled sample is 3.68, indicating that respondents exhibited less than half of the recommended nutritional behaviours on average. The standard deviation of the index is 1.69, and the reliability is 0.48.[5]

*Independent variables*

The primary independent variable of interest in this analysis is respondent's race, derived from a multicategorical measure of race in the CDPS data. For the purposes of this analysis, I consider only the dichotomy of Blacks versus Whites, excluding other racial/ethnic groups from the analytical sample. It should however be noted that the gross Black-White dichotomy employed in this study, and common in many prior studies, ignores ethnic distinctions in the historical origins and cultural contexts of respondents, thereby potentially masking important differences (Livingston and Carter 2004, Livingston *et al.* 2004,

Luke *et al.* 2001, McBarnette 1996, Nazroo 1998, Smaje 1995). While this is an unfortunate limitation of the data employed in this study and a matter to be considered in future research on the topic, it is consistent with the practice of prior research to make generalisations concerning Black-White differences in nutritional behaviour (Blocker and Forrester-Anderson 2004).

In order to distinguish the relationship between race and nutritional behaviour from the relationship between SES and nutritional behaviour, two measures of SES are included in the analysis: annual household income (measured on an eight-point ordinal scale) and educational attainment (measured on a five-point ordinal scale). In the interest of parsimoniousness, household income has been converted here into a continuous variable by calculating the midpoint of the income range indicated at each value of the ordinal scale. The large number of values of the income variable and the effective linearity of the relationship between average index score and income (as evidenced in Table 1) make this conversion feasible, and the net effect is improved model fit.

In addition to race and SES, three control variables are included in the models: sex, age (measured in years), and household size (total number of persons). The latter control is included to account for the divisionary effect of household size on household income (Kawachi 2000), which is important in this study because Black families tend to be larger than White families (Myers *et al.* 2004).

Measures of race (Black = 1; White = 0) and sex (female = 1; male = 0) are entered in the models as dichotomous variables. Household income, age, and household size are entered as continuous variables. Educational attainment is entered as a set of categorical variables with the comparison category of 'high school graduation'.

Note that several characteristics of the CDPS make it appropriate for use in identifying racial differences in health-related nutritional behaviour while controlling for SES, including the large sample sizes, probabilistic sampling method, numerous measures of nutritional behaviour, and dual measures of SES. However, the data do not contain measures of health and, therefore, cannot be used to determine if racial differences in nutritional behaviour contribute to racial disparities in health outcomes. Therefore, this analysis relies upon the existing body of literature supporting relationships between nutritional patterns and health outcomes to supply evidence for the importance and relevance of identified dietary differences between Blacks and Whites.

## Methods

My analysis involves four phases. First, I examine the bivariate relationships between each of the independent variables and the EHEPI. Secondly, I examine the bivariate relationships between race and each of the nutritional behaviours composing the EHEPI. Thirdly, I use nested random coefficient linear regression (Raudenbush and Bryk 2002) to examine the relationship between race and global nutritional healthfulness, first without, and then with, adjustment for SES.[6] Finally, I use random coefficient logistic regression to identify which of the eight health-related nutritional behaviours underlie the racial gap in overall nutritional practice.

Cases with missing data on any of the independent variables other than income (n = 68) or lacking sufficient information to assess the EHEPI (n = 213) are excluded, resulting in the loss of 281 cases (7.7% of the sample).[7] Cases for which income is missing (n = 277) had the missing datum replaced with an imputed value based on respondent's race, sex, age, household size, education, and year of data collection. A dummy variable indicating

Table 1 *Bivariate analysis of the Expanded Healthy Eating Practices Index (n = 3,350)*

| | | *Expanded Healthy Eating Practices Index* | | |
|---|---|---|---|---|
| | | *n* | *mean* | *std dev* |
| Race | White | 2,859 | 3.82 | 1.67 |
| | Black | 491 | 2.84 | 1.55 |
| | *t* | | 12.83*** | |
| Education | less than H.S. grad. | 219 | 3.26 | 1.66 |
| | H.S. graduate | 752 | 3.30 | 1.64 |
| | some college | 1,218 | 3.59 | 1.67 |
| | college graduate | 736 | 3.99 | 1.66 |
| | post graduate | 425 | 4.26 | 1.68 |
| | *F* | | 33.55*** | |
| Household income | <$10,000 | 330 | 3.28 | 1.73 |
| | $10,000–15,000 | 286 | 3.38 | 1.69 |
| | $15,001–20,000 | 257 | 3.53 | 1.79 |
| | $20,001–25,000 | 375 | 3.47 | 1.66 |
| | $25,001–35,000 | 359 | 3.70 | 1.76 |
| | $35,001–50,000 | 489 | 3.91 | 1.70 |
| | $50,001–65,000 | 327 | 3.90 | 1.57 |
| | >$65,000 | 650 | 3.85 | 1.62 |
| | missing income | 277 | 3.77 | 1.67 |
| | *F* | | 7.20*** | |
| Sex | male | 1,259 | 3.55 | 1.68 |
| | female | 2,091 | 3.75 | 1.70 |
| | *t* | | 3.38*** | |
| Age | 18–24 | 299 | 3.32 | 1.63 |
| | 25–34 | 584 | 3.43 | 1.60 |
| | 35–44 | 841 | 3.62 | 1.67 |
| | 45–54 | 559 | 3.64 | 1.70 |
| | 55–65 | 407 | 3.68 | 1.72 |
| | 65+ | 660 | 4.16 | 1.72 |
| | *F* | | 16.44*** | |
| Household size | 1 | 933 | 3.73 | 1.76 |
| | 2 | 1,071 | 3.75 | 1.68 |
| | 3 | 553 | 3.61 | 1.66 |
| | 4 | 468 | 3.62 | 1.65 |
| | 5 | 203 | 3.36 | 1.68 |
| | 6+ | 122 | 3.63 | 1.61 |
| | *F* | | 2.30* | |
| Year of data collection | 1993 | 788 | 3.87 | 1.72 |
| | 1995 | 688 | 3.78 | 1.72 |
| | 1997 | 1,003 | 3.51 | 1.64 |
| | 1999 | 871 | 3.61 | 1.69 |
| | *F* | | 7.90*** | |

*Notes*: *p ≤ 0.05; ***p ≤ 0.001.

Table 2 *Proportion of Whites versus Blacks exhibiting each of the nutritional behaviours composing the Expanded Healthy Eating Practices Index* ($n_{Whites}$ = 2,859; $n_{Blacks}$ = 491)

|  | One fruit and one vegetable | Five fruits and/or vegetables | Dairy products | Low fat dairy products | Wholegrain products | High fibre cereals | Beans | Deep-fried foods and snacks |
|---|---|---|---|---|---|---|---|---|
| White | 0.644 | 0.354 | 0.804 | 0.402 | 0.489 | 0.211 | 0.238 | 0.322 |
|  | (0.479) | (0.478) | (0.397) | (0.490) | (0.500) | (0.408) | (0.426) | (0.467) |
| Black | 0.507 | 0.255 | 0.613 | 0.173 | 0.479 | 0.071 | 0.218 | 0.481 |
|  | (0.500) | (0.436) | (0.488) | (0.379) | (0.500) | (0.258) | (0.413) | (0.500) |
| t | 5.78*** | 4.30*** | 9.38*** | 9.70*** | 0.44 | 7.30*** | 0.96 | 6.84*** |

*Notes*: ***p ≤ 0.001; standard deviations in parentheses.

this imputed condition is included in the models. The final analytical sample includes 3,350 respondents, of which 491 (14.7%) are Black.

## Analysis

### Bivariate analysis
Bivariate analyses of the relationships between the EHEPI and each of the independent variables are presented in Table 1. The relationship between race and the EHEPI is of primary interest, and this relationship is consistent with the hypothesis that Blacks differ significantly and negatively from Whites in terms of nutritional behaviour. While the mean index scores of both Whites and Blacks are less than half the possible range of the index (indicating nutritional practices that differ substantially and negatively from recommended guidelines), the mean EHEPI score for Blacks is 25.7 per cent less than the mean EHEPI score for Whites. Statistically significant variation in EHEPI scores also is observed across categories educational attainment, household income, sex, age, household size, and survey year.

Bivariate analyses of Black-White differences in the unadjusted probability of exhibiting each of the nutritional behaviours composing the EHEPI are presented in Table 2. The results indicate that Whites are more likely, on average, to exhibit six of the eight healthy nutritional behaviours. These include the consumption of one fruit and one vegetable, at least five fruits and/or vegetables, dairy products, high-fibre cereals, and lowfat/nonfat dairy products, and avoiding the consumption of deep-fried foods and snacks. Significant differences are not observed between Blacks and Whites in the probability of consuming wholegrain products nor in the probability of consuming beans.

### Regression analysis of the EHEPI
The results of the nested random coefficient linear regressions of the EHEPI on race, SES, sex, age, and household size are presented in Table 3. In Model 1, I regress the EHEPI on race, sex, age, and household size in order to estimate the average nutritional gap between Blacks and Whites, net of controls. In Model 2, I add education and household income to the variables included in Model 1 in order to determine if a residual racial gap in nutritional behaviour persists after the additional adjustment for SES.

The results presented in Model 1 reveal a substantial average difference in EHEPI scores between Blacks and Whites, net of sex, age, and household size. The average EHEPI score

Table 3 *Estimated coefficients and standard errors for two nested random coefficient linear regressions of the Expanded Healthy Eating Practices Index on selected variables (n = 3,350)*

| | | Expanded Healthy Eating Practices Index | |
| --- | --- | --- | --- |
| | | Model 1 | Model 2 |
| Race | Black (vs. White) | −0.888*** | −0.771*** |
| | | (0.098) | (0.095) |
| Education | <H.S. grad. (vs. H.S. grad) | | −0.049 |
| | | | (0.146) |
| | some college (vs. H.S. grad) | | 0.349*** |
| | | | (0.089) |
| | college grad. (vs. H.S. grad) | | 0.691*** |
| | | | (0.127) |
| | >college grad. (vs. H.S. grad) | | 0.882*** |
| | | | (0.164) |
| Household income | ×10$^3$ dollars | | 0.001 |
| | | | (0.002) |
| | missing income | | 0.004 |
| | | | (0.139) |
| Sex | female (vs. male) | 0.226* | 0.307** |
| | | (0.092) | (0.103) |
| Age | years | 0.013*** | 0.015*** |
| | | (0.002) | (0.002) |
| Household size | persons | 0.015 | 0.023 |
| | | (0.023) | (0.023) |
| Intercept | | 3.013*** | 2.437*** |
| | | (0.151) | (0.148) |

*Notes*: *p ≤ 0.05; **p ≤ 0.01; ***p ≤ 0.001; standard errors in parentheses.

of Blacks is estimated to be 0.89 points less than that of Whites, net of controls but prior to the introduction of SES. In Model 2, a net reduction in the race-nutrition relationship is observed following the introduction of SES. However, the average difference in health-related nutritional behaviour between Blacks and Whites continues to be significant and substantial, after adjustment for SES and the controls. The average EHEPI score of Blacks is estimated to be 0.77 points less than that of Whites, net of controls. In addition, the effect of educational attainment is strong and positive, with respondents who completed some college coursework, respondents who graduated from college, and respondents who participated in graduate school having average EHEPI scores that are 0.35, 0.69, and 0.88 points higher than that of respondents who attained only a high school diploma, respectively. Household income does not have a statistically significant relationship to the EHEPI, net of controls, nor is a significant difference in EHEPI scores observed for respondents who did not report income.

The consequential weight of the differences in nutritional behaviour between Blacks and Whites becomes evident when one accounts for the average index score across the sample. As mentioned earlier, the average EHEPI score in the sample is 3.68, indicating that respondents are accomplishing less than half of the recommended healthful nutritional recommendations. Given the globally low scores on the index, the estimated average discrepancy of 0.77 points between Blacks and Whites appears to be a substantively important nutritional difference.

*Regression analysis of the EHEPI components*
To explore which specific health-related nutritional behaviours underlie the significant difference in EHEPI scores between Blacks and Whites, I used random coefficient logistic regression to identify significant racial differences in each of the index component variables. All component variables were dichotomised to replicate the manner in which the variables are used to construct the EHEPI, and each variable was regressed on the set of independent variables employed in Model 2 (Table 3). The results are presented in Table 4.

Consistent with the findings on the global index of nutritional behaviour, Blacks vary significantly and negatively from Whites on five of the eight index components, after adjustment for SES, age, sex, and household size. Specifically, the estimates indicate that Whites are 169 per cent, 172 per cent, 77 per cent, and 38 per cent more likely than are Blacks to consume dairy products, lowfat/nonfat dairy products, high fibre cereals, and at least one serving each of fruits and vegetables, respectively. Conversely, Blacks are 75 per cent more likely to consume deep-fried foods and snacks than are Whites. Significant differences are not observed in the likelihood of consuming wholegrain products, beans, and at least five servings of fruits and/or vegetables.

The finding of a significant difference in the likelihood of consuming one fruit and one vegetable is surprising given the finding of no significant difference in the likelihood of consuming at least five servings of fruits and/or vegetables. In part, this discrepancy may be due to the low probability generally of consuming five fruits and/or vegetables. On average, only 33.9 per cent of all respondents consumed at least five fruits and/or vegetables, with 35.4 per cent of Whites and 25.5 per cent of Blacks meeting this health-related objective. However, to explore further this incongruity, I separately regressed (using random coefficient linear regression) total fruit consumption and total vegetable consumption on the set of independent variables employed in Model 2 (Table 3). The results, which are presented in Table 5, indicate that Blacks differ significantly and negatively from Whites in total number of servings of vegetables consumed, but not in total number of servings of fruit consumed. On average, Blacks consume 0.35 fewer servings of vegetables and vegetable juices per day than do Whites, after adjustment for SES and controls. Given the low level of vegetable consumption in the sample ($\bar{x}_{Total} = 1.99$; $\bar{x}_{Blacks} = 1.58$; $\bar{x}_{Whites} = 2.06$), it then is not surprising to find a significant difference between Blacks and Whites in the likelihood of consuming at least one serving of fruit and one serving of vegetables per day.

*Supplementary analysis*
As discussed earlier, the differences between Blacks and Whites in nutritional healthfulness could be attributed to one or more of several mechanisms, including culturally-based dietary practices, residential segregation, differences in nutritional knowledge, and the disproportionate number of single-parent Black households. While it is not possible to test these mediating mechanisms in a comprehensive fashion with the CDPS data, additional supporting evidence for several of these explanations can be found in these data. Specifically, evidence for the roles of culture and nutritional knowledge in explaining racial differences in nutritional behaviour can be found in differences between Blacks' and Whites' explanations for food choices.

To elaborate, in the 1999 wave of the CDPS a question was added to the interview schedule addressing the one main reason why each respondent does *not* eat more fruits and vegetables. The responses, which are collapsed here into six categories, include: *cost* (respondent indicates that fruits and vegetables are too expensive), *practice* (respondent is unsure how to determine quality of fruits and vegetables or unsure how to prepare them), *preference* (respondent does not like the taste of fruits and vegetables or respondent's family does not like them), *time* (respondent indicates that fruits and vegetables take too much

Table 4 Estimated coefficients and standard errors for the random coefficient logistic regressions of each component of the Expanded Health Eating Practices Index on selected variables (n = 3,350)

| | | One fruit and one vegetable | Five fruits and/or vegetables | Dairy products | Low fat dairy products | Wholegrain products | High fibre cereals | Beans | Deep-fried foods and snacks |
|---|---|---|---|---|---|---|---|---|---|
| Race | Black (vs. White) | -0.324* | -0.198 | -0.988*** | -1.001*** | -0.015 | -0.571*** | -0.154 | 0.557*** |
| | | (0.138) | (0.128) | (0.134) | (0.208) | (0.162) | (0.151) | (0.156) | (0.149) |
| Education | < H.S. grad. | -0.051 | 0.042 | -0.080 | -0.034 | 0.009 | -0.126 | 0.194 | 0.128 |
| | (vs. H.S. grad) | (0.206) | (0.245) | (0.283) | (0.198) | (0.242) | (0.347) | (0.308) | (0.192) |
| | some college | 0.410*** | 0.397*** | 0.079 | 0.339* | 0.221 | -0.011 | 0.187 | 0.045 |
| | (vs. H.S. grad) | (0.107) | (0.114) | (0.197) | (0.138) | (0.129) | (0.158) | (0.144) | (0.138) |
| | college grad. | 0.743*** | 0.582** | 0.254 | 0.597*** | 0.378** | 0.073 | 0.340* | -0.176 |
| | (vs. H.S. grad) | (0.148) | (0.189) | (0.191) | (0.232) | (0.123) | (0.186) | (0.144) | (0.132) |
| | > college grad. | 0.801** | 0.919*** | 0.216 | 0.663*** | 0.562*** | 0.170 | 0.399* | -0.271 |
| | (vs. H.S. grad) | (0.265) | (0.209) | (0.163) | (0.175) | (0.138) | (0.162) | (0.168) | (0.173) |
| Household income | ×10$^3$ dollars | 0.004 | 0.003 | -0.001 | 0.003 | -0.002 | -0.002 | -0.002 | 0.001 |
| | | (0.003) | (0.004) | (0.003) | (0.002) | (0.002) | (0.002) | (0.003) | (0.002) |
| | missing income | -0.010 | -0.197 | 0.045 | -0.045 | 0.040 | 0.027 | -0.030 | -0.165 |
| | | (0.154) | (0.307) | (0.277) | (0.219) | (0.187) | (0.249) | (0.282) | (0.156) |
| Sex | female (vs. male) | 0.438*** | 0.370* | -0.008 | 0.278** | -0.049 | 0.065 | -0.050 | -0.379*** |
| | | (0.084) | (0.148) | (0.089) | (0.097) | (0.116) | (0.155) | (0.142) | (0.106) |
| Age | years | 0.017*** | 0.015*** | -0.005 | 0.003 | 0.009** | 0.019*** | -0.006 | -0.016*** |
| | | (0.003) | (0.003) | (0.006) | (0.003) | (0.003) | (0.003) | (0.003) | (0.003) |
| Household size | persons | 0.038 | 0.041 | 0.071 | -0.076* | 0.054 | 0.065 | 0.030 | 0.079** |
| | | (0.033) | (0.032) | (0.058) | (0.037) | (0.029) | (0.044) | (0.036) | (0.030) |
| Intercept | | -1.144*** | -2.140*** | 1.423*** | -1.022*** | -0.760*** | -2.309*** | -1.059*** | 0.070 |
| | | (0.200) | (0.200) | (0.265) | (0.282) | (0.183) | (0.358) | (0.306) | (0.203) |

Notes: *p ≤ 0.05; **p ≤ 0.01; ***p ≤ 0.001; standard errors in parentheses.

Table 5 *Estimated coefficients and standard errors for the random coefficient linear regressions of total fruit consumption and total vegetable consumption on selected variables (n = 3,350)*

|  |  | Total fruit consumption | Total vegetable consumption |
|---|---|---|---|
| Race | Black (vs. White) | −0.005 | −0.347** |
|  |  | (0.186) | (0.114) |
| Education | <H.S. grad. (vs. H.S. grad) | −0.055 | −0.129 |
|  |  | (0.247) | (0.153) |
|  | some college (vs. H.S. grad) | 0.231* | 0.194* |
|  |  | (0.096) | (0.083) |
|  | college grad. (vs. H.S. grad) | 0.463*** | 0.345** |
|  |  | (0.124) | (0.128) |
|  | >college grad. (vs. H.S. grad) | 0.554** | 0.591*** |
|  |  | (0.170) | (0.154) |
| Household income | $\times 10^3$ dollars | 0.003 | 0.002 |
|  |  | (0.002) | (0.003) |
|  | missing income | 0.044 | −0.177 |
|  |  | (0.161) | (0.154) |
| Sex | female (vs. male) | 0.219* | 0.173* |
|  |  | (0.092) | (0.071) |
| Age | years | 0.016*** | 0.004* |
|  |  | (0.003) | (0.002) |
| Household size | persons | 0.024 | 0.049 |
|  |  | (0.026) | (0.028) |
| Intercept |  | 0.567*** | 1.357*** |
|  |  | (0.171) | (0.169) |

*Notes*: *p ≤ 0.05; **p ≤ 0.01; ***p ≤ 0.001; standard errors in parentheses.

time to prepare), *habit* (respondent is not in the habit of, or not used to, eating fruits and vegetables), and *knowledge* (respondent believes that he/she already consumes enough fruits and vegetables). Given the literature addressing Black-White differences in nutritional behaviour, several preliminary hypotheses concerning this variable may be posited. On the one hand, if poverty is the primary reason for Black-White differences in nutritional behaviour (Blocker 1994, Kittler and Sucher 1989, Leigh 1995, Siewe 1999, Wickrama *et al.* 1999), and if the controls for SES addressed in this study are insufficient, one would expect to find that Blacks are more likely than are Whites to report that the *cost* of fruits and vegetables is prohibitive, even after accounting for household income and educational attainment. On the other hand, if culturally based food practices contribute to Black-White differences in nutritional behaviour (Semmes 1996), one would expect to find that Blacks are more likely to report *preference* and *habit* as the primary reasons for not eating more fruits and vegetables. In other words, to the extent that personal taste and food preparation habits are a product of culture, a finding of racial differences in the likelihood of reporting preference and habit as primary reasons for not consuming more fruits and vegetables represents evidence for culture as an obstacle to healthy nutritional behaviour. Lastly, if differences in nutritional *knowledge*, which may be, in part, a consequence of racially targeted advertising (Pratt and Pratt 1996), contribute to Black-White differences in nutritional behaviour, one would expect to find that Blacks are more likely than are Whites to report that they believe they eat enough fruits and vegetables, net of actual consumption.

Table 6 *Estimated coefficients and standard errors for the multinomial logistic regression of respondent's one main reason for not eating more fruits and vegetables on selected variables (n = 726; comparison category = Cost)*

|  |  | Practice | Preference | Time | Habit | Knowledge |
|---|---|---|---|---|---|---|
| Race | Black (vs. White) | −0.075 | 1.216* | 0.051 | 0.849* | 0.914* |
|  |  | (0.747) | (0.480) | (0.451) | (0.423) | (0.449) |
| Education | < H.S. grad. | −0.879 | 0.706 | −0.388 | −0.168 | 0.228 |
|  | (vs. H.S. grad) | (1.161) | (0.613) | (0.592) | (0.546) | (0.574) |
|  | some college | 0.436 | 0.270 | 0.409 | 0.401 | 0.561 |
|  | (vs. H.S. grad) | (0.571) | (0.485) | (0.401) | (0.393) | (0.424) |
|  | college grad. | 0.107 | 0.267 | 0.430 | 0.455 | 0.459 |
|  | (vs. H.S. grad) | (0.713) | (0.610) | (0.513) | (0.509) | (0.548) |
|  | > college grad. | 0.168 | 0.828 | 0.828 | 0.411 | 1.310 |
|  | (vs. H.S. grad) | (1.070) | (0.925) | (0.832) | (0.843) | (0.848) |
| Household income | ×10³ dollars | 0.041** | 0.038** | 0.042*** | 0.042*** | 0.031** |
|  |  | (0.014) | (0.012) | (0.011) | (0.011) | (0.011) |
|  | missing income | −0.359 | −0.490 | −0.352 | −0.111 | −0.757 |
|  |  | (0.790) | (0.681) | (0.565) | (0.547) | (0.608) |
| Sex | female (vs. male) | −0.391 | −0.277 | 0.042 | −0.426 | −0.466 |
|  |  | (0.487) | (0.415) | (0.362) | (0.354) | (0.374) |
| Age | years | 0.015 | −0.005 | 0.000 | 0.000 | 0.029** |
|  |  | (0.013) | (0.011) | (0.009) | (0.009) | (0.010) |
| Household size | persons | −0.067 | −0.134 | 0.017 | −0.008 | 0.045 |
|  |  | (0.172) | (0.135) | (0.113) | (0.111) | (0.118) |
| Consumption | total servings | 0.016 | −0.001 | 0.051 | −0.033 | 0.125* |
|  | of f&v | (0.082) | (0.070) | (0.059) | (0.060) | (0.060) |
| Intercept |  | −2.086* | −0.528 | −0.398 | 0.221 | −2.147** |
|  |  | (1.037) | (0.811) | (0.687) | (0.668) | (0.750) |

*Notes*: *p ≤ 0.05; **p ≤ 0.01; ***p ≤ 0.001; standard errors in parentheses.

To explore these preliminary hypotheses, I present in Table 6 a multinomial logistic regression of the primary reason for not eating more fruits and vegetables on race, education, household income, sex, age, household size, and total fruit and vegetable consumption. The results indicate that, relative to the likelihood of reporting that fruits and vegetables are 'too expensive', Blacks are significantly more likely than are Whites to report that they, or their families, do not like the taste (*preference*), that they are not in the habit of eating fruits and vegetables (*habit*), and that they believe they consume enough fruits and vegetables (*knowledge*). These findings indicate that cost is not the primary reason for Black-White differences in nutritional behaviour, at least as far as the consumption of fruits and vegetables is concerned. Rather, the evidence supports the argument that culture and knowledge are primary reasons for Black-White differences in consumption.[8]

## Discussion

In comparing Blacks and Whites in California, the findings presented here indicate that health-related nutritional behaviours differ significantly and in a direction consistent with the well-documented differential in health outcomes between the two groups, independent of SES.

Blacks exhibit less healthy nutritional practice, relative to Whites, both globally and across a range of specific nutritional behaviours, after adjustment for the effects of educational attainment, household income, sex, age, and household size. Blacks do not exhibit nutritional behaviours that are healthier than those of Whites on any of the variables addressed in this study. In a supplementary analysis, I find that, at least as far as fruit and vegetable consumption is concerned, Blacks are more likely than are Whites to offer explanations for their nutritional choices that do not include the issue of cost, which adds to the credibility of a finding of a race-nutrition relationship that is independent of SES. Instead, the evidence suggests that culture and knowledge are the primary reasons Blacks eat fewer fruits and vegetables than do Whites, which is consistent with deductions drawn from the literature (e.g. Airhihenbuwa et al. 1996, Bock et al. 1998, Kiple and King 1981, Pratt and Pratt 1996, Semmes 1996, Witt 1999). Thus, considered globally, the findings presented here suggest that a relationship between race and nutritional healthfulness exists that is independent of SES.

Additionally, my findings provide indirect evidence of the causal role of residential segregation in racial differences in nutritional behaviour, specifically in the types of foods for which Blacks and Whites are found to differ in consumption. As discussed earlier in this paper, Blacks tend to be subjected to intense residential segregation into neighbourhoods often characterised by limited nutritional infrastructure (e.g. Bullard 1994, Cheadle et al. 1991, Emmons 2000, Hwang et al. 1985, Krebs-Smith and Kantor 2001, Leigh 1995, McKinnon 2003, Morland et al. 2002, Steinmetz and Iceland 2003). Consistent with this, significant differences were not identified between Blacks and Whites in the consumption of wholegrain products and beans, which are relatively inexpensive foods that require little special handling or storage, that have extended shelf lives, and that are subject to wide distribution across a diverse range of retail establishments. Blacks were found to consume significantly more deep-fried foods and snacks, which also require little special handling, are relatively inexpensive, are widely distributed, and represent a substantial proportion of the available nutritional choices at fast food restaurants and convenience stores. Conversely, the foods Blacks were found to be less likely to consume all require either special handling or special storage arrangements (e.g. dairy products and vegetables) and, therefore, are less widely distributed across a range of retail establishments, or are somewhat specialised items (e.g. high fibre cereals) confined primarily to supermarkets and large grocery stores. The absence of significant differences in fruit/fruit juice consumption may be explained by the wider availability of fruits and fruit juices relative to vegetables and vegetable juices. Thus, the findings of this analysis are consistent with the argument that racial residential segregation and neighbourhood nutritional infrastructure play a role in Black-White differences in health-related nutritional behaviour.

This study has, however, a number of important limitations. First, the data do not contain measures of SES other than educational attainment and household income. While these are well-established and useful measures of SES (Williams and Collins 1995), they do not allow for the 'fine grain' distinctions in social class discussed by Bartley and colleagues (1998) or account for other potentially important aspects of SES, such as accumulated wealth, income source, labour market position, or material deprivation (e.g. Cooper 2002, Huie et al. 2003, Macintyre et al. 2003, Smaje 1995, Smith and Kington 1997b). Thus, this study faces the same methodological problem that arises in all studies involving race and SES as primary independent variables, and perhaps to an even greater degree due to the limitations of the measures of SES available in these data. Namely, one cannot be certain if the observed residual racial differences (in this case, in nutritional behaviour) are a product of forces other than SES (as I argue) or simply a consequence of the operationalisation of SES (Cooper and Kaufman 1998, Kaufman et al. 1997, Nazroo 1998). In other words, the documented residual gap in nutritional healthfulness between Blacks and Whites yet may be a consequence of differences in SES between Blacks and Whites, albeit aspects of SES that are not addressed in this study.

Secondly, while my findings indicate what appears to be a sizeable residual racial gap in nutritional healthfulness, and while prior evidence suggests that nutritional healthfulness is strongly correlated with health outcomes, the absence of direct measures of health in the data does not allow for a determination concerning whether the nutritional differences identified here are of sufficient magnitude to explain the residual health differences between Blacks and Whites documented in previous studies. Moreover, the threshold at which poor nutritional behaviour begins to affect health outcomes is unclear. Thus, it is uncertain if the Black-White gap in nutrition documented here is large enough to make it a plausible explanation for the health gap.

Thirdly, while the results of this study are generalisable to California, caution must be exercised in generalising these findings to other populations. In particular, the wide availability and comparably low prices of fruits and vegetables in California generally would be expected to attenuate differences in EHEPI scores across strata of SES, leading to smaller coefficients than would be expected in geographic locales with higher prices. The other nutritional components of the EHEPI would be expected to vary less in availability and price, and therefore should have associated coefficients that are more stable vis-à-vis locale. Perhaps more importantly, the intervening mechanisms posited here to explain racial differences in nutrition, particularly culture and residential segregation, do vary regionally. Dietary practices associated with culture are not homogenous throughout the US, nor is the degree of residential segregation. Thus, considered globally, the generalisability of the findings is uncertain.

## Conclusion

The findings I present here suggest that previous studies, which have depended largely upon SES and correlates of SES as explanations for health differences between Blacks and Whites, may have excluded a potentially important variable that may aid in explaining racial disparities in health outcomes. However, these results cannot verify conclusively that nutritional behaviour explains the 'unexplained' racial gap in health outcomes left after adjustment for socioeconomic status. Such a conclusion would require a comparative longitudinal study of health outcomes that monitors nutritional behaviour, as well as other health risk behaviours, socioeconomic status, and demographic characteristics. Nevertheless, with due consideration to the limitations of this study, my findings support a conclusion in favour of the potential scientific fruitfulness of nutritional behaviour, independent of socioeconomic status, for explaining racial disparities in health outcomes. Given the well-established relationship between nutritional quality and chronic disease, the significant racial differences in nutritional behaviour identified here indicate that nutritional behaviour should be considered in future empirical work focused on explaining racial differences in health outcomes. Moreover, these findings constitute a step forward in the study of nutrition and inequalities, as recommended in prior work (Murcott 2002).

## Acknowledgements

I am grateful for the assistance of the following individuals: Diana Cassidy, Rodney Clark, Diane Felmlee, Susan Foerster, Christopher Gardner, Jennifer Gregson, Janet Hankin, Willard Hom, Renato Littaua,

Monica Martin, Michelle Oppen, Mark Regnerus, Xiaoling Shu, and Sharon Sugerman. I thank the Public Health Institute and Freeman, Sullivan & Company for access to the California Dietary Practices Survey data, and Mark Hudes for his assistance in preparing the data. Finally, I thank the editors and anonymous referees of *Sociology of Health & Illness* for their insightful recommendations concerning improving this work. This research was made possible by funds received from the Cancer Research Fund under grant agreement No. 98-16026 with the Department of Health Services, Cancer Research Program.

## Notes

1   Chronic obstructive pulmonary disease, suicide, and Alzheimer's are the three major causes of mortality in the US for which Whites are disadvantaged relative to Blacks.
2   As noted by one referee, socioeconomic status is a complex and sometimes contested concept. In the interest of clarity, the phrase *socioeconomic status*, used at numerous points in this paper, refers to the concept marked by the intersection of education, occupation, income, and prestige (Hauser and Warren 1997).
3   For a recent and particularly comprehensive discussion of the pathways connecting SES to health, please see Crimmins *et al.* (2004).
4   Kumanyika (1993) argues that the nutrition-health relationship may be defined along three differing dimensions: undernutrition, the treatment of conditions that respond to dietary adjustments, and the increased risk of developing chronic diseases associated with poor nutrition. The primary theoretical focus of this paper as it pertains to the nutrition-health relationship is the last of the three.
5   This reliability score indicates a moderate intercorrelation among the items. However, the theoretical foundation of the items selected for the index is of substantially greater importance for this analysis than the interrelationship of the items, so the moderate reliability is of minor concern.
6   Random coefficient regression is appropriate in this case to account for variation in nutritional behaviour across the several waves of the biennial survey.
7   The mean EHEPI scores of respondents who were included and those who were excluded due to missing data on the independent variables were found to not differ significantly ($\bar{x}_{excluded} = 3.53$; $\bar{x}_{included} = 3.68$; t = 0.655).
8   The finding that *knowledge* is a primary reason for deficient fruit and vegetable consumption among Blacks is opposed to some extent by prior findings of no difference between Blacks and Whites in the accuracy of perceptions of dietary healthfulness (Airhihenbuwa *et al.* 1996, Variyam *et al.* 2001). Although the finding presented here does not contradict precisely the findings of prior studies, the discrepancy is worthy of further consideration in future research.

## References

Airhihenbuwa, C.O., Kumanyika, S., Agurs, T.D., Lowe, A., Saunders, D. and Morssink, C.B. (1996) Cultural aspects of African American eating patterns, *Ethnicity and Health*, 1, 245–60.
Bal, D.G., Foerster, S.B., Backman, D.R. and Lyman, D.O. (2001) Dietary change and cancer: challenges and future direction, *Journal of Nutrition*, 131, 181–5.
Bartley, M., Blane, D. and Smith, G.D. (1998) Introduction: beyond the Black Report, *Sociology of Health and Illness*, 20, 5, 563–77.
Berkman, L.F. and Kawachi, I. (2000) A historical framework for social epidemiology. In Berkman, L.F. and Kawachi, I. (eds) *Social Epidemiology*. Oxford: Oxford University Press.
Birch, L.L. (1999) Development of food preferences, *Annual Review of Nutrition*, 19, 41–62.
Blair, S.N., Horton, E., Leon, A.S., Lee, I.M., Drinkwater, B.L., Dishman, R.K., Mackey, M. and Kienholz, M.L. (1996) Physical activity, nutrition, and chronic disease, *Medicine and Science in Sports and Exercise*, 28, 335–49.

Blocker, D.E. (1994) Nutrition concerns of Black Americans. In Livingston, I.L. (ed.) *Handbook of Black American Health*. Westport: Greenwood Press.

Blocker, D. and Forrester-Anderson, I.T. (2004) Nutrition concerns of Black Americans. In Livingston, I.L. (ed.) *Praeger Handbook of Black American Health, Volume 1*. Westport: Praeger.

Bock, M.A., Read, M., Bruhn, C., Auld, G., Gabel, K., Lauritzen, G., Lee, Y., McNulty, J., Medeiros, D., Newman, R., Nitzke, S., Ortiz, M., Schutz, H. and Sheehan, E. (1998) Gender and ethnic differences in factors that influence food intake, *Journal of Consumer Studies and Home Economics*, 22, 25–37.

Brondolo, E., Rieppi, R., Kelly, K.P. and Gerin, W. (2003) Perceived racism and blood pressure: a review of the literature and conceptual and methodological critique, *Annals of Behavioral Medicine*, 25, 55–65.

Browning, C.R. and Cagney, K.A. (2003) Moving beyond poverty: neighborhood structure, social processes, and health, *Journal of Health and Social Behavior*, 44, 552–71.

Bullard, R.D. (1994) Urban infrastructure: social, environmental, and health risks to African Americans. In Livingston, I.L. (ed.) *Handbook of Black American Health*. Westport: Greenwood Press.

Byrd, W.M. and Clayton, L.A. (2002) *An American Health Dilemma: Race, Medicine, and Health Care in the United States 1900–2000, Volume 2*. New York: Routledge.

Cheadle, A., Psaty, B.M., Curry, S., Wagner, E., Diehr, P., Koepsell, T. and Kirstal, A. (1991) Community-level comparisons between the grocery store environment and individual dietary practices, *Preventive Medicine*, 20, 250–61.

Christenson, B.A. and Johnson, N.E. (1995) Educational inequality in adult mortality: an assessment with death certificate data from Michigan, *Demography*, 32, 215–29.

Clark, R. (2003) Self-reported racism and social support predict blood pressure reactivity in Blacks, *Annals of Behavioral Medicine*, 25, 127–36.

Clark, R. and Adams, J.H. (2004) Moderating effects of perceived racism on John Henryism and blood pressure reactivity in Black female college students, *Annals of Behavioral Medicine*, 28, 126–31.

Clark, R., Anderson, N.B., Clark, V.R. and Williams, D.R. (1999) Racism as a stressor for African Americans: a biopsychological model, *American Psychologist*, 54, 805–16.

Colditz, G.A., Atwood, K.A., Emmons, K., Monson, R.R., Willett, W.C., Trichopoulos, D. and Hunter, D.J. (2000) Harvard report on cancer prevention, Volume 4: Harvard cancer risk index, *Cancer Causes and Control*, 11, 477–88.

Cooper, H. (2002) Investigating socio-economic explanations for gender and ethnic inequalities in health, *Social Science & Medicine*, 54, 693–706.

Cooper, R.S. and Kaufman, J.S. (1998) Race and hypertension: science and nescience, *Hypertension*, 32, 813–16.

Crimmins, E.M., Hayward, M.D. and Seeman, T.E. (2004) Race/ethnicity, socioeconomic status, and health. In Anderson, N.B., Bulatao, R.A. and Cohen, B. (eds) *Critical Perspectives on Racial and Ethnic Differences in Health in Late Life*. Washington, D.C.: The National Academics Press.

Emerson, M.O., Chai, K.J. and Yancey, G. (2001) Does race matter in residential segregation?: Exploring the preferences of White Americans, *American Sociological Review*, 66, 922–35.

Emmons, K.M. (2000) Health behaviors in a social context. In Berkman, L.F. and Kawachi, I. (eds) *Social Epidemiology*. Oxford: Oxford University Press.

Erbe, B.M. (1975) Race and socioeconomic segregation, *American Sociological Review*, 40, 801–12.

Eyre, H., Kahn, R. and Robertson, R.M. (2004) Preventing cancer, cardiovascular disease, and diabetes: a common agenda for the American Cancer Society, the American Diabetes Association, and the American Heart Association, *CA: a Cancer Journal for Clinicians*, 54, 190–207.

Farley, R. (1977) Residential segregation in urbanized areas in the United States in 1970: an analysis of social class and racial differences, *Demography*, 14, 497–518.

Farley, R. and Frey, W.H. (1994) Changes in the segregation of Whites and Blacks during the 1980s: small steps towards a more integrated society, *American Sociological Review*, 59, 23–45.

Ferraro, K.F. and Farmer, M.M. (1996) Double jeopardy to health hypothesis for African Americans: analysis and critique, *Journal of Health and Social Behavior*, 37, 27–43.

Ferraro, K.F., Farmer, M.M. and Wybraniec, J.A. (1997) Health trajectories: long-term dynamics among Black and White adults, *Journal of Health and Social Behavior*, 38, 38–54.

Fields, J. (2004) America's families and living arrangements: 2003, *Current Population Reports, P20-553*. Washington, D.C.: U.S. Census Bureau.

Foerster, S.B., Wu, S., Gregson, J., Hudes, M. and Fierro, M.P. (1999) *California Dietary Practices Survey: Overall Trends in Healthy Eating among Adults, 1989–1997, a Call to Action, Part 2.* Sacramento: California Department of Health Services.

Fremont, A.M. and Bird, C.E. (2000) Social and psychological factors, physiological processes, and physical health. In Bird, C.E., Conrad, P. and Fremont, A.M. (eds) *Handbook of Medical Sociology.* New Jersey: Prentice Hall.

Gillum, R.F. (2004) Trends in cardiovascular diseases: an overview of evolving disparities. In Livingston, I.L. (ed.) *Praeger Handbook of Black American Health, Volume 1.* Westport: Praeger.

Harvard School of Public Health (1996) Harvard report on cancer prevention, Volume I: Causes of human cancer, *Cancer Causes and Control*, 7.

Hauser, R.M and Warren, J.R. (1997) Socioeconomic indexes for occupations: a review, update, and critique, *Sociological Methodology*, 27, 177–298.

Hayward, M.D., Crimmins, E.M., Miles, T.P. and Yang, Y. (2000) The significance of socioeconomic status in explaining the racial gap in chronic health conditions, *American Sociological Review*, 65, 910–30.

Hu, F.B., Rimm, R., Smith-Warner, S.A., Feskanich, D., Stampfer, M.J., Ascherio, A., Sampson, L. and Willett, W.C. (1999) Reproducibility and validity of dietary patterns assessed with a food-frequency questionnaire, *American Journal of Clinical Nutrition*, 69, 243–9.

Hu, F.B., Rimm, E.B., Stampfer, M.J., Ascherio, A., Spiegelman, D. and Willett, W.C. (2000) Prospective study of major dietary patterns and risk of coronary heart disease in men, *American Journal of Clinical Nutrition*, 72, 912–21.

Hughes, M. and Thomas, M.E. (1998) The continuing significance of race revisited: a study of race, class, and quality of life in America, 1972 to 1996, *American Sociological Review*, 63, 785–95.

Huie, S.A.B., Hummer, R.A. and Rogers, R.G. (2002) Individual and contextual risks of death among race and ethnic groups in the United States, *Journal of Health and Social Behavior*, 43, 359–81.

Huie, S.A.B., Krueger, P.M., Rogers, R.G. and Hummer, R.A. (2003) Wealth, race, and mortality, *Social Science Quarterly*, 84, 667–84.

Hunt, M.O., Jackson, P.B., Powell, B. and Steelman, L.C. (2000) Color-blind: the treatment of race and ethnicity in social psychology, *Social Psychology Quarterly*, 63, 352–64.

Hwang, S.S., Murdock, S.H., Parpia, B. and Hamm, R.R. (1985) The effects of race and socioeconomic status on residential segregation, 1970–80, *Social Forces*, 63, 732–47.

Iceland, J. and Wilkes, R. (2006) Does socioeconomic status matter? Race, class, and residential segregation, *Social Problems*, 53, 248–73.

Joshipura, K.J., Ascherio, A., Manson, J.E., Stampfer, M.J., Rimm, E.B., Speizer, F.E., Hennekens, C.H., Spiegelman, D. and Willett, W.C. (1999) Fruit and vegetable intake in relation to risk of ischemic stroke, *Journal of the American Medical Association*, 282, 1233–9.

Kant, A.K. (2000) Consumption Of energy-dense, nutrient-poor foods by adult Americans: nutritional and health implications. The third national health and nutrition examination survey, 1988–1994, *American Journal of Clinical Nutrition*, 72, 929–36.

Karlsen, S. and Nazroo, J.Y. (2002) Agency and structure: The impact of ethnic identity and racism on the health of ethnic minority people, *Sociology of Health and Illness*, 24, 1, 1–20.

Kaufman, J.S., Cooper, R.S. and McGee, D.L. (1997) Socioeconomic status and health in Blacks and Whites: the problem of residual confounding and the resiliency of race, *Epidemiology*, 8, 621–8.

Kawachi, I. (2000) Income inequality and health. In Berkman, L.F. and Kawachi, I. (eds) *Social Epidemiology*. Oxford: Oxford University Press.

Kiple, K.F. and King, V.H. (1981) *Another Dimension to the Black Diaspora: Diet, Disease, and Racism.* Cambridge: Cambridge University Press.

Kittler, P.G. and Sucher, K. (1989) *Food and Culture in America*. New York: Van Nostrand Reinhold.

Kong, S.B., Kong, W. and McAllister, S.B. (1994) Politics and health: the coming agenda for a multiracial and multicultural society. In Livingston, I.L. (ed.) *Handbook of Black American Health*. Westport: Greenwood Press.

Krebs-Smith, S.M. and Kantor, L.S. (2001) Choose a variety of fruits and vegetables daily: understanding the complexities, *Journal of Nutrition*, 131, 487–501.

Krieger, N. (2000) Discrimination and health. In Berkman, L.F. and Kawachi, I. (eds) *Social Epidemiology*. Oxford: Oxford University Press.

Krieger, N., Rowley, D.L., Herman, A.A., Avery, B. and Phillips, M.T. (1993) Racism, sexism, and social class: implications for studies of health, disease, and well-being, *American Journal of Preventive Medicine*, 9, 82–122.

Kristenson, M., Eriksen, H.R., Sluiter, J.K., Starke, D. and Ursin, H. (2004) Psychobiological mechanisms of socioeconomic differences in health, *Social Science and Medicine*, 58, 1511–22.

Kumanyika, S.K. (1993) Diet and nutrition as influences on the morbidity/mortality gap, *Annals of Epidemiology*, 3, 154–8.

Kumanyika, S. and Adams-Campbell, L.L. (1991) Obesity, diet, and psychosocial factors contributing to cardiovascular disease in Blacks, *Cardiovascular Clinics*, 21, 47–73.

Lantz, P.M., House, J.S., Lepkowski, J.M., Williams, D.R., Mero, R.P. and Chen, J. (1998) Socioeconomic factors, health behaviors, and mortality: results from a nationally representative prospective study of US adults, *Journal of the American Medical Association*, 279, 1703–08.

Leigh, W.A. (1995) The health of African American women, *Health Issues for Women of Color: a Cultural Diversity Perspective*. Thousand Oaks: Sage.

Lindquist, C.H., Gower, B.A. and Goran, M.I. (2000) Role of dietary factors in ethnic differences in early risk of cardiovascular disease and type 2 diabetes, *American Journal of Clinical Nutrition*, 71, 725–32.

Liu, S., Manson, J.E., Stampfer, M.J., Rexrode, K.M., Hu, F.B., Rimm, E.B. and Willett, W.C. (2000a) Whole grain consumption and risk of ischemic stroke in women: a prospective study, *Journal of the American Medical Association*, 284, 1534–40.

Liu, S., Manson, J.E., Lee, I.M., Cole, S.R., Hennekens, C.H., Willett, W.C. and Buring, J.E. (2000b) Fruit and vegetable intake and risk of cardiovascular disease: the women's health study, *American Journal of Clinical Nutrition*, 72, 922–8.

Livingston, I.L. (1994) Social status, stress, and health: Black Americans at risk. In Livingston, I.L. (ed.) *Handbook of Black American Health*. Westport: Greenwood Press.

Livingston, I.L. and Carter, J.J. (2004) Eliminating racial and ethnic disparities in health: a framework for action. In Livingston, I.L. (ed.) *Praeger Handbook of Black American Health, Volume 2*. Westport: Praeger.

Livingston, I.L., Brown, R.M. and Livingston, S. (2004) Vulnerability of African Americans to adverse health: the importance of social status and stress. In Livingston, I.L. (ed.) *Praeger Handbook of Black American Health, Volume 1*. Westport: Praeger.

Luke, A., Cooper, R.S., Prewitt, T.E., Adeyemo, A.A. and Forrester, T.E. (2001) Nutritional consequences of the African diaspora, *Annual Review of Nutrition*, 21, 47–71.

Macintyre, S. and Ellaway, A. (2000) Ecological approaches: rediscovering the role of the physical and social environment. In Berkman, L.F. and Kawachi, I. (eds) *Social Epidemiology*. Oxford: Oxford University Press.

Macintyre, S., McKay, L., Der, G. and Hiscock, R. (2003) Socio-economic position and health: what you observe depends on how you measure it, *Journal of Public Health Medicine*, 25, 288–94.

Massey, D.S., Condran, G.A. and Denton, N.A. (1987) The effect of residential segregation on Black social and economic well-being, *Social Forces*, 66, 29–56.

McBarnette, L.S. (1996) African American women. In Bayne-Smith, M. (ed.) *Race, Gender, and Health*. Thousand Oaks: Sage.

McCullough, M.L., Feskanich, D., Rimm, E.B., Giovannucci, E.L., Ascherio, A., Variyam, J.N., Spiegelman, D., Stampfer, M.J. and Willett, W.C. (2000a) Adherence to the dietary guidelines for Americans and risk of major chronic disease in men, *American Journal of Clinical Nutrition*, 72, 1223–31.

McCullough, M.L., Feskanich, D., Stampfer, M.J., Rosner, B.A., Hu, F.B., Hunter, D.J., Variyam, J.N., Colditz, G.A. and Willett, W.C. (2000b) Adherence to the dietary guidelines for Americans and risk of major chronic disease in women, *American Journal of Clinical Nutrition*, 72, 1214–22.

McGinnis, J.M. and Foege, W.H. (1993) Actual causes of death in the United States, *Journal of the American Medical Association*, 270, 2207–12.

McKinnon, J. (2003) The Black population in the United States: March 2002. *U.S. Census Bureau, Current Population Reports, Series P20-541*. Washington, D.C.

Morland, K., Wing, S., Roux, A.D. and Poole, C. (2002) Neighborhood characteristics associated with the location of food stores and food service places, *American Journal of Preventive Medicine*, 22, 23–9.

Murcott, A. (2002) Nutrition and inequalities: a note on sociological approaches, *European Journal of Public Health*, 12, 203–07.

Murphy, S.L. (2000) Deaths: final data for 1998, *National Vital Statistics Reports*, 48.

Mutchler, J.E. and Burr, J.A. (1991) Racial differences in health and health care service utilization in later life: the effect of socioeconomic status, *Journal of Health and Social Behavior*, 32, 342–56.

Myers, H.F., Echiverri, A.T. and Odom, B.N. (2004) The role of the family in African American health. In Livingston, I.L. (ed.) *Praeger Handbook of Black American Health, Volume 2*. Westport: Praeger.

Nazroo, J.Y. (1998) Genetic, cultural or socio-economic vulnerability? Explaining ethnic inequalities in health, *Sociology of Health and Illness*, 20, 5, 710–30.

Popkin, B.M., Siega-Riz, A.M. and Haines, P.S. (1996) A comparison of dietary trends among racial and socioeconomic groups in the United States, *New England Journal of Medicine*, 335, 716–20.

Potter, L.B. (1991) Socioeconomic determinants of White and Black males' life expectancy differentials, 1980, *Demography*, 28, 303–21.

Pratt, C.A. and Pratt, C.B. (1996) Nutritional advertisements in consumer magazines: health implications for African Americans, *Journal of Black Studies*, 26, 504–23.

Raudenbush, S.W. and Bryk, A.S. (2002) *Hierarchical Linear Models: Applications and Data Analysis Methods*. Thousand Oaks: Sage.

Robert, S.A. (1998) Community-level socioeconomic status effects on adult health, *Journal of Health and Social Behavior*, 39, 18–37.

Robert, S.A. and Lee, K.Y. (2002) Explaining race differences in health among older adults, *Research on Aging*, 24, 654–83.

Rogers, R.G. (1992) Living and dying in the U.S.A.: Sociodemographic determinants of death among Blacks and Whites, *Demography*, 29, 287–303.

Schlundt, D.G., Hargreaves, M.K. and Buchowski, M.S. (2003) The eating behavior patterns questionnaire predicts dietary fat intake in African American women, *Journal of the American Dietetic Association*, 103, 338–45.

Schnittker, J. (2004) Education and the changing shape of the income gradient in health, *Journal of Health and Social Behavior*, 45, 286–305.

Schulz, A., Williams, D., Israel, B., Becker, A., Parker, E., James, S.A. and Jackson, J. (2000) Unfair treatment, neighborhood effects, and mental health in the Detroit metropolitan area, *Journal of Health and Social Behavior*, 41, 314–32.

Semmes, C.E. (1996) *Racism, Health, and Post-Industrialism: a Theory of African-American Health*. Westport: Praeger.

Siewe, Y.J. (1999) Stages of limiting dietary-fat intake: implications for African Americans, *Journal of Black Studies*, 29, 731–46.

Smaje, C. (1995) *Health, 'Race' and Ethnicity: Making Sense of the Evidence*. London: King's Fund Institute.

Smaje, C. (2000) Race, ethnicity, and health. In Bird, C.E., Conrad, P. and Fremont, A.M. (eds) *Handbook of Medical Sociology*. New Jersey: Prentice Hall.

Smith, J.P. and Kington, R.S. (1997a) Race, socioeconomic status, and health in late life. In Martin, L.G. and Soldo, B.J. (eds) *Racial and Ethnic Differences in the Health of Older Americans*. Washington, D.C.: National Academy Press.

Smith, J.P. and Kington, R. (1997b) Demographic and economic correlates of health in old age, *Demography*, 34, 159–70.

Stampfer, M.J., Hu, F.B., Manson, J.E., Rimm, E.B. and Willett, W.C. (2000) Primary prevention of coronary heart disease in women through diet and lifestyle, *New England Journal of Medicine*, 343, 16–22.

Steinmetz, E. and Iceland, J. (2003) Racial and ethnic residential housing patterns in places: 2000. Presented at the annual meeting of the Population Association of America. Minneapolis.

Subramanian, S.V., Acevedo-Garcia, D. and Osypuk, T.L. (2005) Racial residential segregation and geographic heterogeneity in Black/White disparity in poor self-rated health in the US: a multilevel statistical analysis, *Social Science and Medicine*, 60, 1667–79.

Tibbits, C. (1937) The socio-economic background of negro health status, *Journal of Negro Education*, 6, 413–28.

Variyam, J.N., Shim, Y. and Blaylock, J. (2001) Consumer misperceptions of diet quality, *Journal of Nutrition Education*, 33, 314–21.

Villemez, W.J. (1980) Race, class, and neighborhood: differences in the residential return on individual resources, *Social Forces*, 59, 414–30.

Weisburger, J.H. (2000) Approaches for chronic disease prevention based on current understanding of underlying mechanisms, *American Journal of Clinical Nutrition*, 71, 1710–14.

Wickrama, K.A.S., Conger, R.D., Wallace, L.E. and Elder, Jr., G.H. (1999) The intergenerational transmission of health-risk behaviors: adolescent lifestyles and gender moderating effects, *Journal of Health and Social Behavior*, 40, 258–72.

Willett, W.C. (1994) Diet and health: what should we eat? *Science*, 264, 532–7.

Williams, D.R. and Collins, C. (1995) US socioeconomic and racial differences in health: patterns and explanations, *Annual Review of Sociology*, 21, 349–86.

Williams, D.R. and Collins, C. (2001) Racial residential segregation: a fundamental cause of racial disparities in health, *Public Health Reports*, 116, 404–16.

Witt, D. (1999) *Black Hunger: Food and the Politics of U.S. Identity*. New York: Oxford University Press.

Wrigley, N. (2002) 'Food deserts' in British cities: policy context and research priorities. *Urban Studies*, 39, 2029–40.

Wrigley, N., Warm, D., Margetts, B. and Whelan, A. (2002) Assessing the impact of improved retail access on diet in a 'food desert': a preliminary report. *Urban Studies*, 39, 2061–82.

# 4

## Describing depression: ethnicity and the use of somatic imagery in accounts of mental distress

## Sara Mallinson and Jennie Popay

### Introduction

Research in the UK suggests that neurotic disorders (a 'medical' category which generally includes anxiety, depression, phobia, obsessive-compulsive disorder and panic disorder) are one of the major causes of debilitating ill-health in the community (Singleton *et al.* 2001). It is also known that there are important differences in the patterning of mental illness across social groups. Where you live, your gender, your socioeconomic status and your ethnic background appear to shape both your likelihood of experiencing mental illness and the likely trajectory or outcome of that illness over time although the finer texture of these patterns is complex (Singleton *et al.* 2001, Weich and Lewis 1998, Nazroo 1997). Furthermore, while structural and social mechanisms appear to affect the patterning of illnesses, it has also been shown that the expression, understanding and interpretation of symptoms varies widely within and across social groups depending on the historical, cultural, and social context in which experiences are framed (Kirmayer and Young 1998, Kirmayer 2001). These variations in lay interpretation may have a significant bearing on the choices people make about the management of their condition and on the way in which others respond to them. This paper presents qualitative data from interviews with people of Pakistani origin and white people[1] in the UK in which we explore the physical dimensions of mental health and illness narratives and in particular the use of somatic imagery, analogy and metaphor. First, we place our research within the context of existing epidemiological research on ethnic patterns in the experience of depressive disorders and current debates about the conceptual and methodological challenges of research on ethnicity and mental distress. The study from which the data are drawn is then described and a summary of the findings from the epidemiological element of the study is given. We then present findings from the qualitative element of the research. Finally, in the concluding section, we discuss the implication of our work for contemporary debates about ethnic differences in the experience of mental ill health.

### Background

In recent years a number of studies have focused on the relationship between ethnicity and mental illness in the British context (for example, Sproston and Nazroo 2002, O'Connor and Nazroo 2002). However, the challenges of researching mental illness in different ethnic groups and all the difficulties associated with conceptualising, translating and operationalising the already 'confused' notion of 'depression' (Pilgrim and Bentall 1999) means that the patterns in these relationships remain far from clear. While some studies have pointed to differences in the rates of depression and anxiety and in the longevity of illnesses in different ethnic groups (Husain *et al.* 1997), others have pointed to rates being broadly similar once adjusted for socioeconomic characteristics (for example Shaw *et al.* 1999, Jenkins *et al.* 1997).

In order to plan effectively and deliver public health policies to improve inequalities in health, we need to understand the mechanisms at work in generating patterns of health and illness in particular groups, places and at particular times and how people interpret and respond to these and to the experience of ill health (Popay *et al.* 2003, Popay *et al.* 1998). In terms of deciphering the patterning of mental illness by ethnicity, three key 'causal' domains (and the relationships between them) need to be explored: socioeconomic disadvantage and other chronic stressors such as racism and how these play out in different places (see for example, Illey and Nazroo 2001, Karlsen, Nazroo and Stevenson 2002, Nazroo 2003, Siegrist and Marmot 2004); access to, quality and uptake of mental healthcare for different ethnic groups (Bhui *et al.* 2001, Njobvu *et al.* 1999, Shaw *et al.* 1999, Sproston and Nazroo 2002, Cornwell and Hull 1998, Miranda and Cooper 2004, Rollman *et al.* 2002); and differences in lay knowledge about the nature and causes of mental health problems and how these shape help-seeking behaviour (Fenton and Sadiq-Sangster 1996). It is to the latter of these areas of interest that this paper directs its attention.

In seeking to interpret the actions people take to protect or improve their wellbeing, comparative research on mental distress in different ethnic groups needs to be sensitive to differences in peoples' theories about, and expressions of, mental health and illness. Research on ethnic experiences of mental illness and utilisation of mental health care has identified weaknesses in the identification and management of depression amongst people of South Asian origin (Husain *et al.* 1997, Bhui *et al.* 2001). While the evidence from community-based research is still somewhat thin and not entirely consistent, it has been suggested that this might partly be explained by under-reporting of depressive illness in primary care because some ethnic groups do not 'recognise' depression or have the language to describe it. There have, however, been studies that challenge this stereotypical generalisation. For example, on the basis of their study of South Asian women in Britain, Fenton and Sadiq–Sangster (1996) argue that there are commonalities in the experience of depression and anxiety across ethnic groups – in terms of feelings, thoughts and symptoms. These might be described differently, and responses might also differ, but this does not mean that people are unable to recognise psychic issues. Similarly, Kirmayer (2001) argues that rather than saying that some groups do not 'experience' depression, we should be exploring more closely the cultural mores and the context of exchanges (whether they are in medical or family settings, or between colleagues or friends) which provide both the 'rules' of emotional expression and the boundaries for presentation, management and social response to mental illness.

The notion that 'non-Western' populations are more likely to 'somatise'[2] their distress has been a persistent theme in debates about ethnicity and depression, but research suggests that somatic 'idioms of distress' are much more widely shared. Bhugra and Mastrogianni (2004), for example, have shown that while earlier theories in trans-cultural psychiatry focused on somatisation as the non-Western equivalent of depression, there is good evidence that somatic symptoms feature in accounts of depression across the world. It has also been observed that, regardless of ethnic origin, people often express distress in physical and functional terms in healthcare environments where they perceive that a physical ailment is more appropriate as a 'ticket' to care (Kirmayer 2001). This does not mean that people are unable to connect their experience of bodily disturbance to an emotional source, and when asked to do so the majority of primary care patients presenting with a somatic symptom will acknowledge a potential psychosocial connection (Bhugra and Mastrogianni 2004). In terms of identifying and understanding the factors shaping peoples' interpretation of a symptom, their representation of it, and the remedies they seek, it is important to note that when 'lay' ideas and images conflict with those embedded in dominant medical discourses, the tendency is for Western biomedical attitudes to the body to prevail. It has been argued that biomedicine tends to label accounts of emotional distress that focus on bodily experience rather than psychological state as 'unsophisticated or primitive' (Kirmayer and Young 1998) and, as a result, different 'idioms of distress' (culturally patterned ways of talking about distress) may be discounted or misinterpreted. In this case it is the preconceptions and prejudices of healthcare professionals that need to be examined (Burr 2002).

These complex questions about the nature and extent of similarities and differences in the language and conceptualisations of mental distress across ethnic groups are not just of academic interest. In an important way, the 'sense' people make of their experience of health and ill health will shape help-seeking behaviour and ultimately access to treatment and care. It was with this policy and practice imperatively in mind that we sought to explore the representation of the experience of depression and anxiety in two ethnic groups as part of a wider comparative study conducted between 2003 and 2005.

## The study

The qualitative research described below was linked to an epidemiological study funded by the MRC that was exploring the prevalence and progression of depressive disorder in white people and people of Pakistani origin. Two research teams were involved: a team based at Manchester University undertook the epidemiological study and a team at Lancaster were responsible for the qualitative strand of work. Initially 1,856 people aged 18–65 years were identified from four general practice registers in an urban area of northern England, and sent the Self Reporting Questionnaire (SRQ) that detects mental distress (Harding *et al.* 1980). People with a score of 7+ (n = 651) then completed the Schedules for Clinical Assessment in Neuropsychiatry (SCAN) (WHO 1994) and the Life Events and Difficulties Schedule (LEDS) (Brown and Harris 1978). The Manchester team then identified people with a depressive disorder or a distressed 'sub-threshold' disorder (defined by a high SRQ score but not meeting the criteria for a diagnosis of a depressive disorder at interview). These formed a sample for prospective follow-up and included 208 people with a depressive disorder (114 of Pakistani origin and 94 white) and 190 people with a 'sub-threshold' disorder (97 of Pakistani origin and 93 white). People in the follow-up sample were re-interviewed six months after the first interview, using the SCAN and LEDS.

The qualitative research strand began in January 2003 – at which point people in the prospective follow-up study were having their second (6-month) interview. We aimed to achieve a sample of 60 people using a purposive sampling strategy that took account of three key factors:

1. Ethnic origins: we aimed to interview 30 white people and 30 people of Pakistani origin.
2. Gender: we aimed to interview 15 men and 15 women from both groups.
3. Age: within each group we also aimed to interview people across the age range of the epidemiological study (18–65)

*The sample*
Fifty-eight people participated in the qualitative study from across the two ethnic groups. Table 1 shows the composition of the sample in terms of our three key sampling variables: ethnic origin, age (at the time of interview) and sex. It also shows the proportions that were assessed as experiencing a depressive disorder at the baseline interview and those assessed as experiencing depression after six months.

Table 1 *Composition of the sample*

|  | *PO women* | *PO men* | *W women* | *W men* |
|---|---|---|---|---|
| Number interviewed | 16 | 15 | 14 | 13 |
| Age range | 19–65 years | 26–64 years | 36–64 years | 28–58 years |
| Depression at baseline | 12/16 | 10/15 | 8/14 | 9/13 |
| Depression at follow-up | 6/16 | 10/15 | 6/14* | 5/13 |

*One person listed as having 'other' outcome. Those not diagnosed with depression had a high level of distress but 'sub-threshold' rating on the SCAN assessment.

Amongst the people of Pakistani origin, 19 were first-generation immigrants to the UK and 12 had been born in the UK. Although almost three-fifths of the sample were born outside the UK, all participants could speak some English and more than half of the group said they were fluent English speakers.

### Conduct of the interviews

The interviewers used a topic guide that outlined key themes and sub-themes to be explored in the interview. These included: a general discussion of interviewees' current concerns about their health; issues around the onset, progression and (if relevant) resolution of episodes of distress; and views on formal and informal help sought and, if appropriate, obtained from a range of sources. Interviews were carried out in the interviewees' own homes by interviewers specially trained in qualitative interviewing techniques.[3] Interviewees were each paid £15 in acknowledgement of the time taken to complete the interview.

Interviews were tape-recorded with the interviewee's permission. All interviewees from the Pakistani-origin sample had the option of completing the interviews in English, Urdu or Punjabi. Six interviewees elected to do their interview in a language other than English and the interviewer translated these tapes.[4] All other tapes were transcribed verbatim by a professional transcriber. On average interviews lasted 45 minutes ranging from 25 minutes to 1.5 hours.

### Ethics and informed consent

The research team based at Manchester obtained ethical approval for the research. They obtained initial verbal consent for the qualitative researcher to contact respondents. Those who agreed to be contacted were sent a letter detailing the purpose of the interview and contact information if they had queries or wished to withdraw. They were also told that a researcher would telephone to arrange the interview. The information letter was translated from English into Urdu and the Pakistani-origin sample was sent information in both languages. The interviews were conducted at a place and time agreed with the interviewee. All interviewees were made aware of their right to withdraw at any stage in the research, and the steps we would take to protect their anonymity were explained. Our decision to train multi-lingual interviewers meant that consent processes could be conducted in the language chosen by the respondent.

### Analysis

Data from the qualitative study have been analysed using a manual content analysis and indexing technique (Spencer and Ritchie 1994). Initially, the verbatim transcripts are read, marked and annotated. This involves marking the transcripts by adding notes in the margins (memos) and colour marking key extracts of text to highlight potential themes and emergent ideas. The themes from the preliminary coding are used to produce a formal coding frame that is systematically applied to the data across all the transcripts. In a manual system this is done using matrices on A3 paper to summarise each transcript by theme. Once all narratives have been coded, cross-case analysis then allows for connections across the narratives to be made and tested and for analysis to move beyond individual 'case-studies' – although these still have value in the qualitative analysis process. In the final stage of analysis patterns and associations in the material can be explored in the context of the research as a whole, and the theoretical framework for the work is refined drawing on the wider literature on the topic. All the narratives were analysed by the first author with a sample of narratives being read and coded by the second author. Similarly, emerging themes were discussed with other members of the wider research team including those involved in interviewing.

There is some debate about the acceptability of any 'counting' in the analysis of data collected in qualitative interviews. Critics suggest that counting the number of people who make similar comments during an interview or who fall into any particular analytical category does nothing to expand our understanding of subjective experience. Rather, they suggest, it begins to fragment and objectify accounts that need to be assessed in their entirety. Others have argued that there is a place for limited counting or 'cautious positivism' (Silverman 1993) where the material lends itself to such practices. In this research we believe that there are some aspects of the data that allow interviewees to be grouped into broad categories, and where to do so adds to the analysis – so where appropriate we provide some limited numerical representations. All interviewees have been given an ID number and this is used in the presentation of quotations and summaries below (PO denotes a person of Pakistani origin and the W means white).

## A summary of the quantitative study findings

The methods used in the epidemiological element of this study and the detailed findings will be reported in a future paper. Here we provide a brief summary of the results as a context for the findings from the qualitative research reported in the next section. In general, depressive disorders were much more prevalent in both groups than recent population-based studies in the UK and elsewhere, reflecting the socially deprived nature of this inner-city sample. However, the most important finding, and contrary to other prospective studies in the UK, was that the prevalence of depressive disorders amongst people of Pakistani origin and white people living in this inner-city area of the UK were broadly similar. The unadjusted prevalence was not significantly different between white men and men of Pakistani origin (12.3% v 9.0%) and adjustment for covariates did not alter these findings. The unadjusted prevalence was higher in women of Pakistani origin than white women (31.1% v 19.3%) but after adjusting for age, marital status, socio-economic status and years of education the difference was no longer significant. Depressive disorder at baseline persisted for six months in a high proportion of both ethnic groups (54%). Also, in those with sub-threshold disorder at baseline, there was a similar incidence of new episodes of depressive disorder (17%). Similarly, the study did not find a higher rate of suicidal ideas in young women of Pakistani origin compared to other age or ethnic groups. The only group with a significantly raised risk of depression compared with their white counterparts were women of Pakistani origin aged 50 years or older – a finding reported in previous studies in the UK and the Netherlands. (Weich *et al.* 2004, van der

Wurff *et al.* 2004) This appears to be related to the ongoing nature of the marked social difficulties in this group particularly problems with close relationships. (Hasin *et al.* 2005)

The study identified differences in the factors correlating with depressive disorder in the two populations. Compared with people of Pakistani origin, a much higher proportion of the white sample had a past psychiatric history, and the subgroup of white men had more seriously limiting physical health problems and less social support. On the other hand, fewer men and women of Pakistani origin had received a formal education, and they were much more likely to be of lower socioeconomic status or unemployed than the white interviewees. The women of Pakistani origin had a higher rate of relationship problems and were more frequently dissatisfied with their social support compared with the white women involved in the study.

In terms of access to primary care the quantitative study found that depressed people in the two ethnic groups made a similar number of visits to their general practitioner for depressive or anxiety symptoms although total GP consultation rates were higher in depressed people of Pakistani origin because they consulted more often for bodily symptoms. There were some differences in medication use with white women being more likely to receive medication for depression than women of Pakistani origin, and more white people receiving psychological therapy in the six months prior to the baseline interview. However, whilst white women were more likely than women of Pakistani origin to have received psychotropic medication at baseline (57% v 26%), this gap had narrowed at the six-month follow up (56% v 44%). Overall, only 15 females and three males reported seeking alternative help, including that from a hakim or a homeopath, with no significant difference between the two ethnic groups.

**Findings from the qualitative study**

The qualitative interviews began by asking people in a very general way 'how [they] were feeling at that moment'. Although the respondents were aware that the qualitative research component was linked to a study of mental distress it was felt important that the interviewers should not directly approach the topic of mental distress or types of mental illness. Instead, they utilised the language and imagery introduced by respondents to lead the discussion format.[5] The interviewees were encouraged to describe their current feelings and if these had changed over time. For some who had experienced improvement in the months leading up to the interview, this means that descriptions are in the past tense; for others, the experience of distress was current at the time of the interview.

In this part of our analyses we wanted to see *what* people talk about when asked to describe how they feel and *how* they talk about it. While we have compared the main topics people talked about across the groups, it is to the language and imagery of the narratives that we will devote most of our attention.

*Telling the story: everyday words and images*
Across the two ethnic groups included in this research and across ages and sexes there appeared to be a shared lexicon of terms to describe feelings and sensations of mental distress. Much of this language was informal and colloquial with the most commonly used words and phrases including: low, down, in the dumps, stressed, under pressure, fed-up, edgy, sad, distressed, moody, miserable, weepy, negative, worried, angry, tense, tired, numb, frustrated or lacking confidence. Some examples of the ways in which people responded to this question are given below.

I'm feeling stressed-out (14 PO female).

Yeah, really low, like I can't be bothered with anything (04 W male).

I was just lethargic, it's just everything seems so worthless (05 PO male).

I felt I hit rock-bottom (14 W female).

The everyday language illustrated above was a prominent feature across the accounts. They used familiar terms to give their experience social and temporal currency and this served the purpose of making their personal experiences seem 'ordinary' and intelligible, even though they were describing things that they themselves often regarded as 'extra-ordinary'. In drawing on what appears to be a cultural cache[6] of terms and ideas to describe depression it helped them to establish common ground with the person they were giving their account to, and demonstrated their connection to socially valid experience. Thus, their personal experiences were recounted in a way that emphasised everyday meanings and these crossed age, sex and ethnic boundaries.

As well as using colourful colloquialisms, people also used other narrative techniques to enhance the meaning and power of their 'stories'. Analogies, metaphors and similes were used across the groups to make potentially alien experiences or feelings familiar for the listener. For instance, water, seas and drowning were commonly used narrative embellishments. Phrases such as '. . . it just crashes over me' and 'it washes over me' use the symbolism of waves to describe the variability in depressed feelings at different times and on different days. Other people used whirlpool similes 'it's like swirling down' and 'sinking' metaphors, whilst yet others used imagery suggesting that they felt 'adrift'. Another common technique was to talk of 'blackness' or 'darkness'. For example, one white man said 'My wife calls it "the black dog, here's the black dog again"' (06 W male).

### Medicalised terms

A large proportion of interviewees also at some point during the interview used what might be called 'medicalised' terms such as: 'depression' and 'anxiety', 'mental illness', 'psychological problems' or 'mental distress' to describe how they were or had been feeling. So for example one respondent noted that she had been feeling:

Very depressed, yeah I was very down (07 PO female).

In general there appears to be little difference between ethnic or gender groups with regard to the use of medicalised terms – they would appear to be just one of the wide-ranging discourses lay people utilise to construct accounts of illness experience. However, the context of the discussion does shape when these terms are used. In both ethnic groups there were several interviews where the 'depression' label arose only at the point where helpseeking or treatments were explored. In particular, talk about pharmacological treatments was often the first point at which respondents began to frame their experiences in medicalised terms, moving from colloquial descriptions to more formal diagnoses such as depression and treatments such as 'anti-depressant'.

There were some respondents who never engaged with 'medicalised' language during their interviews. The numbers were somewhat higher in the Pakistani-origin sample with four out of 15 men and five out of the 16 women interviewed not using the term 'depression' (or anything similar) at any time during their interviews, instead relying on descriptions of emotional distress that used colloquial language and familiar imagery. Of the five women of Pakistani origin who did not use medicalised terms four talked about mental distress in terms of feeling 'slightly stressed but not enough to make me down' (16), 'worried and on edge' (15), 'really down and weak' (08), and 'very low' (09), without mentioning terms such as depression, anxiety or mental illness. In the accounts of two of these women (16 and 09) even the general references to emotional distress were fleeting and guarded as this extract illustrates. This respondent (09) was an older woman with painful arthritis and high blood pressure. At various points she alludes to feeling 'frightened' and 'sorry for myself' because of the pain and her limitations:

Once the pain's around, you know, very bad, very bad. Sometimes I cry, you know. Doctor says it's good to cry.

She links her distress to the impact of pain and yet a few minutes later says:

I don't show them . . . because they'd get upset, you know. They always ask, 'How are you feeling?' Alright thank you.

She did not expand this any further, other than to say she liked to do things herself. About 10 minutes later there was another exchange:

Interviewer: How would you say you are at the moment? Do you say that you are feeling quite happy and content at the moment? Are you managing?

Respondent: Managing very hardly. Unbearable pain when it comes, you know. Very hard to take it.
Interviewer: And how do you feel then? Is that a time when you feel quite low?
Respondent: Yeah, very low. Very low.
Interviewer: And what do you feel then?
Respondent: What I say, you know, have to cope. Take medicine and sit down (09 PO female).

In the white sample by contrast, only four interviewees (three men and one woman) made no reference to medical terms at any stage during their interview. For example, the white female interviewees talked about feeling 'frightened' and that 'life is so pointless'. The three men talked about feeling 'stressed-out, crabby and snappy' (13), 'up and down' (03), and 'irritable and moody' (08).

Finally, a small number of women from both groups referred to specific medical diagnoses during their interviews. In the white group two women spoke about phobias and panic attacks whilst two women from the Pakistani origin group defined their distress as post-natal depression following a difficult birth and a miscarriage (14 and 01).

*Somatic experiences*
Although there has been a tendency in the literature to claim that physical or somatic presentation of emotional distress is more common in 'non-Western' populations, there was no clear distinction in this study. In trying to give a grounded and 'realistic' description of their experiences people searched for symbols which explained both the type of feeling and its impact upon them. Thus there was a process of translation between essentially psychic events and functional or physical consequences as people proceeded with their explanations.

For example, in both ethnic groups the physical, functional impacts of mental health problems were described in terms of lethargy ('I feel like a druggie'), sleeplessness ('mind is still working – like there's a film playing'), lack of quality sleep ('No matter how much sleep I get, I'm constantly tired'), appetite loss ('I just forget to get my dinner') and loss of concentration ('I think, what am I doing?'). These changes in bodily experience are widely associated with depressed states and feature in many lay accounts of depression. Indeed, changes in sleep patterns, appetite, energy level and concentration are used in the clinical diagnosis of depression. They relate to the organisation and conduct of everyday life and are keenly felt as a limitation on social participation.

Although there was a considerable degree of similarity in the imagery used by respondents in both ethnic groups, and in the tendency to 'somatise' feelings as part of the narrative process, there were some images, analogies and metaphors which were distinctive to the narratives of people in the Pakistani-origin sample. For example, talk about chills or feeling hot and faint:

> I felt I had a chill all the time. I had a temperature, I felt dizzy (05 PO female).

Similarly feelings of paralysis, lifelessness and being 'gripped' by emotion were also only made in one of the interviews with a Pakistani-origin woman:

> When I am not well my body starts to shake. I experience blackouts. I feel lifeless and I cannot move (13 PO female).

There were also some distinctive elements to the way in which some of the Pakistani-origin sample described mental pressure – for example 'pressure in the head' (04 PO male), 'too much thinking' (01 PO female) or a 'heavy-head' (01 PO male). These particular images have been described in other research on ethnic differences in mental illness (Nazroo and O'Connor 2002). There were, however, comparable forms of somatic imagery and metaphors in the accounts of men and women from the white sample – such as a 'banging head' (08 W male). In this instance we did not have the opportunity to explore whether the difference between the images was simply semiotics or a more substantive conceptual contrast. Even so, what we can say is that across the groups describing anxiety and depression in terms of problems that are experienced as pressure, pain, or weight on the mind is shared, even if there is some difference in the language used to represent these experiences.

Finally, the interviewees of Pakistani origin were more likely to explore the relationship between the body and mind than white interviewees. These included narratives exploring the possibility that pains led to depressed mood or suggesting a reverse causal pathway with 'mental tension' having caused pains as well as those where the relationship between pain and mental distress was unclear. For example, one respondent talked about going for lots of tests for pain, generalised pains, aching and feelings of distress without crystallising any particular theories about their connection to emotional distress.

In the white sample, while there were fewer references to aches and pains, people did talk about headaches and muscular tension and when they did, as in the Pakistani-origin sample, they developed a clear relationship between their experience of both chronic and acute health problems and the onset or deepening of a depressed state.

*Narrating extreme emotions*
The data suggest that there are some differences in the expression of emotional distress between the ethnic groups in relation to more severe experiences such as suicidal thoughts. In particular, the Pakistani-origin interviewees did not discuss suicidal feelings to the same

extent as the W sample. The difference applies to both the number of people expressing suicidal thoughts and, at a more qualitative level, the vividness of the imagery used to describe such feelings. Overall, four of the Pakistani-origin sample alluded to feelings that could be interpreted as suicidal – one woman and three men. This extract from a tearful interview with a woman whose husband had died two years previously illustrates the guarded references to extreme hopelessness she made:

> I think if I have to live alone I will die . . . Sometimes I feel healthy but other times I feel 'what is this life?' (03 PO female).

In the male sub-sample, there were more references to feelings of worthlessness and hopelessness, and three men made explicit reference to suicidal thoughts. One man said he often asked:

> What is the point of living? (14 PO male).

Another noted:

> I feel like taking my own life (01 PO male).

Whilst the third was more guarded, commenting that:

> I think to myself 'what is the point of coming into this world?' . . . I have lots of questions about life and everything but no answers (03 PO male).

In all these cases the interviewees did not wish to elaborate further.

The contrast between the cautious allusions to suicidal thoughts illustrated above and the more direct images and illustrations used by the white group is marked:

> I can't cope. There's days, I'm afraid sometimes to peel an onion because I'm just ready to, I've been like this for a long, long time, I feel like either cutting my throat or stabbing myself with a knife (04 W female).

> I used to put tablets on the bed and think 'Should I or shouldn't I?' (09 W female).

> When I get like that I think 'what's the point of carrying on?' Even ethically, I've been examining it ethically. It's gone that far . . . At the time, I can't see any reason why I shouldn't just end it (09 W male).

Across the groups people's accounts of extreme distress shared the image of hopelessness. What was different was that in the white narratives people went on to give often vivid descriptions of actual events and points of crisis, whereas the Pakistani-origin interviewees never moved past general allusions.


## Discussion

The accounts people give of their experience of health and illness are an important mediator of the action they take to protect their health or to respond to ill health (Popay *et al.* 2003, Williams 2003). In this research we interviewed a sample of men and women living in a locality of northwest England, who were diverse in terms of their ethnic origin, to explore perceptions and experiences of mental distress. We have considered whether the language used to 'represent' emotional or mental distress in people's accounts differed between groups and what factors might explain the differences. In terms of the composition of the study sample, there are some features which one needs to be sensitive to when appraising the findings. Almost three-fifths of the group who had Pakistani origins had been born outside the UK, but of these a large proportion had been UK residents for many years. Almost all the interviewees could speak some English and two-thirds said they were fluent, which may mean the group had a mastery of and willingness to use Western language of depression and mental illness which non-English speaking groups could not.

There is a persistent notion that significant and distinctive differences exist in the language and representation of mental distress in different ethnic groups and that this may be part of the explanation for different patterns of help seeking and health outcomes. However, we found that much of the language, and in particular the type of somatic metaphors and similes drawn upon to enrich and enliven the storytelling, were shared across the ethnic groups, even where people chose to be interviewed in a language other than English.

There were some points of departure in the everyday language of distress that need to be flagged. Men were more likely than women to refer to low self-esteem and worthlessness and the sample of Pakistani origin in general used the idea of 'too much thinking' more often than their white counterparts. There were also some somatic images that were unique to the Pakistani-origin sample (in particular heavy headedness, numbness, and emptiness). The Pakistani-origin sample also specifically linked the experience of mental distress and pain more often than the white sample, particularly among older women of Pakistani origin. However, in general somatic imagery, that is images that are essentially about physical experience, were a feature of accounts across the sample. Men and women of Pakistani origin were less likely than the white sample to use medicalised terms to describe their mental state. In other ways, however, the interchanging of colloquial and medicalised terms at different points in the account-giving process, was a feature of narratives from across the groups.

The one notable dimension of difference between groups was in relation to descriptions of extreme emotional distress. White men and women had a greater tendency than those in the Pakistani-origin sample to express suicidal thoughts. This was apparent in terms of both the numbers willing to speak openly about such thoughts and the vividness and directness of the accounts given. While this may be a reflection of more severe problems amongst the white sample, there may also be a cultural dimension to the narratives such that the white people are more willing to describe suicidal thoughts. Although other research has indicated that young South Asian women have a higher incidence of attempted suicide than young women in other ethnic groups (Bhugra *et al.* 1999), there is also evidence showing that suicidal feelings are unlikely to be expressed directly by South Asian women. This is a finding supported by both the quantitative and qualitative elements of the study reported here (Nazroo 1997). The literature suggests that this may be to do with religiosity (O'Connor and Nazroo 2002). So, for example, one study of cultural expressions of distress showed that women of South Asian origin only talked about suicide in the third party, creating a social distance between themselves and suicidal thoughts (Burr and Chapman 2004). By contrast, it has been suggested that suicidal thoughts have cultural meaning in Western dialogues as a symbol of extreme distress and have potentially less stigma for people without strong religious affiliations.

Overall, the analysis supports the contention that people of Pakistani origin living in the UK do not misunderstand or feel unfamiliar with the concept of depression because the relationship between the conceptualisation and the embodiment of emotions is much more complex than this assumption would suggest. Neither of the ethnic groups appeared to use narrative approaches that were exclusive to that group, even though we acknowledge some differences in the particular images or terms people chose by which to make their story meaningful. We would argue that these particularistic linguistic elements are therefore more appropriately conceptualised as part of a wider repertoire of concepts and 'symbolic systems' available to respondents irrespective of ethnic origin, rather than representing defining features of the accounts of mental distress given by a particular ethnic group.

While we argue that all our story-tellers showed considerable fluency across different symbolic domains and have the capacity to select metaphors and images which best serve the context of their narrative, we are sensitive to the need to explore the link between language, imagery and action in more depth. That has not been feasible in this paper, which is the first of several based on the interviews described here. In addition to the descriptive narratives of emotional distress and its personal impact presented in this paper, respondents also provided often complex multi-faceted theories of causality and attribution and accounts of help-seeking strategies including their perceptions of the appropriateness and efficacy of medical and non-medical 'treatments' and talking therapies. The relationships between these and the symbolic systems people draw on, the visible face of which is the language of distress, will be the focus of future papers.

### Acknowledgements

The research reported here is part of a larger study funded by the Medical Research Council entitled 'Anxiety and Depression in people of Pakistani Family origin and white Europeans' MRC G9900569.

### Notes

1   The difficulty in finding suitable terms to describe the ethnic groups involved in this work is a source of concern. The term 'South Asian' is acknowledged to be too wide and possibly inappropriate in its application, just as the term 'white' is. They both mask a wealth of cultural diversity. Nevertheless, we are obliged to find some way of writing about 'groups' in a way that is manageable and we have used these summary terms in this paper. Where we refer to people of Pakistani origin it indicates a specific ethnic group.

2   The term 'somatisation' is generally used to describe patterns of illness behaviour where physical symptoms are identified without any reference to psychosocial ones, and there are three main uses: medically unexplained symptoms (as in DSM-IV), hypochondriacal worry or somatic preoccupation, and somatic clinical presentations of affective anxiety or other disorder (Kirmayer and Young 1998).

3   During the fieldwork several different interviewers were involved in data collection. This was partly due to the extended period of fieldwork and low turnover of cases. Three interviewers were trained for the WE sample. Unfortunately, one of our female colleagues died in the early months of the work. The interviews were then shared between two other female interviewers. Initially we contracted two interviewers to complete the interviews with the Pakistani-origin sample: a multi-lingual male and female (both speaking English, Urdu and Punjabi). After conducting three interviews the male interviewer was unable to continue. The female interviewer agreed to conduct all the interviews. She checked with male participants that they were happy to be interviewed by a woman and reported no difficulties. Although gender issues are perceived to be more salient in fieldwork with a Pakistani (Muslim) sample than a white-British one, the evidence for this is unclear. Female interviewers are generally used with both genders in qualitative research, perhaps because of womens' over-representation in research support roles in the health and social care research arena, but also because of their perceived empathetic skills. After discussion within the team and with other academics working in the field of ethnicity and health, we concluded that the skill and 'approachability' of our interviewer were more important than gender and that using a female with Pakistani-origin men would not adversely affect our fieldwork.

4   There are technical and theoretical difficulties in the translation and interpretation of interview recordings in the context of a project exploring meaning and representation. Our approach was to be as reflexive and open about translation as possible. Prior to the interviews the research team met and agreed a translation protocol for a range of words and terms that the multi-lingual researchers, and the psychiatry team involved in the epidemiology strand of the study, thought might appear. This protocol listed agreed meanings and flagged the need for prompts where clarity was required in the interview context. Post-interview team reviews suggested that there were no terms used which we had not previously discussed.

5   We appreciate that people were sensitised to the psychological orientation of the research because of our connection to the team from the Department of Psychiatry at Manchester. However, we informed interviewees that we had no access to their previous interview data at this stage and were operating independently.

6   We use the term of culture cautiously because of the complexity and diversity of 'cultures' which operate in any population at any one time. In this specific instance when we talk about a cultural cache we are referring to symbolic webs of meaning built on contemporary and historical legacies, social systems and discourses which act as a framework for the interpretation and agency of people at different times and in different contexts.

## References

Bhugra, D., Desai, M. and Baldwin, D.S. (1999) Attempted suicide in west London, I. Rates across ethnic communities, *Psychological Medicine*, 29, 1125–30.

Bhugra, D. and Mastrogianni, A. (2004) Globalisation and mental disorders. Overview with relation to depression, *British Journal of Psychiatry*, 184, 10–20.

Bhui, K., Bhugra, D., Goldberg, D., Dunn, G. and Desai, M. (2001) Cultural influences on the prevalence of common mental disorder, general practitioners' assessments and help-seeking among Punjabi and English people visiting their general practitioner, *Psychological Medicine*, 31, 815–25.

Brown, G.W. and Harris, T. (1978) *Social Origins of Depression*. London: Tavistock.

Burr, J. (2002) Cultural stereotypes of women from South Asian communities: mental health care professionals' explanations for patterns of suicide and depression, *Social Science and Medicine*, 55, 5, 835–45.

Burr, J. and Chapman, T. (2004) Contextualising experiences of depression in women from South Asian communities: a discursive approach, *Sociology of Health and Illness*, 26, 4, 433–52.

Cornwell, J. and Hull, S. (1998) Do general practitioners prescribe antidepressants differently for South Asian Patients? *Family Practice*, 15, S16–S18.

Fenton, S. and Sadiq-Sangster, A. (1996) Culture, relativism and the expression of mental distress: South Asian women in Britain, *Sociology of Health and Illness*, 18, 1, 66–85.

Harding, T.W., de Arango, M.V., Baltazar, J., Climent, C.E., Ibrahim, H.H., Ladrido-Ignacio, L., Murthy, R.S. and Wig, N.N. (1980) Mental disorders in primary health care: a study of their frequency and diagnosis in four developing countries, *Psychological Medicine*, 10, 231–41.

Hasin, D.S., Goodwin, R.D., Stinson, F.S. and Grant, B.F. (2005) Epidemiology of major depressive disorder, *Archives of General Psychiatry*, 62, 1097–106.

Husain, N., Creed, F. and Tomenson, B. (1997) Adverse social circumstances and depression in people of Pakistani origin in the UK, *British Journal of Psychiatry*, 171, 434–8.

Illey, K. and Nazroo, J. (2001) Ethnic inequalities in mental health: a critical examination of the evidence. In Culley, L. and Dyson, S. (eds) *Sociology, Ethnicity and Nursing Practice*. Basingstoke: Palgrave.

Jenkins, R., Lewis, G., Bebbington, P., Brugha, T., Farrell, M., Gill, B. and Meltzer, H. (1997) The National Psychiatric Morbidity surveys of Great Britain–initial findings from the household survey, *Psychological Medicine*, 27, 775–89.

Karlsen, S., Nazroo, J.Y. and Stephenson, R. (2002) Ethnicity, environment and health: putting ethnic inequalities in health in their place, *Social Science and Medicine*, 55, 9, 1647–61.

Kirmayer, L.J. and Young, A. (1998) Culture and somatization: clinical, epidemiological and ethno-graphic persepctives, *Psychosomatic Medicine*, 60, 420–30.

Kirmayer, L.J. (2001) Cultural variations in the clinical presentation of depression and anxiety: implications for diagnosis and treatment, *Journal of Clinical Psychiatry*, 62, Supplement 13, 22–30.

Miranda, J. and Cooper, L.A. (2004) Disparities in care for depression among primary care patients, *Journal of General Internal Medicine*, 19, 120–6.

Nazroo, J. (1997) *Ethnicity and Mental Health*. London: Policy Studies Institute.

Nazroo, J. (2003) The structuring of ethnic inequalities in health: economic position, racial discrimi-nation, and racism, *American Journal of Public Health*, 93, 2, 277–84.

Nazroo, J. and O'Connor, W. (2002) Idioms of mental distress. In O'Connor, W. and Nazroo, J. (eds) *Ethnic Differences in the Context and Experience of Psychiatric Illness: a Qualitative Study*. London: The Stationery Office.

Njobvu, P., Hunt, I., Pope, D. and Macfarlane, G. (1999) Pain amongst ethnic minority groups of South Asian origin in the United Kingdom: a review, *Rheumatology*, 38, 1184–87.

O'Connor, W. and Nazroo, J. (eds) (2002) *Ethnic Differences in the Context and Experience of Psychiatric Illness: a Qualitative Study*. London: The Stationery Office.

Pilgrim, D. and Bentall, I. (1999) The medicalisation of misery: a critical realist analysis of the concept of depression, *The Journal of Mental Health*, 8, 3, 261–74.

Popay, J., Williams, G., Thomas, C. and Gatrell, A. (1998) Theorising inequalities in health; the place of lay knowledge, *Sociology of Health and Illness*, 20, 6, 619–44.

Popay, J., Thomas, C., Williams, G., Bennett, S., Gatrell, A. and Bostock, L. (2003) A proper place to live: health inequalities, agency and the normative dimensions of space, *Social Science and Medicine*, 57, 1, 55–69.

Rollman, B.L., Hanusa, B.H., Belnap, W. and Gardner, L.A. (2002) Race, quality of depression care, and recovery from major depression in a primary care setting, *General Hospital Psychiatry*, 24, 6, 381–90.

Seigrist, J. and Marmot, M. (2004) Health inequalities and the psychosocial environment – two scientific challenges, *Social Science and Medicine*, 58, 8, 1463–73.

Shaw, C.M., Creed, F., Tomenson, B., Riste, L. and Cruickshank, J.K. (1999) Prevalence of anxiety and depressive illness and help seeking behaviour in African Caribbeans and white Europeans: two phase general population survey, *British Medical Journal*, 318, 302–05.

Silverman, D. (1993) *Interpreting Qualitative Data: Methods for Analysing Talk, Text and Interaction*. London: Sage.

Singleton, N., Bumpstead, R., O'Brien, M., Lee, A. and Meltzer, H. (2001) *Psychiatric Morbidity among Adults Living in Private Households*. London: The Stationery Office.

Spencer, J. and Ritchie, L. (1994) Qualitative data analysis for applied policy research. In Bryman, A. and Burgess, R.G. (eds) *Analysing Qualitative Data*. London: Routledge.

Sproston, K. and Nazroo, J. (eds) (2002) *Ethnic Minority Psychiatric Illness Rates in the Community (EMPIRIC)*. London: The Stationery Office.

van der Wurff, F.B., Beekman, A.T., Dijkshoorn, H., Spijker, J.A., Smits, C.H., Stek, M.L. and Verhoeff, A. (2004) Prevalence and risk-factors for depression in elderly Turkish and Moroccan migrants in the Netherlands, *Journal of Affective Disorders*, 83, 33–41.

Weich, S. and Lewis, G. (1998) Material standard of living, social class and the prevalence of the common mental disorders in Britain, *Journal of Epidemiology and Community Health*, 52, 8–14.

Weich, S., Nazroo, J., Sproston, K., McManus, S., Blanchard, M., Erens, B., Karlsen, S., King, M., Lloyd, K., Stansfeld, S. and Tyrer, P. (2004) Common mental disorders and ethnicity in England: the EMPIRIC study, *Psychological Medicine*, 34, 1543–51.

Williams, G.H. (2003) The determinants of health: structure, context and agency, *Sociology of Health and Illness*, 25, Silver Anniversary Issue, 131–54.

World Health Organisation (1994) *Schedules for Clinical Assessment in Neuropsychiatry*. Geneva: WHO.

# 5

## Hospice or home? Expectations of end-of-life care among white and Chinese older people in the UK

## Jane Seymour, Sheila Payne, Alice Chapman and Margaret Holloway

### Introduction

In the developed world death is an event concentrated in older age: cancer has its highest incidence among older people, particularly those aged over 85, and the incidence of respiratory, circulatory and nervous disease is weighted towards older people (Franks *et al.* 2000). In the UK, contemporary policy is directed at trying to increase the proportions of death that occur at home both because this is seen as an 'ideal' environment in which to die and because cost savings are anticipated once a shift occurs from secondary to community care (Department of Health 2006). This policy may be criticised for being based on untested ethnocentric assumptions about the preferences of dying people and their informal caregivers for place of care and also for being somewhat blind to the problems (and household costs) with which older people and their informal carers may be confronted in accessing help and support during a final illness. It is well known that all older people access health and social support services either at home or in hospices less than might be anticipated. Access by older adults from black and minority ethnic groups is particularly low (NCHSPCS 1995, 2001, Ahmed *et al.* 2004). The factors that lie behind this are not fully understood and little is known about the perspectives of older adults in the diverse ethnic groups that constitute the oft cited category of 'black and minority ethnic' (Department of Health 1999). A review of the literature on the palliative care needs of black and ethnic minority groups has highlighted the paucity of research on the views and needs of Chinese people in this area (NCHSPCS 2001).

The aim of this paper is to present a comparison of findings from two linked studies of white (n = 77) and Chinese (n = 92) older adults living in the UK, in which we sought their views about end-of-life care. We focus particularly on experiences and expectations in relation to the provision of end-of-life care at home and in hospices. The findings show that white elders perceived hospices in idealised terms which resonate with a 'revivalist' discourse of the 'good death' (Walter 1994, Seale 1998, Long 2004). In marked comparison, for those Chinese elders who had heard of them, hospices were regarded as repositories of 'inauspicious' care in which opportunities for achieving an appropriate or good death were limited. They instead expressed preferences for the medicalised environment of the hospital. Among both groups these different preferences for instutitional death seemed to be related to shared concerns about the demands on the family that may flow from having to manage pain, suffering and the dying body within the domestic space. These concerns, which appeared to be based on largely practical considerations among the white elders, were expressed by Chinese elders as beliefs about 'contamination' of the domestic home (and, by implication, of the family) by the dying and dead body.

### The studies

The paper is based on an understanding of 'ethnicity' as denoting shared cultural ideas, values and traditions in relation to fundamental aspects of life experience (see for example,

Barot 1996). Ethnicity involves dynamic self-identification with a range of identities, and to this extent it is a resource for living, rather than a prescriptive code (Ahmad 1996, Karlsen and Nazroo 2002: 3), with choices related to ethnic identity bounded by social structural factors (Karlsen and Nazroo 2002). In the context of choices about end-of-life care, these mean that the range of options available is influenced not only by perceptions of 'cultural appropriateness' but also by a complexity of other factors such as access to formal and informal health and social care resources, and availability and utility of information and knowledge.

*Comparing Chinese and white older adults living in the UK*
People of Chinese origin made up about 0.4 per cent of the population in the UK (ONS 2003), following an influx from Hong Kong during the 1990s. Patterns of settlement in distinct but dispersed areas and of employment (largely in the family catering trade) have been reported as contributing to the social and political exclusion of Chinese people in the UK (Chau and Yu 2001), although a comparison of white and ethnic minority groups has shown that Chinese and white older people have broadly similar health and income status, similar family structures – with both unlikely (in comparison with all other ethnic groups) to have an adult child still living at home – and similar employment status among the people aged under 55 years (Nazroo *et al.* 2004). Chinese people living in the UK are less likely to use community medical services such as GPs, probably for language-related reasons (Sprotson *et al.* 1999). Our study of Chinese and white elders was concentrated in two major UK cities: Sheffield and Manchester, where respondents lived in similar environments typical of such major urban conurbations.

*Places of care at the end of life*
Specialist palliative care services in the UK are now designed to predominately support home care at the end of life, working to the principle that admissions to specialist units such as hospices should only be for those patients with 'distressing symptoms and other complex needs which are not readily relieved in the home and other care settings' (NICE 2004). The direction of policy seems to be supported by evidence from cross sectional surveys which suggest that most people will express a preference for a home death if asked on any one occasion (Higginson 2003). However, the numbers who actually achieve this wish are small, with the majority of people having a final admission to hospital in the days immediately preceding death (Addington-Hall and McCarthy 1995).

A range of constraints has been identified in epidemiological research that prevents people from dying at home: haematological malignancy, disease of rapid progression, older age, low socioeconomic status and lack of access to palliative care services, are the most commonly identified (see for example: Grande *et al.* 1998), with the degree to which palliative care needs can be met successfully in the home environment shown to depend most closely upon the close involvement and availability of an informal carer for the dying person: whether a family member or a close friend (Gomes and Higginson 2006). The extent to which different cultural beliefs about death and dying, the role of the family, or of the relative perceived values of places of care, might influence these patterns has been little explored, with some notable exceptions. Data from a cross-sectional survey of 256 white people aged 55–75 show that hospice is generally preferred as a place of death in comparison with home (Catt *et al.* 2005), while a survey from the Netherlands of bereaved carers' recollections of the last three months of life for older dying people suggests that perceived carer burden is strongly associated with whether death takes place at home (Visser *et al.* 2004). Factors which might shape expressed preferences for hospice care and shape the experience of 'burden' during dying are indicated by qualitative data from a longitudinal study among 41 older white people with terminal cancer and 14 of their family caregivers. Thomas (2004) reports that a stronger preference for hospice care was expressed by respondents than the researchers anticipated, and that this preference was shaped dynamically by experiential and existential factors during the illness trajectory relating to perceived service quality, informal care-giving relationships and expectations and struggles in caring for the body. The factors reported by Thomas *et al.* (2004) resonate with a growing body of research which shows how white older adults engage in a struggle to balance a desire for independence with a need for care and support during any final illness (Kelner 1995, Howarth 1998, Wilson 2000, Vig and Pearlman 2003, Hallberg 2004, Lloyd 2004, Calnan *et al.* 2006).

There have been no UK-based studies of older Chinese people on these issues, but a number of studies outside the UK are of relevance. Among older Chinese people in Singapore, Yaw *et al.* (2005) report observations from clinical practice which suggest that patients are increasingly opting for institutional death, suggesting a range of practical and environmental reasons for this shift. In a survey of Chinese caregivers of dying people in Hong Kong, younger caregiver age was found to be related to greater difficulty with the tasks required to give care to the dying person and in managing interpersonal family relationships (Chan and Chang 1999). Evidence from other developed countries where Chinese people have settled during the 20th century (Crain 1996, Fielding and Hung 1996, Waddell and McNamara 1997, Bowman and Singer 2001) suggests that the traditional beliefs and practices of Chinese people, which are shaped by many influences such as Confucianism, Buddhism and Taoism, are undergoing adaptation as acculturation to life in Western societies occurs. This makes the task of trying to understand experiences of illness and expressed preferences for end-of-life care extraordinarily complex.

Our study of 'white' elders took place in Sheffield between 2001 and 2003. Opportunities were then sought to conduct similar studies among other cultural groups, with funding gained to examine the views of older Chinese people living in Sheffield and Manchester. This took place between 2003 and 2005. Due to different funding streams, the studies had different emphases: the study of white elders was focused on beliefs about end-of-life care technologies; while the study of Chinese elders examined views and knowledge about cancer and cancer screening, as well as end-of-life care. Some aspects of Study One have been previously published, and we draw on aspects of previous publications in summary throughout, as well as previously unpublished data from Study One (Gott *et al.* 2004, Seymour *et al.* 2002).

## Methods

Here, attention is drawn to the main methodological features of the studies. Further detail about the methods employed in the study (including the third-party vignettes employed) of white elders is available at (http://www.esrcsocietytoday.ac.uk) and from the final report of the study of Chinese elders (available from the authors on request). In both cases, Research Ethics Committee approval was gained prior to the commencement of fieldwork.

### Study design
Both studies used the same design of participatory qualitative research and liaised closely with community groups representing older people. In each case, the research was conducted in two phases over 24 months. Phase 1 consisted of focus groups with participants drawn

from community groups. Phase 2 involved interviews in which 'vignettes' were used to prompt discussion of end-of-life care (available from the authors on request). The first study involved 77 older people from three socio-economically contrasting areas of Sheffield, UK. The very large majority of these reported their ethnicity as 'white'. The second study involved 92 older adults from the Chinese communities in Sheffield and Manchester, with interviews and focus groups conducted by a multi-lingual researcher of Chinese ethnicity in Cantonese, with Mandarin or Hakka used as necessary. Participants in Study Two reported their ethnicity as 'British Chinese' or 'Mainland Chinese' or 'Hong Kong Chinese'.

The focus groups were guided by an aide memoire which covered: the role of life-prolonging treatment, hospice and palliative care, care decision-making, caregiving and place of care. The interviews were based on third party vignettes covering similar themes. While the use of third-party vignettes distances participants' responses both from their own personal circumstances and from any concrete choice of action, their use can enhance the comparability of data gathered, and allows insights to be developed into the 'general imagery' (Finch 1987) that may be associated with the phenomenon under study.

In both studies, the focus groups were conducted over the course of up to two hours, and each interview lasted for approximately one hour. The process of explanation prior to data gathering, and the process of debriefing afterwards, added two or three hours to each interaction.

*Sampling*

Purposive and snowballing sampling methods were used to generate a range of study participants in Sheffield and in Manchester. In the study of white elders, 32 participants in six focus groups were invited via links with local voluntary groups representing older people in Sheffield. In the second interview phase of the study, three general practices in different localities within Sheffield were asked to draw a sample of patients in the age categories: 65–74 years, 75–84 years and over 85 years. The sample was checked by GPs to ensure the inclusion of people of different marital status and place of residence. Forty-five people took part in interviews in this study. In the study of Chinese elders, interaction with the local Chinese communities in Sheffield and Manchester enabled the recruitment of participants, and enabled the generation of helpful insights into the issues at hand during the whole study process. Forty-six people took part in focus groups (32 from Manchester and 14 from Sheffield); and 46 people took part in interviews (37 in Manchester and nine in Sheffield). In both studies, exclusion criteria were: inability to give informed consent, experience of close bereavement in the last year, or the recent diagnosis of a life-limiting illness. It therefore needs to be noted that the participants were not facing these issues in 'real time'. Many, however, reported having thought about these issues at length prior to their participation in this study, having personal experience of caring for dying relatives, or living with one or more long-term conditions as well as, for some, the frailty often associated with late old age.

*Participants' characteristics*

The age range of participants across the two studies varied, partly because of differences in self-identification of participants as 'older', and partly because we decided to recruit people aged from 50 and over in the study of Chinese elders, because of some evidence that the health of Chinese adults deteriorates faster with ageing than the same-aged groups in wider society (Owen 1994). Table 1 gives details of the characteristics of participants in each study.

Table 1 *Demographic characteristics of participants*

| | Study 1 6 Focus groups (n = 32) | Study 2 7 Focus groups (n = 46) | Study 1 Interviews (n = 45) | Study 2 Interviews (n = 46) |
|---|---|---|---|---|
| *Gender* | | | | |
| Male | 9 | 13 | 16 | 13 |
| Female | 23 | 33 | 29 | 33 |
| *Age bracket* | | | | |
| <55[1] | 2 | 7 | 0 | 6 |
| 55–64 | 7 | 11 | 2 | 10 |
| 65–74 | 15 | 22 | 16 | 21 |
| 75–84 | 5 | 5 | 15 | 6 |
| 85+ | 2 | 1 | 12 | 3 |
| Missing | 0 | 0 | 0 | 0 |
| *Marital status* | | | | |
| Married | 14 | 28 | 25 | 24 |
| Single | 2 | 4 | 2 | 2 |
| Widowed | 13 | 8 | 16 | 14 |
| Divorced/separated | 2 | 6 | 2 | 6 |
| Missing | 1 | 0 | 0 | 0 |
| *Ethnic origin* | | | | |
| White British | 26 | | 45 | |
| White Irish | 2 | | 0 | |
| Black Caribbean | 2 | | 0 | |
| Black British | 1 | | 0 | |
| Missing | 0 | | 0 | |
| British Chinese | | 22 | | 17 |
| Hong Kong Chinese | | 12 | | 10 |
| Mainland Chinese | | 12 | | 19 |
| Taiwan Chinese | | 0 | | 0 |
| Malaysian Chinese | | 0 | | 0 |
| Singapore Chinese | | 0 | | 0 |
| Vietnamese Chinese | | 0 | | 0 |
| *Description of health* | | | | |
| Excellent | 4 | 5 | 1 | 2 |
| Very Good | 6 | 5 | 4 | 5 |
| Good | 13 | 14 | 13 | 19 |
| Fair | 7 | 21 | 24 | 20 |
| Poor | 1 | 1 | 3 | 0 |
| Missing | 1 | 0 | 0 | 0 |
| *Strong religious beliefs* | | | | |
| Yes | 21 | | 31 | |
| No | 10 | 20 | 14 | 26 |
| Missing | 1 | 0 | 0 | 0 |
| Buddhism | | 13 | | 9 |
| Christian | | 7 | | 7 |
| Catholic | | 6 | | 4 |

Table 1 *Continued*

|  | Study 1 6 Focus groups (n = 32) | Study 2 7 Focus groups (n = 46) | Study 1 Interviews (n = 45) | Study 2 Interviews (n = 46) |
|---|---|---|---|---|
| *Social class based on last reported occupation* |  |  |  |  |
| I Professional | 1 | 2 | 2 | 8 |
| II Managerial/Technical | 11 | 0 | 6 |  |
| III Skilled occupations | 6 |  | 11 |  |
| (N) Non-manual | 3 |  | 11 |  |
| (M) Manual | 4 |  | 7 |  |
| IV Partly skilled occupations | 4 | 37 (Catering) | 5 | 34 (Catering) |
| V Unskilled occupations | 3 |  | 3 |  |
| Missing |  | 1 |  |  |
| Housewife |  | 6 |  | 4 |
| *Living arrangements* |  |  |  |  |
| Own home | 31 | 15 | 38 | 19 |
| Nursing/residential home | 1 | 0 | 7 | 0 |
| Rented flats-Council or Housing association |  | 31 |  | 27 |

[1]There was no lower age limit on participation in the focus groups, rather we included anyone who self-defined as older, meaning that two participants in Study 1 and 13 participants in Study 2 were aged <55 years.

## Data analysis

Both focus group data and interview data were audio taped and transcribed verbatim, and analysed as freestanding data sets. Focus group analysis provided an initial coding frame for the analysis of the interview data and informed the development of vignettes for Phase 2 interviews. In both studies, the vignettes were discussed with members of dedicated project advisory groups, who were relevant community-group representatives or key informants. The vignettes comprised unfolding stories which allowed participants to reflect on the situation of a fictional 'third party'. In both studies, the analysis process involved study of the variety of ways in which participants positioned themselves in relation to the vignettes (for example, some focused exclusively on the situation of the character in the story presented to them, while others preferred to talk about their own experiences) as well as the content and meaning of their responses. The research teams were involved in the interpretive activities that followed sorting and coding of data. In the study of Chinese elders, all the interviews and focus groups were transcribed into Chinese and then translated into English with consistency checked by a Chinese researcher. We did not have the resources for back translation, and readers should be aware that the process of translation can distort concepts and understandings embedded in Chinese languages.

## A note about comparability

The different funding streams, the demands of constructing culturally sensitive interview and focus group aide memoires, and the desire to collaborate with community groups to ensure the latter, means that the data from the two studies cannot be regarded as comparative in any simplistic sense. What it was possible and acceptable to ask varied in the two studies. However, this afforded interesting comparison in itself. The approach taken in the study of Chinese elders tended to be more 'open' since it became clear that to some extent interviewing and focus group discussions can be experienced as counter cultural (Payne *et al.* 2005). We were also aware that we had perhaps taken an overly structured approach in the study of white elders because of our anxieties to make the data collection process as 'safe' as possible for those taking part (Seymour *et al.* 2002). The same key concerns, however, underpinned both studies, and data analysis raised some interesting common themes. Reflection on these has helped us to understand more clearly why particular issues were of importance to all the respondents involved. Below, we report on respondents' expectations and experiences of hospice and palliative care and their concerns about care of the dying at home.

## Results

### The meaning of hospice and palliative care
Both studies aimed to explore expectations and experiences of hospice and palliative care, and the meaning these terms had for participants. The term palliative care was not known by any respondents, although the white respondents were familiar with the role of GPs and Macmillan nurses in providing end-of-life care for people with advanced cancer, and almost everyone had heard of hospices. However, most of the white elders expressed underlying concerns about what was perceived as the obvious relationship of hospices with death. This was especially prominent among those respondents living in the more deprived areas of Sheffield. For example, Eddie, a man who had witnessed the painful death of his father from cancer, said the following:

> It's a place to stop permanent, it's like St [local hospice] . . . So if you, well, you see, once people start saying, 'We're going to put you in this hospice', then they know they're going to die, don't they? So I think you'd want to spend your last few months with your family, wouldn't you? (Interview 5, Man aged 65–74)

Because hospice care was seen as clearly linked to inevitable death it was spoken about cautiously and warily by the white respondents but, at the same time, it was often referred to by them in highly idealised terms. These invoked what were perceived to be the essential elements of hospice care for the dying: 'wonderful' or 'special' staff; the ability to transform death from the expected bad experience to a good one, and the provision of care, comfort and 'ease'. Thus hospice care seemed to be symbolic of the hope for the 'good death' among the white elders. These perceptions were especially notable among those who had had personal experience of hospice care, something that was markedly lacking among the Chinese sample. For example, Sally, a 90-year-old woman living near the local hospice where she had visited a number of friends who had died there, said:

> . . . And a hospice would . . . I think the hospices must help people. That . . . I mean I've only been up to St [local hospice], I've never been in another one, but it's such a wonderful atmosphere and it, there's no, there must be, it's so quiet and so beautiful up there, it must be a great help to anybody who's ill. And I think that must help a lot. And they must have special nurses in these places, have they? (Interview 34, Woman aged over 85).

Another younger woman, who played an active part in a local community support network and had visited the hospice many times, echoed this view:

> Audrey: Er, my opinion is if I was ill like that, personally, I would like to be in a hospice, er, for the simple reason that the comfort is there, you cannot always get comfortable at home, where in a hospice they spend all of their time making you comfortable and. . . . once they are comfortable, they are at peace and that is what they need I think, to me that is the reason, that is the reason of a hospice, that's what it is there for (Focus group 1, woman aged 75–84).

Among the Chinese elders, only one person said that they had heard of a Macmillan nurse, and only one quarter of the interview respondents (n = 12) said that they had heard of the term 'hospice'. Of these, two people said that they had visited a hospice and four had known friends of relatives who had received care in a hospice. As with the white respondents, those Chinese elders who had heard of hospice made a link with imminent death. One relatively young woman, who described herself as 'Westernised Chinese' explained it in the following way:

> But I think the Chinese would find it difficult to accept this; as when you are in there, they are people who are about to die . . . Entering a hospice means you're proclaiming to the world . . . I am not going to come out of it (Interview 31, woman aged 58).

The 'proclamation' of imminent death made by entering a hospice was regarded in highly negative terms for several reasons. Being surrounded by others who were dying was perceived to be unhelpful and discouraging for the ill person, who would not be encouraged to maintain their daily activities for as long as possible and would lose hope of recovery. It also seemed to contradict assumptions about the right way to die: carrying on with life and maintaining good spirits until the end, as one woman, who had lived in the UK for over 30 years but had very limited English, explained:

> I don't think the Chinese would prefer to go there. . . . they would not like the word 'death' . . . staring at it all the time . . . staring at it as they [try to] carry on with their life. Yes [otherwise] you might die without knowing or it is possible that you might just die; but if you were in a hospice, well you definitely would die; it seems that the word death would be thrown in your face all the time (Interview 22, woman aged 62).

Entering a hospice would also demonstrate that one had become a 'burden' to one's family and that there was no other option for care at the end of life. To this extent, hospice care was not seen as a positive 'choice' that one might make for care at the end of life. Instead it seemed to contradict important notions about family care and support during death. These were expressed clearly by Mrs Cho, a widow who lived near her adult children and who had strong views about the role of children in caring for their parents. She had cared for her own mother during a final illness many years earlier:

> Mrs Cho: [people] would not have much opinion if they were 'put' there.
> Interviewer: Right, what did the family think? Those who visited.
> Mrs Cho: The family wouldn't have much response; if you really cared, you would have taken the elder home to stay; well, it is because the children did not care so they ended up there.
> Interviewer: So they could not look after him and they would put him there?

Mrs Cho: They could not look after him and that was why they dropped him at that sort of place. . . . if you could afford it of course you don't want your parents to go to that sort of place, right? Unless you have no choice (Interview 29; Woman, aged 65).

As we shall see below, end-of-life care at home was not, however, a preferred option for Chinese elders; rather it was perceived that being cared for in hospital would allow the dying person to maintain a sense of hope, thus contributing to a sense of peacefulness. It was also perceived that in hospital it would be easier for the family to visit and provide the essential support and care that a person required. The relatively young, 'Westernised Chinese' woman described it thus:

The hospital would let you keep him company . . . the hospital would let the family have the convenience to spend more time with him; it is vital (Interview 31, woman aged 58).

Additional perceptions related to contamination and cleanliness of the home were also voiced: we examine these in more detail below.

In contrast to the Chinese elders, many of the white respondents expressed a preference for a hospice death over and above death in any other location, including home. The white elders reported that, while hospitals had the potential to provide high-quality technical care, their experiences of inadequate 'basic' care especially in relation to hand feeding and the provision of adequate pain relief and comfort, made hospitals a poor option for end-of-life care. Hospitals were also reported by the white elders as invoking 'strangeness' or 'impersonal' care; one woman referred to the problem of being perceived by care staff as '*just a body*' (Interview 34, woman aged 85+).

Among some of the white female respondents, hospices were especially preferred because of their perceived ability to provide a 'familial' standard of care: a standard that they perceived was becoming hard to achieve with the rapid demographic and social changes they had experienced. For example, in one focus group a woman who had lived in a small rural community in her youth recalled the management of illness and death in her childhood and contrasted this with the present:

Catherine: Oh yes, not many people died away from home and they were laid out and everything at home, they were, I never laid one out mind you (laughter) They didn't give me that job, but er no and they need somewhere where they can finish their days in quiet and comfort and loving care 24 hours a day not just when somebody has got time to go and look at them, and that's what they get in [hospice] my own husband and lots of friends I know have been in [hospice] and they are absolutely wonderful there should be more hospices like that, and er, like I say, before not a lot of wives did full-time work so you were more or less expected to look after the family . . . 1 mean if we have [to look] after any one like that I don't think our age would er be upset by it, because we are used to it – but I don't think our young people are really used to it . . . yes; we lived with the dead as well as the living. But now no, er, life's too busy and so there needs to be proper care for the elderly (Focus group 2, women aged 75–84).

Such perceptions were not however limited to women. In another focus group in the study of white elders, two men debated the meaning of hospice, making it clear that for them it was associated with familiarity, comfort and care:

Frank: See I haven't any first-hand experience of [hospice] but I would think there are people there who you know [and] comfort you, you know if someone is in there you've got proper caring people who try to put your mind at ease. I'm quite happy with that Gordon: it's got a very good name, it's got a very good name for that hasn't it? (Focus group 3, part 1, men aged 65–74)

As we shall see below, one of the factors that seemed to underpin the attitudes expressed in both studies was that respondents were concerned about the impact on their children's lives of caregiving at the end of life: both Chinese and white men and women expressed worries about being a burden on their adult children and other relatives, and expressed a range of other similar concerns about care of the dying at home.

*Dying at home*
In the study of white elders, respondents tended initially to identify home as the preferred place to be cared for at the end of life in ideal circumstances because of its symbolic meanings: the presence of loved ones, independence, familiarity and as a repository of memories with which to support one's sense of 'self' (Gott *et al.* 2004). However, a range of practical and moral problems associated with care at home was recognised as the focus groups and interviews unfolded. These included: fears about dying alone; worries about being a 'burden' to family; and concerns about the caring skills of family carers and the risk of receiving inadequate pain relief. Many respondents were facing their own or their partner's illness, or had experienced bereavement in the recent past. Clearly, their concerns and perceptions were shaped by these. For example, one man who lived in deprived area of Sheffield, had experienced both a heart attack and a mild stroke, and lived with his second wife who was moderately disabled with arthritis. They had no support from health or social care services. He had previously experienced the death of his first wife from cancer and had been recently hospitalised with a heart attack:

Fred: That's when I would want to go in hospital, when I thought I was being too much of a trouble, you know, if you get incontinent and if you get . . . well having to wash beds and things everyday . . . in our situation we haven't got a dryer, but there's only two of us, we manage all right. But I don't know how we go on if we . . . and this would worry me, it would kill me if I were waking up every morning to a problem like that and knowing Fay had got to try wash the sheets and things, day after day, no drying weather and things like that (Interview 6, Man aged 65–74).

This view was echoed by a man living in a similarly poor area of Sheffield, who was divorced and who had one daughter:

Eddie: If he were incontinent he wouldn't want to put his wife through that lot; er, and in pain a lot, tha' know, and I, I mean, again he wouldn't want, you don't want your loved one to see you suffering – I don't think so anyway. And I don't want to see my loved ones suffering (Interview 5, man aged 65–74).

As reported above, women especially emphasised how they did not want their adult children to have to engage in caring in the way that they themselves (and their mothers) had done. This was in spite of many of the respondents having traditional family structures with grown up children living locally and a wide extended family network. For some, this was clearly related to experiences of caring for dying relatives themselves in the fairly recent past:

Emma: I think circumstances vary, er, like if, if you are a, if you are an older person on your own, you know, you are better off in a hospital or a hospice or something obviously, but if you've a family they might want, you know, decide to want to have you at home. Like we had me mother, I mean er, me mother died a terrible death of er, lung cancer and we wouldn't let her go into, into care, we had her and nursed her at home and everything, but having said that, if I were in that position I wouldn't let my kids do that for me (Focus group 3, part 1 woman aged 55–64).

Carol: Yeah, yeah, your family's **very** important. But I don't think they'd be able to give you t' nursing that a nurse would or your own doctor . . . (Interview 3, woman aged 65–74, respondent's emphasis).

Another aspect of the 'burden' of care which participants perceived as important was the personal and intimate nature of the caring that may be required. Many reported that while it was 'right' or 'natural' that spouses cared for each other in this way, they did not want, and could not envisage, their adult children delivering this sort of care to them (Gott *et al.* 2004). Among the Chinese respondents, many of these themes recurred, with worries expressed about: burdening younger members of the family (this was often presented as a wish not to interrupt the working schedules of one's adult children), providing continuous care, ensuring that the dying person was always accompanied and that death did not happen when someone was alone; and controlling pain and other symptoms adequately. There were also concerns expressed about the ability of younger family members to provide nursing care which would be sufficient to provide comfort. For example, three women with grown-up children who did not live near them, said the following:

If you were at home and anything happened, the young ones would not know how to deal with it . . . for example, with bathing. In the old days when the elders stayed at home they would have other folks to give them a wash; now you would have the nurses in the hospital to do this (Interview 26, woman aged 61).

. . . it would be clean and tidy to go to hospital. Don't burden the youngsters (Interview 20, woman aged 68).

. . . I would not burden my family: I would definitely not burden my family because they have enough to worry [about] . . . (Interview 24, woman aged 65).

The views of the Chinese women were echoed by the male respondents. For example, this man, who lived alone and had been in England for many years, expressed the following view:

If there is pain and suffering, it would be good to go to hospital; they would have people there to help you any time [and] give you medicine and so on (Interview 17, man aged 71).

As with the white respondents, there was a particular concern with the management of the dying body and of ensuring cleanliness, comfort and containing incontinence. Among some Chinese respondents these concerns took a more developed form, with worries expressed about the 'contamination' of home by death which would make it lose its resale value; or of fears of 'contagion' or 'scaring' of the family by illness. The following views were expressed by women who had lived in England for many years following emigration. The older woman spoke good English, while the younger woman's English was very limited. Both drew on a range of previous experiences of death, as well as their knowledge about the attitudes of their friends and acquaintances in the Chinese community, in shaping their responses:

And if you die in the house, you know, the house is not a good house any more. When you've had an accident in the car, no Chinese would buy a car that had been in an accident (Interview 27, woman aged 76).

[It] would cast this shadow on you; and they say if you die at home it would make the home 'dirty' . . . (Interview 25, woman aged 54).

Again, the views of the women were echoed by the male respondents. For example, this man, who spoke limited English, had lived in England for many years, and who lived in a Chinese Housing Association flat, expressed the following perception:

. . . the family do not want [them] to stay at home. Scared it would be contagious; this would be the most important problem. Because they worry it could infect the family (Interview 15, man aged 70).

**Limitations**

In presenting these findings, we are mindful of the methodological difficulties that we encountered in studying views about end-of-life care. Respondents were engaged in discussions about topics that were often avoided in day-to-day conversation, and the use of the vignette technique was to try to make it easier for them to consider what were potentially upsetting and difficult subjects. We were particularly concerned that the older Chinese respondents might see the interviews and focus groups as entering 'inauspicious' territory. Such a response could occur because traditional beliefs associated with death would tend to suggest that raising it as a topic of discussion would be perceived as bringing bad luck (Chow et al. 2000, Chan 2000). However, we found that working with the Chinese community in designing the aide memoires and vignette scenarios used in the focus groups and interviews made it possible to explore some complex views and experiences with regard to end-of-life care. Subsequent high attendance and enthusiastic participation in dissemination meetings with the participating Chinese communities (which involved people asking questions about cancer and end-of-life care, and voicing their own experiences) highlighted that our earlier fears about broaching these topics were at least partly unfounded. It should be noted, however, that some of our findings in relation to the Chinese community, may be attributable to the fact that the subjects of hospice and palliative care that we introduced to them were, in many cases, completely new.

Three further potential weaknesses can be identified in relation to both studies. First, the samples were necessarily somewhat limited in the sense that only those people who felt able to talk about the subject of the study took part, although attempts were made to maximise socioeconomic diversity. Secondly, the participants were not 'patients' and, as such, not facing these choices about end-of-life care imminently, although many (especially in the study of white elders) reported having thought about these issues at length prior to their participation in this study, or had personal experience of caring for dying relatives. Lastly, as Thomas and colleagues have noted in their reflections on a study of similar issues, presenting views and preferences about end-of-life care is fraught with difficulty

'... preferences for place of final care and death were not simple choices ... but took the form of a stronger or weaker leaning in one direction, qualified by speculation about how things might change with events' (Thomas *et al.* 2004).


## Discussion

The data collection for these studies took place at a time when the policy rhetoric surrounding end-of-life care in the UK began to focus strongly on increasing the numbers of home deaths from cancer and other diseases. This rhetoric is underpinned by three assumptions: first, that home is the preferred place of care and death for most people; secondly, that there exists a monolithic family culture in which members prefer and are willing to give and receive care from one another; and lastly, that if there are differences between subgroups within the population, these are unlikely to run counter to the dominant discourse surrounding death, in which death at home tends to be held up as one of the key factors in achieving death with dignity. None of these assumptions have been adequately empirically evaluated. This paper makes a contribution to this gap in knowledge by presenting findings from studies of older adults from very different cultural backgrounds but who were living in the UK in similar urban environments.

Although most older people expressed an immediate preference for being at home during a final illness, this view was quickly moderated during discussion and reflection which the interviews and focus groups allowed. The findings particularly contradicted our expectations that the Chinese respondents would favour death at home. These expectations were formed in the context of a literature which suggests that traditional cultural values mean that death at home is regarded as vitally important. For example, in a review article about the cultural importance of death at home in Taiwan, Tang (2000) notes:

> When death occurs at home, the spirit of the dead can reunite with the forebears. Thus, 'the fallen leaves can return to their roots'. This is an important traditional concept of Chinese religious beliefs. When an individual dies at home, the spirit of the dead has a place to rest, and the dead will not be a 'koo'un'ia' kui' (spirit wanderer), which is a solitary soul with no one on whom to depend (2000: 368).

Our study took place in city environments and it seems that one possible explanation for the different position taken on this issue is to do with the tendency for transient inhabitancy or ownership of modern urban housing. Unlike many years ago in Chinese ancestral villages, homes are no longer retained by one family for generation after generation. Nor is home one dwelling insulated from contact with others. Wee (1997) has observed how this trend in Hong Kong has resulted in a change in preferences for dying at home for practical reasons of space and convenience; an observation supported by Yaw *et al.* (2005), as reported above. Our data seem also to suggest that death at home, or the passage of a dead body past the living spaces of others, risks making those dwellings unattractive to future buyers, thus bringing misfortune to family and neighbours. It seems that deeply held notions of collective responsibility, in which one's personal interests (wishing to die at home) are secondary to protecting the wellbeing of one's family (by protecting the value of the dwelling the family may wish to sell), come into play here, showing a pragmatic adaptation to the trends of the late-modern era (Chen 1996).

The concerns of the Chinese elders to protect the value of family assets from contamination, were linked to the expression of other views which they shared with the white elders. Both groups of respondents perceived similar difficulties with regard to the practicalities of care and not wanting to be a burden on others, especially when this might interrupt the lives of their adult children. Among the white women, this was expressed as a desire for their children to avoid the trap of expectation that had confined them, while among older Chinese people there were concerns not to interrupt the heavy working schedules of the younger generation. Research into attitudes to family care suggests that white communities seem to prefer to maintain a degree of independence from their adult children who, in turn, do not automatically see themselves as first port of call for assistance (Walker 1993, Finch 1995, McGlone et al. 1996, Calnan et al. 2006). It is often assumed that, in contrast, people from minority ethnic groups prefer and are able to seek help with personal care from within the extended family. However, research among eight different ethnic groups living in the UK, including 11 Chinese older people, suggests that it is relatively uncommon for personal care to be provided by anyone other than a very close relative, usually a spouse (Moriarty and Butt 2004). In the same study, it was observed that the Chinese respondents were, like the white respondents, unlikely to have a child living within a 20-mile radius and that they had not had an opportunity to develop non-familial social networks because of their history of working in occupations with long and unsocial hours (2004: 196).

Our respondents were pragmatic and realistic about the impact of social change on the family's skills in caring, acknowledging that care provision during death and illness was no longer a common experience and reflecting that better-quality care was likely to be provided out of the home environment where access to those with specialist training for the purpose was possible. However, beyond these pragmatic issues, many concerns about home and family care, which were expressed by both groups, took the form of worries about containment of what Lawton (2000) has called the 'unbounded body': that which can no longer maintain control over bodily functions, or threatens incontinence or the expression of overwhelming pain and suffering. Neither Chinese nor white older people wanted their children to have to deal with the bodily consequences of dying, reflecting what Twigg (2000) (drawing on Ungerson (1983)) observes is the powerful influence of the incest taboo: 'people are disturbed by activities that violate this norm; personal care can literally mean uncovering a parent's nakedness' (2000: 71). Twigg argues that it is for this reason that older people will often prefer a stranger, particularly a nurse, to deliver intimate care. Nurses are culturally sanctioned to deal with the body and moreover, are expected to behave in a manner which provides comfort and emotional support to the recipient of their care within a bounded set of expectations (Twigg 2000: 74). Our respondents' preferences for care in hospices or in hospitals during dying can be better understood in the light of this interpretation, since it is in these environments that older people are most likely to come in close contact with nurses who can manage the 'dirty work' (Lawton 2000) associated with the body without risking sexual transgression and with the possibility of doing so in an emotionally supportive manner which mirrors notions of what is 'ideal' familial care.

Among both groups of respondents, hospices were strongly associated with death and dying. White elders perceived hospices in idealised terms almost synonymous with the 'good death', and tended to express a preference for death in hospice over and above either home or hospital care. In contrast, for those Chinese elders who had heard of them, hospices were regarded as repositories of 'inauspicious' care contravening the circumstances believed to contribute to achieving the 'good death': maintaining the good spirits necessary to live as death approached, and demonstrating the duty and value of family care during dying. Unlike the white elders, the Chinese respondents appeared to have a strong preference for hospital care, linking this to the availability of nursing care and the possibility of maintaining hopefulness in the face of illness.

One way of interpreting the white elders' idealised preferences for hospice care is to set them in the context of what Walter (1994) and Seale (1998) have described as a discourse of revivalism, in which personal knowledge and awareness of dying, choice, and the emotional accompaniment of the dying are central features. This ideology has arguably permeated the public consciousness about the best way to die as a result of its widespread representation in a range of media (Seale 1998) and through the extensive fundraising activities of the voluntary hospice movement. As Long (2004) has observed in a comparative study of the US and Japan, the revivalist discourse of the hospice movement is of essentially Western origin, and usually entails an implicit critique of the 'medicalised' death of the hospital. Long reports that although elements of a revivalist discourse can be found in expressions about the good death in Japan, it is much less widely known and accepted as a model for dying than in the US. Instead, Japanese people tend to focus on dilemmas of disclosure and informed consent, emphasising these against a backdrop of strongly held beliefs about the responsibilities of caregivers for maintaining an atmosphere of calm and hope. In this context, open awareness of dying is seen as an unnecessary cruelty (2004: 921–2). These issues seem to be similarly played out in the views of the Chinese respondents reported here, most of whom had little or no access to English media because of language barriers.

## Conclusion and implications for service provision

Much palliative care policy assumes the existence of a family culture in which members prefer and are willing to give and receive care from one another. Social research into attitudes to family care among white and ethnic minority communities does not support this supposition. Few older adults of all ethnicities have family carers readily available to care, and yet it has been observed that the 'sustainability of keeping terminally ill people at home depends on how close their families are and how able they are to give care to their loved ones' (Gomes and Higginson 2006: 517).

While there are differences in the findings from these two studies, it is the similarities that are perhaps most noteworthy. The shared concerns raised by older white and Chinese people have much to say about the position of older adults in UK society and provide an important pointer to the need for changes in service provision to ensure that their worries and fears with regard to end-of-life care are addressed. Such concerns are rooted in a reality of enduring marginalisation in relation to good quality end-of-life care: attention has been drawn to this in a report by the Healthcare Commission on the progress of the National Service Framework for Older People in the UK (Healthcare Commission 2006).

The findings presented here suggest that there needs to be a new focus of attention on the ageing and dying body in a way that recognises that personal and intimate care is not merely a set of tasks, but is inextricably bound up with feelings of value, dignity and personal identity both for the dying individual and their companions. This means any 'preferences' expressed for care are mediated by a range of complex social, interpersonal and pragmatic considerations (Morris 2003), and cannot be regarded as culturally determined or 'scripted' (Gunaratnam 1997). The shared preferences for institutional care at the time of death, although differently expressed as hospice or hospital, can be understood by reference to shared ideas about the best ways of caring for the body during dying, especially the central role that nurses are perceived to have in this process. The preferences expressed by white elders for hospice care are a particular challenge to the trends for shorter patient stays in hospices and for increasing age to make it less likely that one's death will occur in a hospice (Seymour *et al.* 2005). Similarly, the apparent rejection of the hospice model by the Chinese elders is a challenge to the voluntary hospice movement's claims of inclusivity, while their preferences for hospital deaths run counter to the assumptions underpinning current policy that death at home is necessarily preferable to all.

## Acknowledgements

We are grateful for funding from the ESRC (award number: L218252047) and from the Health Foundation, which made this research possible. We thank all those who took part in the studies reported and the community groups who enabled our contact with respondents. We acknowledge with thanks the contributions of Sam Ahmedzai, Gary Bellamy, David Clark and Merryn Gott in the study funded by the ESRC. We are grateful for the assistance of Professor Cecilia Chan from Hong Kong University who helped us to make sense of the data from the study of Chinese elders.

## References

Addington-Hall, J.M. and McCarthy, M. (1995) Regional study of care for the dying: methods and sample characteristics, *Palliative Medicine*, 9, 27–35.
Ahmad, W.I.U. (1996) The trouble with culture. In Kelleher, D. and Hillier, S. (eds) *Researching Cultural Differences in Health*. London: Routledge.
Ahmed, N., Bestall, J.C., Ahmedzai, S.H. *et al.* (2004) Systematic review of the problems and issues of accessing specialist palliative care by patients, carers and health and social care professionals, *Palliative Medicine*, 18, 525–42.
Barot, R. (ed.) (1996) *The Racism Problematic: Contemporary Sociological Debates on Racism and Ethnicity*. Lewsiton, New York: The Edwin Mellen Press.
Bowman, K.W. and Singer, P.A. (2001) Chinese seniors' perspectives on end-of-life decisions, *Social Science and Medicine*, 53, 455–64.
Calnan, M., Badcott, D. and Woolhead, G. (2006) Dignity under threat? A study of the experiences of older people in the United Kingdom, *International Journal of Health Services*, 36, 2, 355–75.
Catt, S., Blanchard, M., Addington-Hall, J.M. *et al.* (2005) Older adults' attitudes to death, palliative treatment and hospice care, *Palliative Medicine*, 2005, 19, 402–10.
Chan, C.L.W. (2000) 'Death awareness and palliative care'. In Fielding, R. and Chan, C.L.W. (eds) *Psychosocial Oncology and Palliative Care in Hong Kong: the First Decade*. Hong Kong: Hong Kong University Press.
Chan, C.W.H. and Chang, A.M. (1999) Managing caregiver tasks among family caregivers of cancer patients in Hong Kong, *Journal of Advanced Nursing*, 29, 2, 484–9.
Chau, R.C.M. and Yu, S.W.K. (2001) Social exclusion of Chinese people in Britain, *Critical Social Policy*, 21, 1, 103–15.
Chen, Y.L. (1996) Conformity with nature: a theory of Chinese American elders' health promotion and illness prevention processes, *Advanced Nursing Science*, 19, 17–26.
Chow, A.Y.M., Koo, E.W.K. and Lam, A.Y.Y. (2000) Turning grief into good separation: bereavement services in Hong Kong. In Fielding, R. and Chan, L.W.C. (eds) *Psychosocial Oncology and Palliative Care in Hong Kong: the First Decade*. Hong Kong: Hong Kong University Press.
Crain, M. (1996) A cross-cultural study of beliefs, attitudes and values in Chinese-born American and non-Chinese frail homebound elderly, *Journal of Long-Term Home Health Care*, 15, 1, 9–17.
Department of Health (1999) *Reducing Health Inequalities: an Action Report*. London: HMSO.
Department of Health (2006) *Our Health, our Care, our Say: a New Direction for Community Services*. London: HMSO.
Fielding, R. and Hung, J. (1996) Preferences for information and involvement in decisions during cancer care among a Hong Kong Chinese population, *Psycho-Oncology*, 5, 321–9.

Finch, J. (1987) Research note: the vignette technique in survey research, *Sociology*, 21, 105–14.

Finch, J. (1995) Responsibilities, obligations and commitments. In Allen, I. and Perkins, E. (eds) *The Future of Family Care for Older People.* London: HMSO.

Franks, P.J., Salisbury, C., Bosanquet, C., Wilkinson, E.K., Kite, S., Naysmith, A. and Higginson, I.J. (2000) The level of need for palliative care: a systematic review of the literature, *Palliative Medicine*, 14, 93–104.

Gomes, B. and Higginson, I. (2006) Factors influencing death at home in terminally ill patients with cancer: systematic review, *British Medical Journal*, 332, 515–21.

Gott, M., Seymour, J.E., Bellamy, G., Clark, D. and Ahmedzai, S. (2004) How important is dying at home to the 'good death'? Findings from a qualitative study with older people, *Palliative Medicine*, 18, 460–7.

Grande, G.E., Addington-Hall, J.M. *et al.* (1998) Place of death and access to home care services: are certain patient groups at a disadvantage? *Social Science and Medicine*, 47, 5, 565–78.

Gunaratnam, Y. (1997) Culture is not enough: a critique of multiculturalism in palliative care. In Field, D., Hockey, J. and Small, N. (eds) *Death, Gender and Ethnicity.* London: Routledge.

Hallberg, I.R. (2004) Death and dying from older people's point of view. A literature review. *Aging, Clinical and Experimental Research*, 16, 2, 87–103.

Healthcare Commission (2006) *Living well in later life. A Review of Progress against the National Service Framework for Older People.* London: Commission for Healthcare Audit and Inspection.

Higginson, I. (2003) *Priorities and Preferences for End of Life Care in England, Wales and Scotland.* London: National Council for Hospice and Specialist Palliative Care Services.

Howarth, G. (1998) Just live for today: living, caring, ageing, dying. *Ageing and Society*, 18, 6, 673–89.

Karlsen, S. and Nazroo, J.Y. (2002) Agency and structure: the impact of ethnic identity and racism on the health of ethnic minority people, *Sociology of Health and Illness*, 24, 1, 1–20.

Kelner, M. (1995) Activists and delegators: elderly patients' preferences about control at the end of life, *Social Science and Medicine*, 41, 4, 537–45.

Lawton, J. (2000) *The Dying Process: Patients' Experiences of Palliative Care.* London: Routledge.

Lloyd, L. (2004) Morality and mortality: ageing and the ethics of care, *Ageing and Society*, 24, 235–56.

Long, S. (2004) Cultural scripts for a good death in Japan and the United States: similarities and differences, *Social Science and Medicine*, 58, 913–28.

McGlone, F., Park, A. and Roberts, C. (1996) Relative values: kinship and friendship. In *Social and Community Research, British Social Attitudes. The 13th Report.* Aldershot: Dartmouth.

Moriarty, J. and Butt, J. (2004) Social support and ethnicity in old age. In Walker, A. and Hennesy, C.H. (eds) *Growing Older: Quality of Life in Old Age.* Maidenhead: Open University Press.

Morris, S. (2003) Emotional and embodied factors relating to preference for place of final care and death among cancer patients and their main carers. Presented at a conference on *Emotional Geographies*, Lancaster University.

National Council for Hospices and Specialist Palliative Care Services (NCHSPCS) (1995) *Opening Doors.* London: National Council for Hospices and Specialist Palliative Care Services.

National Council for Hospices and Specialist Palliative Care Services (NCHSPCS) (2001) *Wider Horizons.* London: National Council for Hospices and Specialist Palliative Care Services.

National Institute for Clinical Excellence (NICE) (2004) *Supportive and Palliative Care Guidance.* London: National Institute for Clinical Excellence.

Nazroo, J., Bajekal, M., Blane, D. and Grewal, I. (2004) Ethnic inequalities at older ages. In Walker, A. and Hennesy, C.H. (eds) *Growing Older: Quality of Life in Old Age.* Maidenhead: Open University Press.

National Institute for Clinical Excellence (2004) *Improving Supportive and Palliative Care for Adults with Cancer.* London: National Institute for Clinical Excellence.

Office for National Statistics (2003) *Census UK 2001.* London: Office of National Statistics. Available: http://www.statistics.gov.uk (accessed 17th February, 2006).

Owen, D. (1994) *Chinese People and 'Other' Ethnic Minorities in Great Britain: Social and Economic Circumstances.* University of Warwick: Centre for Research in Ethnic Relations.

Payne, S.A., Chapman, A., Chau, R., Holloway, M. and Seymour, J.E. (2005) Chinese community views: promoting cultural competence in palliative care, *Journal of Palliative Care*, 21, 2, 111–16.

Seale, C. (1998) *Constructing Death: the Sociology of Death, Dying and Bereavement*. Cambridge: Cambridge University Press.

Seymour, J.E., Bellamy, G., Gott, M., Ahmedzai, S. and Clark, D. (2002) Using focus groups to explore older people's attitudes to end of life care, *Ageing and Society*, 22, 517–26.

Seymour, J.E., Witherspoon, R., Gott, M, Ross, H. and Payne, S. (2005) *End of Life Care: Promoting Comfort, Choice and Well Being among Older People Facing Death*. Bristol: Policy Press.

Sproston, K., Pitson, L, Whitfield, G. and Walker, E. (1999) *Health and Lifestyles of the Chinese Population in England*. London: Health Education Authority.

Tang, S.T. (2000) Meanings of dying at home for Chinese patients in Taiwan with terminal cancer. A literature review, *Cancer Nursing*, 23, 5, 367–70.

Thomas, C., Morris, S.M. and Clark, D. (2004) Place of death: preferences among cancer patients and their carers, *Social Science and Medicine*, 58, 12, 2431–44.

Twigg, J. (2000) *Bathing – the Body and Community Care*. London: Routledge.

Ungerson, C. (1983) Women and caring: skills, tasks and taboos. In Garmarnikow, E., Morgan, J., Purvis, J. and Taylorson, D. (eds) *The Public and the Private*. London: Heinemann.

Vig, E.K. and Pearlman, R.A. (2003) Quality of life while dying: a qualitative study of terminally ill older men, *Journal of American Geriatric Society*, 51, 11, 1595–601.

Visser, G., Klinkenberg, M., van Groenou, M.I.B. *et al.* (2004) The end of life: informal care for dying older people and its relationship to place of death, *Palliative Medicine*, 18, 5, 468–77.

Waddell, C. and McNamara, B. (1997) The stereotypical fallacy: a comparison of Anglo and Chinese Australians' thoughts about facing death, *Mortality*, 2, 2, 149–61.

Walker, A. (1993) Old people in Europe: perceptions and realities. In Kaim-Caudle, P., Keithley, J. and Mullender, A. (eds) *Aspects of Ageing: a Celebration of the European Year of Older People and Solidarity between Generations*. London: Whiting and Birch.

Walter, T. (1994) *The Revival of Death*. London: Routledge.

Wee, B. (1997) Palliative care in Hong Kong, *European Journal of Palliative Care*, 4, 6, 216–18.

Wilson, D.M. (2000) End of life care preferences of Canadian senior citizens with caregiving experience, *Journal of Advanced Nursing*, 31, 6, 1416–21.

Yaw, W.H., Kei, A.L.O., Onn, I.L.Y., Hwang, M.K.Y. and Chan, S. (2005) Older adults' attitudes to death, palliative care and hospice care: a view from Singapore (letter), *Palliative Medicine*, 20, 117–18.

# 6

# Contextualising accounts of illness: notions of responsibility and blame in white and South Asian respondents' accounts of diabetes causation

## Julia Lawton, Naureen Ahmad, Elizabeth Peel and Nina Hallowell

### Introduction

Type 2 diabetes has recently received a high profile within biomedical, public health and social science forums because of mounting concerns about its increasing prevalence. Despite epidemiological evidence that the risk of the disease increases with age and social disadvantage (Roper 2001), has associations with stress (see Schoenberg et al. 2005), and is greater amongst particular ethnic minority groups, biomedical understandings tend to focus upon individual-level risk factors. According to biomedicine, whilst type 2 diabetes may have a genetic component, the disease's growing prevalence can be attributed to lifestyle changes (poor diet, low levels of physical activity), which can themselves lead to an additional risk factor: being overweight/obese. In Britain, attention has also started to focus upon ethnic minority groups, especially those with ancestral origins in the Indian subcontinent (who are often termed 'South Asian' in the literature to which we refer), since they are at least four times more likely to develop type 2 diabetes than their white counterparts (D'Costa et al. 2000). From a biomedical perspective, a genetic predisposition has been held to be partly responsible for South Asian people's greater disease susceptibility. However, individual risk factors have also been implicated; specifically, a 'Westernisation' of lifestyle following migration (Greenhalgh 1997).

Given the individualised focus of biomedical paradigms, diabetes prevention and management strategies tend to target individuals and emphasise lifestyle modification. Yet many people struggle to follow lifestyle advice, even when given extensive information and advice (Sullivan and Joseph 1998, Snoek 2002). Though the reasons for non-adherence are likely to be complex (and, indeed, the concept of 'non-adherence' may itself need to be problematised – see Lutfey 2005), it has been suggested that differences between patients' explanatory models and biomedical understandings of type 2 diabetes are likely to be very salient (Cohen et al. 1994). Hence, there is a growing interest in looking at patients' own perceptions and understandings of diabetes causation, and whether, and in what ways, these might differ from biomedical paradigms.

A wealth of sociological work has already examined people's general understandings of disease causation (Blaxter 1983, Pill and Stott 1985), and their perceptions of specific conditions such as coronary heart disease (Davison et al. 1991, Emslie et al. 2001), stroke (Pound et al. 1998) and osteoarthritis (Sanders et al. 2002). These studies suggest that biomedical teaching may partly inform people's disease perceptions. Furthermore, they also draw upon other contextual factors and experiences to account for (ill-)health in themselves and others, be these their personal and social histories (Blaxter 1983), the media, and/or observation of people within personal networks and public arenas (Davison et al. 1991).

By highlighting the ways in which understandings of health and illness are contextually informed, such studies have been important in bringing the life-worlds of lay people centre stage. However, with some notable exceptions (e.g. Williams 1990), they have also tended to treat context in relatively restricted ways. 'Context', in these studies, tends to be concerned with individual biographies and experiences which are, at the most, grounded in respondents' socioeconomic circumstances (Backett 1992, Blaxter 1983, Pill and Stott 1985) and/or stage in the lifecourse (Pound *et al.* 1998, Sanders *et al.* 2002). What seems to have been left out, or under-explored, is the role of culture (or the macro-context more broadly), an absence which, arguably, may have arisen from these pivotal studies being conducted 'at home' rather than 'abroad'. It is possible that culture has formed such a fundamental part of researchers' and respondents' lives that it has been experienced as an 'absent presence', in much the same way bodies constitute experiential absences when they function in taken-for-granted ways (Leder 1990).

Indeed, when studies have been conducted with 'exotic' people, the reverse situation seems to be true: analyses have tended to focus on the broader socio-cultural (*i.e.* macro-context), rather than biographies and the minutiae of everyday experience (*i.e.* the micro-context). This is particularly apparent in studies of lay understandings of diabetes causation. Not only have these tended to focus on supposedly marginalised, disadvantaged and/or ethnic minority groups, findings have, in general, been interpreted in terms of folk models which are culturally and historically-bound (Schoenberg *et al.* 2005). Notable in this respect are Thompson and Gifford's (2000) and Garro's (1995) studies of aboriginal populations in Australia and Canada respectively. In both, the authors found that respondents tended to perceive diabetes as a condition 'imposed' from the 'outside', specifically as a result of white settlement, an observation which prompted them to interpret respondents' accounts as serving a broader political, ideological and communicative role. Garro, for instance, speculated that respondents used such accounts to make statements about 'the disruption and destruction of the Anishinaabe way of life which has been on-going since first contact with the Europeans' (1995: 45). Thompson and Gifford (2000) similarly concluded that the emphasis their respondents placed on external (rather than self-imposed) events conveyed a sense of disenfranchisement arising from the historically-specific circumstances of white settlement. In their study of Guadalajara Mexicans, Mercado-Martinez and Ramos-Herrera (2002) similarly observed that respondents tended to see their diabetes as being 'imposed' by negative emotions such as 'anger', 'fright' or 'fear', and to interpret this lay theorising as being 'logical' in light of prevailing cultural paradigms (see also Schoenberg *et al.* 1998).

These diabetes studies stand in notable contrast to the sociological work presented earlier. Whereas the former has drawn heavily upon culturally and historically specific interpretations, the latter has tended to ground people's disease accounts in the more immediate contexts of their personal experiences and individual biographies. Whether such differences in emphasis (and the different interpretations arising as a consequence) are valid and useful, reflecting differences (*i.e.* cross-cultural variations) in lay perceptions, or whether they should be better understood as an artefact of specific kinds of research encounters (researchers may, for instance, 'see' their data differently if they are conducting research within their own rather than a 'different' cultural group) remains a matter for debate.

To engage in this debate, and contribute to the literature on lay understandings of diabetes causation, we capitalised on an opportunity to undertake a secondary analysis of data from complementary studies involving an ethnic minority and an ethnic majority group in the Lothian region of Scotland, and to draw upon the perspectives of an ethnically-mixed research team. One study focused on Indians and Pakistanis with type 2 diabetes, the other on white patients. Both were concerned with looking at respondents' perceptions and experiences of their disease (in order to inform health service delivery), a key component of which was their understandings of why they had originally developed diabetes.

These causal accounts provide the focus for this paper. We should emphasise here that at no point did we assume that the perspectives of either group of participants were more 'normal' than those of the other, although, as described below, our ways of seeing and understanding their accounts did evolve as a result of bringing the two datasets together.

As both studies were Lothian-based, respondents had often attended the same clinics and structured education classes. In theory, this should have led to their receiving similar information about type 2 diabetes, although the reliance some Indian and Pakistani respondents' had on interpreters may have led to this information being simplified, edited and/or miscommunicated (Lawton *et al.* 2006b).

*Bringing the studies together*
Full details of the studies' aims, methodologies, recruitment procedures and sampling strategies are provided elsewhere (Lawton *et al.* 2005a, 2005b, 2005c, 2006a). Briefly, respondents who took part in the first study were recruited via general practices and face-to-face within Edinburgh's Pakistani and Indian communities and were purposively selected on the basis of their ethnic/religious group, age, sex and diabetes duration. The sample comprised 15 males and 17 females, of whom 23 were Pakistani (22 Muslims, 1 Christian) and 9 Indian (4 Hindus, 5 Sikhs). The age range was 33–78 years (mean = 59 years), and disease duration varied from 1–30 years. All originated from the West or East Punjab. Since risk of diabetes increases with age, the majority (n = 26) were first-generation migrants, and many (n = 19) described their ability to speak/understand English as being very poor or limited. Whilst social class was not used as a selection criterion, given the well-recognised difficulties of classifying members of ethnic minority groups, there was diversity in the sample in terms of occupation and residence (Lawton 2006a). Respondents were interviewed in their first language (Punjabi or English) by NA from 2003 to 2004. Interviews were informed by topic guides, translated into English when necessary, and transcribed in full.

The second study involved 40 white patients newly diagnosed with type 2 diabetes recruited from general practices and hospital clinics. To capture a diversity of experiences and views, and to reflect the demography of (white) Scottish patients with the disease, sampling took age, gender and socioeconomic status into account (see Lawton *et al.* 2005a). Data were collected by EP by means of in-depth interviews, informed by topic guides, between 2002 and 2003, which were transcribed in full. For the purposes of the analysis reported in this paper, 32 respondents were selected who matched our 32 Pakistani and Indian respondents as closely as possible in terms of age and sex. This yielded a sample with an age range of 36–77 years (mean = 56 years), comprising 15 men and 17 women.

The analysis was undertaken by JL, a white, British researcher, and NA, a Pakistani of Punjabi descent. JL and NA read all interviews before jointly coding for any talk which captured: respondents' understandings of diabetes causation in themselves and others; causes of health and illness in general; and any factors and considerations underlying and informing their causal accounts (the software package NUDIST was used to facilitate data coding and retrieval). These coded data formed the focus for further, in-depth analysis, with JL and NA meeting regularly to identify themes, troubleshoot ideas, and reach agreement on the interpretation. All coded material was initially analysed as one dataset. Differences and similarities in respondents' accounts were identified, and linked to respondent characteristics, issues and experiences which were grounded in, and emerged from, the data. After notable differences were observed in the ways in which the two respondent groups accounted for their disease, we decided to treat material from the two studies as distinctive datasets in a final analysis which was comparative. As these group-based differences appeared to transcend other (potential) differences, such as those relating to religious beliefs and practices (Ismail *et al.* 2005), diabetes duration (Hunt *et al.* 1998) or the experience of having, or not having, a family history of the disease (see Hunt *et al.* 2001), they form the focus of the findings reported below.

*A methodological note*
The experience of bringing together data from different respondent groups, and drawing on the perspectives of ethnically heterogeneous researchers led, we believe, to richer analysis than would have been possible had just one dataset and/or researcher(s) from one background been involved. This situation particularly applied to the ways JL and NA initially perceived the data from their own cultural/ethnic group, and how their 'ways of seeing' these data evolved during the analysis. Initially, both regarded aspects of the data from their own group as being obvious, banal and in need of little explication, beyond attempting to situate and understand the nuances of individuals' accounts in relation to their personal histories and everyday experiences (*i.e.* the micro-context). By contrast, data from the 'other' respondent group was perceived as 'exotic', unfamiliar and intriguing, particularly as far as notions of responsibility and control were concerned. Encountering exoticness and difference in this way prompted, and enabled, both researchers to 'see' the broader backdrop which underpinned the accounts of respondents who shared their cultural/ethnic backgrounds. Thus, combining the two datasets created 'presences' where there had hitherto been 'absences' from each researcher's perspective, prompting the erstwhile implicit role of the macro-context to enter the analysis.

## Findings

Respondents of both studies presented diverse and multifaceted accounts to explain their diabetes onset. These accounts often appeared to derive from their personal experiences of the disease, observations of its presence or absence within their family and other networks, and information gained from the media (a situation most commonly described by white respondents), healthcare professionals, family members and acquaintances (*i.e.* micro-contextual experiences). Yet, we also observed some striking, but subtle, differences between the two groups' accounts, suggesting that culturally-informed meanings, experiences and interpretations were at least partly at play. As we shall now show, while there were some differences in the *kinds* of explanations offered (*i.e.* whether respondents made recourse to lifestyle, genetics and/or other factors), more salient and telling were the differences in the *ways* in which respondents presented and involved themselves in the processes by which they had become unwell. To set the scene, we begin with two very different responses to a question we asked respondents about why they thought they had developed diabetes. The first comes from a white, 51-year-old retail assistant, Christine.[1] The second is from Bushra, 58, a Pakistani Muslim who had migrated to Scotland in the late 1960s to join her husband. Bushra's sister had accompanied her and, for a time, their families ran a small business together before a feud occurred.

### The role of self in the onset of diabetes

Christine:  Probably the lack of exercise n' eating the wrong stuff I would think that's probably what's caused it. Plus, as I say, I was having chocolate, which was the wrong thing.

Bushra:  I got blood pressure because of worry, because my son, when he was married, he was married into my sister's home. My sister lives here, and then we had a bit of conflict. We also had a shop together and then divorce was given to the girl, and then my son and my sister and I were separated because of that, and that's why I got blood pressure. My sister was very good to me. We got married at the same time and we came here together. Our businesses were together, everything was. She used to come and go from our house everyday because I was quite ill and she would come and find out how I was doing. She was younger than me and now she does not see me, now we are separated. That's the reason why I got blood pressure. And that's how I got sugar.

Both respondents attributed their diabetes to a wrongdoing in their lives. However, how they chose to represent this wrongdoing (in terms of what went wrong and why) differs notably. On the face of it, Christine provided a fairly straightforward explanation in which she linked her own lifestyle, specifically 'eating the wrong stuff' and a 'lack of exercise', to her diabetes onset. Bushra, by contrast, made no recourse to lifestyle; rather, she accounted for her diabetes in terms of severed social networks. For her, several factors were interrelated: social and contextual factors gave rise to emotional and psychological strain which, in turn, manifested itself as hypertension and caused her diabetes. Bushra's explanation thus focuses on 'external' causes over which she appears to have had little or no control; namely, on a disharmony inflicted by her life circumstances. Christine's account, in contrast, centres upon her own actions and behaviours. Thus, whereas Christine identifies herself as being to blame, Bushra pointed to her circumstances, and not herself, in accounting for her disease.

The next comparative example brings these group-based differences further to the fore. Pauline, a 58-year-old Scottish shop assistant, and Manzoor, 61, an Indian Hindu, employed as an administrator, both attributed their diabetes to an excessive consumption of chocolate. Both thus appear to have highlighted the same cause; the nuances of their accounts, however, as we shall now see, are quite different.

Pauline:  Well I thought it was eating so many sweeties . . . I thought maybe this [diabetes] is making up for all the years of, I'll give you an example, when I was having my . . . third child n' I told my mum I was expecting, she went absolutely ballistic right cos a third child. My granny had 13 and she says 'what, are you trying to up yer granny..?' [laugh] I was about 28 then, y'know, n' eh 'how did you fall pregnant?' I says 'well how everybody falls pregnant', 'but you were taking the pill' n' I says 'I forgot the pill' . . . She says 'if there was a bloody Mars Bar you wouldna have forgot that would you'. So that'll give you an idea o' how much sweeties I used tae eat. When I was younger, I'd rather have a Mars Bar than a meal.

Manzoor:  It's the result of eating the wrong kind of food. You see I was a vegetarian for most of my life . . . It's funny because when I first came to the UK . . . I used to live on Mars Bars because there was nothing that I could eat, right, in a student sort of environment. They were only catering for non-veg[etarians]. I mean nowadays it's much different because veg[etarianism] is sort of, in this era, a lot of people are on that sort of diet. But in those days there was nothing. And so the landladies couldn't make stuff for me, so I was forced to eat sugary things.

Pauline's account contains detailed talk about the conception of her third child which, superficially, seems to have nothing to do with her diabetes onset, but, rather, is an example chosen to convey her love of chocolate. However, her way of metaphorically describing her uncontained desire for chocolate seems to be indicative of a particular mindset, one pervaded by guilt. Indeed, by comparing missing a pill and falling pregnant with eating far too much chocolate and getting diabetes, Pauline presents herself as being irresponsible, and as now having to live with the consequences.

Whilst Manzoor also claimed to have consumed an excess of Mars Bars, he made recourse to external factors to account for this. For him, it was the circumstances arising from his migration in the 1960s that presented him with a lack of opportunities to make 'healthy' dietary choices. Indeed, Manzoor's vegetarianism was not a matter of personal preference, as his Hindu faith places prohibitions on meat consumption. Hence, by moving to a meat-oriented society (as Britain was in the 1960s), he was left with no choice but to eat the limited, non-meat alternatives available, principally chocolate. By presenting matters in this way, Manzoor thus inferred that, had more vegetarian food been available, he would not have had to consume an abundance of sugary foods and, hence, he would not have become a diabetic. Thus, he appears to project the blame for his diabetes onto a culturally unaccommodating environment, rather than himself.

### Attributing blame: contextualising responsibility and control

*Internalising responsibility: causal accounts and the risky self*
Many white respondents, like Christine and Pauline, seemed to draw upon a common discourse to account for their diabetes, one which resonates with 'Western' public health ideology, which emphasises personal responsibility for health, achieved through discipline, self-control and adherence to a healthy lifestyle (Lupton 1993; Petersen and Lupton 1996). Indeed, not only did these respondents tend to implicate biomedically-recognised risk factors (*e.g.* a poor diet, overweight/obesity, physical inactivity, and/or genetics), many also indicated a strong sense of personal culpability, by pointing to an 'unhealthy', pre-diabetes lifestyle and, associatedly, a lack of self-control. For instance, Vera, a 58-year-old retail manager, attributed her diabetes to 'eating all of the sugar and stuffing myself', a perspective echoed by Andy, a 40-year-old manager, who put his diabetes down to: 'gluttony n' no exercise whatsoever'.

In striking contrast to Indian and Pakistani respondents, such as Manzoor above, white respondents rarely sought external explanations and/or presented mitigating circumstances to account for their 'unhealthy', pre-diabetes lifestyles. On the contrary, they talked extensively about personal failings and weaknesses, such as being 'a complete glutton', 'being sweet-toothed', and having 'a weak spot'. In so doing, most presented themselves as being to blame for their diabetes, an issue which Andy (who weighed 19 stone at diagnosis), conveyed explicitly when he described how he had 'had to work very hard at staying very overweight'. Allan, a 65-year-old retired tradesman, similarly made his sense of culpability (and subsequent self-chastisement) apparent when, after highlighting his former propensity for 'drinking brandy n' smoking n' eating all the rubbish', he claimed that, 'I cannot blame anything else bar myself for being so stupid'.

By presenting themselves as being responsible for their diabetes onset, white respondents also expected others to judge them negatively. For instance, Ellen, a 40-year-old former healthcare assistant, blamed her diabetes on being overweight – an attribution which had partly arisen from her observation that, in the nursing home where she had previously worked, 'I never nursed a diabetic who was slim'. As well as chastising herself for 'abusing myself with sweets and everything over the years', Ellen shared the sense of embarrassment she felt every time she attended her diabetes clinic, where: 'I go in and say "I'm diabetic", n' I think, "look at myself, no wonder you're diabetic cos you're fat"'. These anxieties were shared by Andy who did not tell his friends he had diabetes until he had successfully lost weight because 'if I was still massive they would judge me even more'. Indeed, Andy seemed willing to shoulder responsibility for the onset of his disease partly because this served as a strategy by which he could present himself as now acting responsibly, fulfilling a socially-sanctioned 'duty' to look after his health. As he put it: 'cos it's been self-inflicted, I've got a duty to myself to do the best I can with it . . . the biggest duty in the world for me is to manage it properly and responsibly'. Other respondents who had young children, likewise, were keen to stress that they were now policing their children's diets as well as their own, thereby presenting themselves as acting as responsible parents.

Even when white respondents considered themselves to have an increased (genetic) risk, arising from a self-identified family history of type 2 diabetes, most still shouldered responsibility for becoming unwell. A good case in point is Callum, a 36-year-old civil servant, who, based on his observation that both maternal grandparents had had the disease, initially speculated that the it might have 'been there in the genes just waiting to happen'. However, the notion of a genetic predisposition (which, arguably, could have absolved him of blame) did not suffice as an explanation. Instead, Callum went on to speculate that 'it might never have happened', had it not been for his 'habit of having consistently over a few years, a bar of chocolate with my morning coffee, a bar of Toffee Crisp with my afternoon coffee, having a big glass of strawberry milk, and two or three biscuits at night'. In Callum's mind, 'that's been enough to kind of trigger things now', his choice of the term 'trigger' conveying the idea that his over-indulgent lifestyle, which he 'put down to my own ignorance', had been responsible for bringing his diabetes out of his genes and into bodily existence.

This notion of individual responsibility seemed so omnipresent that on occasions when white respondents did not perceive themselves as fulfilling the criteria of 'candidacy', derived from their own 'lay epidemiology' (see Davison *et al.* 1991), they were left floundering for an explanation. For instance, Helen, a 70-year-old 'homemaker' (as she described herself), neither regarded herself as having a family history of type 2 diabetes, nor did she consider her pre-diabetes lifestyle to have been 'unhealthy', particularly in comparison to that of her sister, who had remained free of the disease. Indeed, she juxtaposed her own self-restraint in which 'I could get a box of chocolates . . . and I could have it for a month before I finished it' with her sister's tendency 'to scoff the lot, you know'. As Helen's experiences of 'living a healthy life and eating a plain, simple diet' contradicted her understandings of disease causation, she concluded that 'I don't know why I've got it'. Mark, a 57-year-old engineer, constitutes a more extreme example. His diabetes was originally diagnosed during a hospital admission for pancreatitis during which his blood glucose levels went 'sky high', although they fell following treatment. Having told the interviewer that he had always adhered to what he saw as a healthy lifestyle, in which 'I was very active' and 'we don't take sugar', he went on to speculate that his high blood glucose levels might have been due to his pancreatitis, and to conclude that: 'I don't know if I'm diabetic or not'.

*Externalising responsibility: causal accounts and risky contexts*
The notion of individual responsibility, central to white respondents' accounts, was notable by its absence from those provided by Pakistani and Indian respondents. Indeed, some of these respondents were dismissive when asked why they thought that they had developed diabetes, which suggested that a line of questioning which implicated the self in the onset of the disease, and the notion of 'candidacy' underpinning it (Davison *et al.* 1991), may

have been ethnocentric. For instance, Zarina, a first-generation Pakistani Muslim (aged 69), responded tersely and simply as follows 'don't know why I got sugar'. Nazish, 67, also a first-generation Pakistani Muslim, provided a similar answer: 'it just happened'.

Narish's notion of diabetes being a disease which 'happened' to her, rather than one she had brought on herself was typical amongst this respondent group. Pakistani and Indian respondents made recourse to a variety of factors to account for their disease (only some of which were concurrent with biomedically-recognised risk factors). Nevertheless, most presented factors outside their control as being directly, or indirectly, to blame. For example, many of those who implicated a family history seemed content to present this as the sole explanation (in contrast to white respondents, such as Callum above, who claimed the disease had also been 'triggered' by something they had done themselves). Balraj, a 55-year-old, British-born Indian Sikh tradesman, is a case in point. He described his disease as coming from 'my father to my oldest brother and then to me . . . and my sister has it, she's my wee sister. It just runs in the tree'. For others, diabetes seemed to have such an all-pervading presence in their families and communities, that they perceived the disease as being an inevitable, 'biographically anticipated' feature of their lives (see Williams 2000). Rahat, a 51-year-old Pakistani Muslim, who had lived in Britain for almost 30 years, and was married to a shopkeeper, recounted how:

. . . almost in every family many members have it. In our family two of my brothers have it, my father had it. I've heard that that maybe my mother had it too. My sister-in-law also has it, one of them does, and in her family everyone has it. It's so common. No one gets away with it.

The attribution of the disease to 'external' factors was also evident amongst those who accorded a central role of Allah's will in dictating their health and destiny. As Javid, 54, a first-generation Pakistani Muslim shopkeeper suggested, 'whatever disease comes about will come from Allah, so what can you do?' This somewhat fatalistic sentiment was echoed by a fellow Pakistani Muslim, Shahbaz, 68, who suggested that 'the coming time's in Allah's hands', and also by Indu, 45, an Indian Sikh who described her disease as being 'what our Master (God) wants to happen'.

Most common, however, were those accounts in which respondents linked their diabetes onset to their migration to Britain. These accounts seemed to capture and convey in deep and powerful ways the dilemmas and pressures respondents had experienced by virtue of transplanting their lives to a country which was culturally and spatially far separated from their own, and which, ultimately, for them, caused them to become unwell. Ali, for instance, was a 48-year-old Pakistani Muslim, who, like other first-generation male immigrants, originally moved to Britain to take up temporary employment in manual and unskilled occupations (in his case, factory employment), in order to earn money for his extended family on the Indian subcontinent. Ali had originally intended his stay to be temporary. However, like others (see Ballard 1994, Shaw 2000), he made Britain his permanent home after his wife and children joined him, and subsequently wanted to settle there. As a consequence, Ali had become geographically separated from other members of his extended family for whom he saw himself as having a continued responsibility. This separation, as his account highlights, gave rise to detrimental consequences to himself:

It [diabetes] is because of stress . . . I had a lot of stress due to the family, like, if I was leaving them behind, how was I to move them forward. And when I did move forward [by migrating] then I thought of how to bring the family I had left behind forward . . . to the same place as I was. Because in our culture, even if you're married you still have to think of your sister and their children, you have to think of your mother and father – I mean there's no old people's home in Pakistan, we have to do everything ourselves . . . So I thought like this a lot, so I think the mistake was made here.

Ali, as we have seen, highlighted the stress arising from the pressures of fulfilling social roles and obligations as causing his diabetes. Specifically, he referred to a culturally-mandated sense of family responsibility which precipitated his migration to Britain, and also meant that, as well as looking after his wife and children in Britain, he felt obligated to care for relatives remaining in Pakistan. Indeed, by making reference to the unavailability of old people's homes in Pakistan and saying 'we have to do everything ourselves', he pointed to a collective concept of personhood, wherein one's own interests are subjugated to those of others. As such, Ali presented himself as being blameless for his diabetes (and the stress he saw as causing it); as being subjected to culturally-dictated circumstances over which he had little control.

This sense that one's life (and health) was dictated by one's circumstances was evident in other accounts. Hameed, a 66-year-old Pakistani Muslim, for instance, had initially moved to Britain to work as a bus driver, although he had subsequently set up and now managed a successful retail business. Despite having only been diagnosed a year earlier, he attributed his disease to the poor post-migration lifestyle he had led in the1960s (and over which he saw himself as having had 'no control'), in order to fulfil his role as family provider.

Hameed:  I think I have sugar because firstly the way we slept was wrong, secondly the way we ate was not right.
Interviewer:  This is when you were driving the buses?
Hameed:  Yes, when driving buses. . . . And there was just no control over life [laughs] we were overworked. We used to work a lot, we used to overwork, like we used to go on the buses and do two shifts before we came back.
Interviewer:  So you're saying it is because of the way your lifestyle was?
Hameed:Yes because the lifestyle was not good, we had no control.

Others perceived their diabetes and/or the factors they saw as giving rise to it, as attributable to the more general experience of being what Hussain and Bagguley (2005) have termed a 'visitor', living in a 'foreign country'. Manzoor (above) is a good case in point – he blamed his diabetes on a high-sugar diet, which, for him, was necessitated by moving to a non-Hindu, meat-oriented culture. Several respondents, in similar ways, held the excessive consumption of a 'Western' product – medications prescribed by their British healthcare professionals – responsible for their disease. For instance, Rashida, a 58-year-old Pakistani Muslim who ran a shop with her husband, pinpointed an occasion eight years earlier, when she was admitted to hospital following a severe asthma attack, and was given a high dosage of steroids:

For my asthma, they gave me tablets and they were sweet tablets [steroids], and I had to take eight tablets all at once . . . I stayed [in hospital] for a week and they gave me all those tablets, and because of that I got sugar . . . I was angry that I got sugar because of their medication.

Rashida, then, like others, attributed her diabetes to an external cause; in her case, medications she had had to take to ameliorate the symptoms of acute asthma. The actual timing of her diagnosis (which, as she later described, occurred during her hospital stay) is salient in understanding her causal account. The sense of anger and injustice she conveyed, and her identification of the steroids as being 'their medication', is also telling. By intimating that 'their [*i.e.* white/British] medication' had had health-damaging effects, she may not simply have been expressing her sense of misfortune at having become unwell through no fault of her own, she may also have been conveying more general, negative, feelings about settling in Britain. Indeed, elsewhere in her account, Rashida talked at length about feeling isolated, the difficulties of navigating the British healthcare system as a non-English speaker, her sadness about being separated from family in Pakistan, and, in common with other respondents, her concerns that sustained exposure to the 'goray' [white people] and their morals was undermining traditional family values in ways she felt powerless to change. Specifically, she expressed her sorrow that her own children wanted more freedom and independence, a situation which (elsewhere) she attributed to the influence of their white peers.

. . . Nowadays [British-born] daughters-in-law want to live separately. Even the sons when they are not married, they want to live separately. My youngest son lives separately.

For Rashida, then, like other Pakistani and Indian respondents, causation accounts may not simply have captured and conveyed a sense of lack of control over, and responsibility for, their own health, but also a lack of control over the broader contours of their past, present and future lives.

## Discussion

Both white and Pakistani and Indian respondents presented varied and multifaceted accounts to explain their diabetes onset. These accounts seemed to be connected to, and informed by, respondents' specific, and sometimes idiosyncratic, circumstances. We also observed remarkable within-group consistencies regarding the ways in which they located and allocated responsibility for their disease onset. Indian and Pakistani respondents placed particular emphasis upon their life circumstances in general, and, in many cases, those arising from moving to Britain in particular. This included not having access to the right kinds of food or medication, having to work too hard, stress arising from family responsibilities, and the disease having an invidious presence amongst family and community members. As such, they often presented their diabetes and/or the factors they saw as giving rise to it as being moulded by their circumstances, and thereby, in some senses, inevitable. By contrast, white respondents tended to implicate their own lifestyle 'choices' and personal 'failings' in their disease onset, and thereby to depict themselves, rather than their circumstances, as being to blame. Indeed, this notion or discourse of individual responsibility seemed to be so powerful that those white respondents who were unable to provide an explanation for their diabetes onset still made recourse to it, if only to refute its relevance in their particular case.

Clearly, the (different) ways in which our respondent groups internalised or externalised responsibility for their diabetes calls for an interpretative approach which moves beyond the micro-context and the minutiae of everyday experience to embrace broader (*i.e.* cultural) paradigms. As Bury contends, when 'lay people construct and present narratives of their experiences they do so within cultural settings which provide specific forms of language, clichés, motifs, references . . . which allow and constrain what is said and expressed' (2001: 278). In other words, within a particular society or context certain culture-bound, 'core narratives' exist, which both reflect and fashion experience, and through which, as Crawford suggests, "[d]ominant values and categories for understanding reality (and the social arrangements they signify) are reaffirmed (1984: 61–2). In support of this kind of broader, interpretive perspective, one can see, for instance, a resonance between the notions of personal responsibility our white respondents expressed and the rhetoric of modern Western individualism, in which people are supposedly the authors of their intentions and agents of their own lives (Lukes 1973, Rose 1990). Indeed, internalising responsibility for one's diabetes should not simply be understood as a culturally-framed admission of failure. On the contrary, as Radley (1993) has pertinently suggested, self-blame could be regarded as one strand in the modern Western discourse of self-legitimation and, as such, may serve to bolster and legitimise the modern Western concept of selfhood.

Conversely, the ways in which Pakistani and Indian respondents externalised responsibility for their disease could be understood as reflecting and reinforcing the tenets and values central to what Dumont (1970) and others working within the anthropological tradition (*e.g.* Mauss 1985, La Fontaine 1985) have termed a 'holistic' culture. According to these commentators, within holistic cultures such as India (which formed the focus of Dumont's analysis), the individual does not exist as a moral or conceptual category as such. Rather, people are enmeshed within kinship structures and political, economic and religious systems which define who and what they are. This situation leads to a 'socio-centric' concept of self (Dumont 1970), to a 'body-self' which, as Kleinman has similarly observed, 'is not a secularised domain'; rather, it is 'an open system linking social relations to self, a vital balance between interrelated elements in a holistic cosmos' (1988: 11). Indeed, as suggested above, by attributing their diabetes to 'external' factors, Indian and Pakistani respondents appear to have been conveying the more general experience of living a life dictated by their circumstances (such as the culturally-mandated obligation to work hard and earn money for kin). Arguably, then, and given the notion of inevitability conveyed in many of their accounts, the onset of their diabetes may have been perceived as a marker of a socio-centric identity, as a form of 'biographical reinforcement' (Carricaburu and Pierret 1995) which signified that one was living a life for the greater good. By contrast, and as already indicated, for white respondents, the disease seemed to be presented as a sign of individual failure, as a 'biographical disruption' (Bury 1982), which necessitated, and enabled, the reflexive construction of a new, morally responsible self (see Giddens 1991).

This 'individualistic'/'holistic' distinction appears to be a useful and plausible way of accounting for different notions of responsibility the two respondent groups expressed. However, we would also caution against embracing simplistic 'us'/'them' dichotomies too wholeheartedly. Not only is the notion of the modern Western 'individual' being subjected to ever greater scrutiny (*e.g.* Hallowell 1999), the dichotomy between individualism and holism has also been challenged. Morris (1994), for instance, has questioned whether the dichotomy may have been over-determined on the grounds that perceptions of self-interest and personal autonomy have been identified in studies of Indian life-histories. As he usefully speculates, because these kinds of perceptions may not have been articulated through the Western 'language' of individualism, they may have previously gone unnoticed by Western researchers.

Other explanations may thus be needed to complement and/or counterbalance those already offered. It is possible, for instance, that the different kinds of accounts we observed may be (partly) an artefact of the different sampling procedures employed in the two studies. As noted earlier, all our white respondents had been recently diagnosed, whereas many Indian and Pakistani respondents had had the disease for many years. Since people's understandings of causation may evolve over time (see Linn *et al.* 1982), it is possible that the two respondent groups' different temporal relationships to their diabetes may have led to different disease perceptions. Indeed, in their interview study, Hunt *et al.* (1998) present a persuasive case for the idea that, rather than simply predicting treatment behaviours (as the Health Belief Model would suggest), diabetes concepts may arise from the perceived success or failure of treatments, such as attempts at dieting. In other words, 'patients' concepts about the relationship between their behaviour and illness may not so much *determine* their self-care activities, as reflect their *experiences* of trying to gain control over their disease' (1998: 964). It is possible, then, that had white respondents had diabetes for longer and, hence, had had more experience of attempting, and failing, to achieve good glycaemic control, they might have made greater recourse to 'external' factors in their causal accounts (one needs to be mindful of the evidence that the body's production of insulin tends to decrease over time, irrespective of self-care attempts). We would not, however, wish to over-emphasise this kind of explanation given the homogeneity we observed in our Indian and Pakistani respondents' perspectives, irrespective of how long they had lived with their condition.

The emphasis Pakistani and Indian respondents placed upon their life circumstances might not simply have arisen from a socio-centric concept of selfhood, but also from a way of 'seeing' the world which itself arose from moving to a 'foreign' country. Many such respondents described encountering unfamiliar lifestyles and values in Britain, and it is possible that this experience of observing 'difference' might have led to their reflexively engaging with erstwhile taken-for-granted values and practices of their own. In other words, Indian and Pakistani respondents might have made greater recourse to context than white respondents because this context was more 'visible' to them, an issue which could be explored further by looking at diabetes accounts amongst those remaining on the Indian subcontinent, as well as undertaking more extensive work with those born and raised in Britain.

Reflecting upon the findings in these kinds of ways returns us to the key question raised for debate; namely, whether the different emphasis researchers have tended to place on micro- or macro-contextual factors should be understood as reflecting cross-cultural variations in the ways lay people perceive and/or account for disease onset, or if, instead, greater attention needs to be paid to the research encounter – that is, to who is looking at whom and in what circumstances – and how this might 'frame' what is seen and understood. (Another area for critical explication might be the disciplinary backgrounds to which researchers belong, and the specific theories and genres informing their perspectives, an issue, regrettably, beyond this article's scope.) Our position should now be fairly clear. Engaging with two datasets simultaneously not only created a way of seeing our data which was multifaceted, but also – and this is key – enabled us to explicate positions salient to our interpretation, even when these were not explicitly articulated by our respondents (for example, the role of 'individualistic' cultural paradigms in informing our white respondents' notions of personal responsibility). Such an experience has thus alerted us to the limitations which may arise when research is confined to one cultural/ethnic group or one setting. In the absence of comparative data, those conducting studies 'at home' (or with people from the same ethnic group as their own) may be more inclined to regard certain (culturally-informed) aspects of their respondents' perspectives as being 'normal' and self-evident, and thus as not requiring, or prompting, critical explication. Conversely, those conducting research 'abroad' may be drawn into looking at what seems 'exotic' and 'unfamiliar' to the detriment of examining the ways in which everyday and/or idiosyncratic experiences also inform people's disease perceptions. As our experience suggests, to do full justice to the richness and complexities of illness accounts, a broad approach is required, one which embraces micro- and macro-contextual factors, explicates multiple positions (including those not immediately 'visible' to us and/or articulated by our respondents), and, ultimately, as Bury (2001) contends, recognises that illness narratives take many forms, have many uses, and serve many purposes.

*Making the research 'useful'*
Finally, whilst endorsing the notion that illness narratives should not be treated as some form of 'unalloyed subjective truth' (Bury 2001), we would also like to take heed of Williams's (1993) suggestion that they should not be thought of as being so abstracted from reality that nothing useful can be said to health professionals and those working in applied disciplines. There may, for instance, be an important lesson to be learnt by those who use behavioural/lifestyle factors as proxy measures of self-responsibility (*e.g.* Blaxter 1997), particularly in analyses involving ethnic minority groups. As our Pakistani and Indian respondents' accounts have usefully highlighted, even if people do implicate lifestyle factors (*e.g.* poor diet, lack of physical activity) in their disease onset, this does not necessarily indicate that they see themselves as being to blame.

We have also highlighted a lack of resonance between the individualistic paradigms contained within Western diabetes education approaches/models which aim to promote self-efficacy (Knight *et al.* 2006), and the socio-centric concept of selfhood conveyed by Pakistani and Indian respondents. Given the sense of inevitability, and lack of self-efficacy, these respondents expressed, current educational approaches are unlikely to strike a responsive chord, an issue which clearly needs consideration by those attempting to develop culturally-competent services. It is also important to recognise that the biomedical perspective is itself a cultural 'way of seeing', one which, like the rhetoric of individualism underpinning it, needs to be subjected to critical scrutiny. Indeed, some commentators have started to question whether biomedicine's emphasis upon individual-level risk factors may lead to patients being positioned poorly in relation to their disease (Parry *et al.* 2006). Frankel *et al.* (1991), for instance, have voiced concerns that, by propagating 'simple messages concerning individual risk factors' which are 'at best only a partial presentation of the epidemiological evidence' (1991: 428), health education/promotion approaches may result in scepticism. Whilst we would contend that the epidemiological perspective, like that of biomedicine, needs to be problematised, we nonetheless share such concerns. Indeed, our findings indicate that diagnosis is one arena where scepticism may arise, since patients may question whether they have diabetes if they are unable to reconcile their own understandings and experiences with discourses which exalt individual risk factors to a central and exclusive domain.

### Acknowledgements

Both studies were funded by the Chief Scientist Office. The opinions expressed in this paper are those of the authors, and not necessarily of the funding body. The authors would like to thank the health-care professionals who assisted with recruitment and the patients who took part. Additional thanks go to Margaret MacPhee for excellent secretarial support, and to Margaret Douglas, Lisa Hanna and Odette Parry, who were grant holders on one or both studies.

### Note

1 All names used are pseudonyms.

# References

Backett, K. (1992) Taboos and excesses: lay health and moralities in middle class families, *Sociology of Health and Illness*, 14, 2, 255–74.

Ballard, R. (1994) The emergence of Desh Pardesh. In Ballard, R. (ed.) *Desh Pardesh: the South Asian Presence in Britain*. London: Hurst and Company.

Blaxter, M. (1983) The cause of disease: women talking, *Social Science and Medicine*, 17, 59–69.

Blaxter, M. (1997) Whose fault is it? People's own conceptions of the reasons for health inequalities, *Social Science and Medicine*, 44, 747–56.

Bury, M. (1982) Chronic illness as biographical disruption, *Sociology of Health and Illness*, 4, 2, 167–82.

Bury, M. (2001) Illness narratives: fact or fiction? *Sociology of Health and Illness*, 23, 3, 263–85.

Carricaburu, D. and Pierret, J. (1995) From biographical disruption to biographical reinforcement: the case of HIV positive men, *Sociology of Health and Illness*, 17, 1, 65–88.

Cohen, M.Z., Tripp-Reimer, Smith, C., Sorofman, B. and Lively, S. (1994) Explanatory models of diabetes: patient-practitioner variation, *Social Science and Medicine*, 38, 1, 59–66.

Crawford, R. (1984) A cultural account of 'health': control, release and the social body. In McKinlay, J.B. (ed.) *Issues in the Political Economy of Health Care*. London: Tavistock.

Davison, C., Smith, G.D. and Frankel, S. (1991) Lay epidemiology and the prevention paradox: the implications of coronary candidacy for health education, *Sociology of Health and Illness*, 13, 1, 1–19.

D'Costa, F.D., Samanta, A. and Burden, A.C. (2000) Epidemiology of diabetes in UK Asians: a review, *Practical Diabetes*, 8, 64–6.

Dumont, L. (1970) *Homo Hierarchicus: the Caste System and its Implications*. London: Weidenfeld and Nicolson.

Emslie, C., Hunt, K. and Watt, G. (2001) Invisible women? The importance of gender in lay beliefs about heart problems, *Sociology of Health and Illness*, 23, 2, 203–33.

Frankel, S., Davison, C. and Smith, G.D. (1991) Lay epidemiology and the rationality of responses to health education, *British Journal of General Practice*, 4, 428–30.

Garro, L.C. (1995) Individual and societal responsibility? Explanations of diabetes in an Anishinaabe (Ojibway) community, *Social Science and Medicine*, 40, 1, 37–46.

Giddens, A. (1991) *Modernity of Self-Identity*. Cambridge: Polity Press.

Greenhalgh, P.M. (1997) Diabetes in British South Asians: nature, nurture and culture, *Diabetic Medicine*, 14, 10–18.

Hallowell, N. (1999) Doing the right thing: genetic risk and responsibility, *Sociology of Health and Illness*, 21, 5, 597–621.

Hunt, K., Emslie, C. and Watt, G. (2001) Lay constructions of a family history of heart disease: potential for misunderstandings in the clinical encounter? *Lancet*, 357, 1168–71.

Hunt, L.M., Valenzuela, M.A. and Pugh, J.A. (1998) Porque me toco a mi? Mexican American diabetes patients' causal stories and their relationship to treatment behaviours, *Social Science and Medicine*, 46, 959–69.

Hussain, Y. and Bagguley, P. (2005) Citizenship, ethnicity and identity: British Pakistanis after the 2001 riots, *Sociology*, 39, 407–25.

Ismail, H., Wright, J., Rhodes, P. and Small, N. (2005) Religious beliefs about the causes and treatment of epilepsy, *British Journal of General Practice*, 55, 26–31.

Kleinman, A. (1988) *The Illness Narratives: Suffering, Healing and the Human Condition*. New York: Basic Books.

Knight, K.M., Dornan, T. and Bundy, C. (2006) The diabetes educator: trying hard, but must concentrate more on behaviour, *Diabetic Medicine*, 23, 485–501.

La Fontaine, J. (1985) 'Person and individual: some anthropological reflections'. In Carrithers, M., Collins, S. and Lukes, S. (eds) *The Category of the Person*. Cambridge: Cambridge University Press.

Lawton, J., Peel, E., Parry, O., Araoz, G. and Douglas, M. (2005a) Lay perceptions of type 2 diabetes in Scotland: bringing health services back in, *Social Science and Medicine*, 60, 1423–35.

Lawton, J., Parry, O., Peel, E. and Douglas, M. (2005b) Diabetes service provision: a qualitative study of newly diagnosed Type 2 diabetes patients' preferences and views, *Diabetic Medicine*, 22, 1246–51.

Lawton, J., Ahmad, N., Hallowell, N., Hanna, L. and Douglas, M. (2005c) Perceptions and experiences of taking oral hypoglycaemic agents amongst people of Pakistani and Indian origin: qualitative study, *British Medical Journal*, 330, 1247–49.

Lawton, J., Ahmad, N., Hanna, L., Douglas, M. and Hallowell, N. (2006a) 'I can't do any serious exercise': Barriers to physical activity amongst people of Pakistani and Indian origin with type 2 diabetes, *Health Education Research*, 21, 43–54.

Lawton, J., Ahmad, N., Hanna, L., Douglas, M. and Hallowell, N. (2006b) Diabetes service provision: a qualitative study of the experiences and views of Pakistani and Indian patients with type 2 diabetes, *Diabetic Medicine*, 23, 1003–07.

Leder, D. (1990) *The Absent Body*. Chicago: University of Chicago Press.

Linn, M.W., Linn, B.S. and Stein, S.R. (1982) Beliefs about causes of cancer in cancer patients, *Social Science and Medicine*, 16, 835–9.

Lutfey, K. (2005) On practices of 'good doctoring': reconsidering the relationship between provider roles and patient adherence, *Sociology of Health and Illness*, 27, 4, 421–47.

Lukes, S. (1973) *Individualism*, Oxford: Basil Blackwell.

Lupton, D. (1993) Risk as moral danger: the social and political functions of risk discourse in public health, *International Journal of Health Services*, 23, 425–35.

Mauss, M. (1985) A category of the human mind: the notion of the person; the notion of the self. In Carrithers, M., Collins S. and Lukes, S. (eds) *The Category of the Person*. Cambridge: Cambridge University Press.

Mercado-Martinez, F.J. and Ramos-Herrera, I.M. (2002) Diabetes: the layperson's theories of causality, *Qualitative Health Research*, 12, 792–806.

Morris, B. (1994) *The Anthropology of the Self: the Individual in Cultural Perspective*. London: Pluto Press.

Parry, O., Peel, E., Douglas, M. and Lawton, J. (2006) Issues of cause and control in patients' accounts of type 2 diabetes, *Health Education Research*, 21, 97–107.

Petersen, A. and Lupton, D. (1996) *The New Public Health: Health and Self in the Age of Risk*. London: Sage.

Pill, R. and Stott, C.H. (1985) Choice or chance: Further evidence of ideas of illness and responsibility for health, *Social Science and Medicine*, 10, 981–91.

Pound, P., Gompertz, P. and Ebrahim, S. (1998) Illness in the context of older age: the case of stroke, *Sociology of Health and Illness*, 20, 4, 489–506.

Radley A. (1993) Introduction. In Radley, A. (ed.) *Worlds of Illness: Biographical and Cultural Perspectives on Health and Illness*. London: Routledge.

Roper, N.A., Bilous, W., Kelly, W.F., Unwin, N.C. and Connolly, V.M. (2001) Excess mortality in a population with diabetes and the impact of material deprivation: longitudinal population based study, *British Medical Journal*, 322, 1389–93.

Rose, N. (1990) *Governing the Soul: the Shaping of the Private Self*. London: Routledge.

Sanders, C., Donovan, J. and Dieppe, P. (2002) The significance and consequences of having painful and disabled joints in older age: co-existing accounts of normal and disrupted biographies, *Sociology of Health and Illness*, 24, 2, 227–53.

Schoenberg, N.E., Amey, C.H. and Coward, R.T. (1998) Stories of meaning: lay perspectives on the origin and management of noninsulin dependent diabetes mellitus among older women in the United States, *Social Science and Medicine*, 47, 2113–25.

Schoenberg, N.E., Drew, E.M., Stoller, E.P. and Kart, C.S. (2005) Situating stress: lessons from lay discourses on diabetes, *Medical Anthropology Quarterly*, 19, 171–93.

Shaw, A. (2000) *Kinship and Continuity: Pakistani Families in Britain*. Amsterdam: Harwood Academic Publishers.

Snoek, F.J. (2002) Breaking the barriers to optimal glycaemic control – what physicians need to know from patients' perspectives, *International Journal of Clinical Practice*, 129, Supplement, 80–4.

Sullivan, E.S. and Joseph, D.H. (1998) Struggling with behaviour changes: a special case for clients with diabetes, *Diabetes Educator*, 21, 533–40.

Thompson, S.J. and Gifford, S.M. (2000) Trying to keep a balance: the meaning of health and diabetes in an urban Aboriginal community, *Social Science and Medicine*, 51, 1457–72.

Williams, G. (1993) Chronic illness and the pursuit of virtue in everyday life. In Radley, A. (ed.) *Worlds of Illness: Biographical and Cultural Perspectives on Health and Disease*. London: Routledge.

Williams, R. (1990) *A Protestant Legacy: Attitudes to Death and Illness among Older Aberdonians*. Oxford: Clarendon Press.

Williams, S.J. (2000) Chronic illness as biographical disruption or biographical disruption as chronic illness? Reflections on a core concept, *Sociology of Health and Illness*, 22, 1, 40–67.

# 7

# Long-term health conditions and Disability Living Allowance: exploring ethnic differences and similarities in access

## Sarah Salway, Lucinda Platt, Kaveri Harriss and Punita Chowbey

### Introduction

An increase in chronic health conditions has been recognised as a feature of demographic and epidemiological transitions of the last century across Western Europe. Yet long-term health conditions are not purely the experience of older people. In the Health Survey for England 2003, 44 per cent of men and 46 per cent of women reported one or more long-standing illnesses and 23 per cent of men and 26 per cent of women reported long-standing illness that limited their daily activities in some way (Joint Surveys Group 2004);[1] while the *Labour Force Survey* for September 2004, using a slightly different series of questions, estimated that around 27 per cent of working-age adults had a long-term health problem with 16 per cent regarding it as activity limiting. Such adults will have substantially reduced chances of employment (Smith and Twomey 2002, Berthoud 2006), and those in work command relatively low wages, increasing their risks of poverty. In such circumstances the role of state welfare benefits in mitigating poverty is crucial. These include benefits aimed at off-setting additional expenditure associated with illness and impairment (primarily Disability Living Allowance [DLA]), which offer an important – even if not a fully adequate (Smith *et al.* 2004) – contribution towards maintaining standards of living and continued engagement with the wider society. UK health and social policy currently places great emphasis on increasing self-reliance and reducing the burden of long-term health conditions to the NHS and social security expenditure (through the promotion of self-care, particularly expansion of lay-led self-management programmes, and welfare-to-work initiatives, including reform of Incapacity Benefit). But despite this emphasis, the ways in which individuals and families with long-term health conditions can be protected against poverty has received less emphasis.

Moreover, regardless of ample evidence that both long-term health conditions and income poverty affect certain ethnic minority groups more seriously than others (Erens *et al.* 2001, Platt 2002, Nazroo 1997), the potential variation in take-up of sickness/disability benefits (including DLA) by ethnic group and the role of such benefits in mitigating poverty across and within ethnic groups has not been subject to investigation. Furthermore, while there is a large and growing body of sociological research exploring the lived experiences of individuals reporting long-term health conditions (see Bury, Newbould and Taylor 2005 and Lawton 2003 for useful reviews), how ethnicity patterns the processes linking long-term health conditions to poverty has not received sustained attention.

This paper aims to address these gaps by integrating national-level quantitative findings on DLA receipt and in-depth qualitative material relating to four ethnic 'groups': Bangladeshis; Pakistanis; White British (White English in the qualitative work); and Black Africans (Ghanaians in the qualitative work). Investigation of DLA provides an opportunity to increase our understanding of the patterning of health-related outcomes by ethnicity. Moreover, it is a particularly pertinent benefit to explore because it is an individual benefit, is health-related, non-means-tested and is available to those in work. The following research questions guided our analyses:

- How is the receipt of DLA distributed across different ethnic groups?
- What factors influence access to DLA?
- In what ways is ethnicity relevant to our understanding of individual access to DLA?

## Background to the research focus

*Ethnicity and benefit take-up*
There is a significant literature on benefit take-up in the UK, which has predominantly taken two forms. On the one hand, systematic comparisons of eligibility criteria with benefit receipt have been used to estimate take-up rates, primarily for means-tested benefits (including tax credits) (*e.g.* Falkingham 1986, Fry and Stark 1993, DWP 2006a). These studies have not considered differentiation by ethnic group, despite a longstanding acknowledgement of the need for such information (Craig 1991). On the other hand, a range of qualitative studies has explored issues in take-up of various benefits, and this literature includes a number that engage with potential variation in take-up by ethnicity (*e.g.* Gordon and Newnham 1985, NACAB 1991, Law *et al.* 1994, Barnard and Pettigrew 2003, Craig 2004).

Between them, these two types of study provide some indication of the factors that may be relevant to ethnic patterns of DLA claims, including those relating to both claimant behaviour and administrative response, though these are not, of course, independent of each other (Platt 2003a). Whether or not a claim for benefit is submitted is likely to depend on a range of factors, including the perceived advantages and disadvantages associated with both the claiming process and receipt of the benefit in question. Anticipated response will shape perceptions of the claiming process, while those administering benefits will be influenced by how they see and understand the claims being brought to them. Moreover, both take place in the wider context of the ways in which state and society construct and legitimate particular ideas of welfare and entitlement.

It is clear that take-up of benefit increases with the amount of entitlement (DWP 2006a, Pudney *et al.* 2004). This suggests that the perceived 'costs' of claiming in terms of time, effort, information needs, 'hassle' and stigma (Pudney *et al.* 2004, Platt 2003a) are weighed up against the potential monetary gains. Moreover, it seems likely that low-income households (and therefore those ethnic groups with a larger proportion of low-income households) would face stronger incentives to claim even small amounts of benefit because of their greater *relative* contribution to household income.

Costs of claiming are unlikely to be constant across individuals and groups. Barnard and Pettigrew (2003) identified a range of potential barriers among older people from minority ethnic groups, including language issues, lack of a National Insurance Number (among South Asian older women), and concerns about the impact of claiming on residence status. Fears of the system and the arduous nature of the claims process, while general issues, were enhanced for minority ethnic group members (see also Scharf *et al.* 2002).

Craig (2004) has drawn attention to the lack of adequate exploration of attitudes towards claiming benefits among minority ethnic groups, and the available evidence suggests significant heterogeneity across groups and contexts. Molloy *et al.* (2003) found that African, Caribbean and Pakistani respondents more commonly raised issues related to pride and avoidance of charity than Whites and Indians. In contrast, Law *et al.* (1994) found positive, rights-based attitudes to claiming among some Bangladeshi respondents alongside more resistant attitudes from others. Craig's (2004) study among older people found that those from South Asian groups, particularly women, were more deferential than those from Black groups who more commonly expressed feelings of entitlement to benefits. In addition, an information deficit relating to both knowledge and familiarity with the 'system' has been identified as a significant issue for certain minority groups (Bloch 1993, Scharf *et al.* 2002, Molloy *et al.* 2003, Craig 2004).

Experience or anticipation of refusal, or requests for additional evidence, also increase costs of claiming (Gordon and Newnham 1985, NACAB 1996), and legitimising or de-legitimising discourses in relation to particular benefits or types of benefit (for example the recent focus on incapacity benefits (DWP 2006b)) or targeted at particular groups (for example, the exclusion of asylum seekers from the mainstream benefits system) also shape the costs and benefits of claims. Such discourses are absorbed and reproduced by potential claimants as our analysis shows.

Those groups, therefore, that stand to gain the greatest proportional increase in income through the receipt of benefits may be the very same ones for whom the costs of claiming are high. It is also important to consider the possibility that those who claim may not be deemed eligible or be awarded benefit. Again, information on ethnic variation in the probability of award is not extensive – though there is some evidence that minority groups are at a disadvantage (Bloch 1997).

### The case of Disability Living Allowance

DLA is intended to offset the additional expenditure that the mobility and 'care' needs associated with long-term health conditions may bring. Eligibility is determined by the extent of need (assessed by a standard assessment tool), as well as additional criteria relating to residence and age (<65 years). Given the two components and their levels (illustrated in Box 1), overall entitlement in 2006 varied between £105.70 and £16.50 per week. The incentive to claim is thus likely to vary substantially with perception of likely award.

Box 1 *Disability Living Allowance, May 2006*

---

*Eligibility criteria:*
Intended for people with 'severe physical or mental illness or disability'.
Two components: mobility and care. Age (<65 years).
Non-means tested (not affected by savings or other income).
Not affected by employment status.

*Weekly amounts, May 2006:*
Total ranges from £16.50 to £105.70

|  | *Care component* | *Mobility component* |
|---|---|---|
| Higher | 62.25 | 43.45 |
| Middle | 41.65 | N/A |
| Lower | 16.50 | 16.50 |

*Claiming process:*
Self-completion of claim form detailing daily activities and capabilities. Claim form asks for permission to contact individual's general practitioner, but no certification from GP needs to be included. Medical examination by a Department for Work and Pensions Examining Medical Practitioner may be needed where a decision cannot be made on the basis of the questionnaire. Renewal of fixed term awards and periodic review take place.

---

The complex (and largely opaque) nature of the eligibility criteria make it impossible to determine from standard surveys or general interviews whether differential receipt of DLA represents variation in eligibility or in take-up among those eligible, though there have been evaluation studies attempting to address whether DLA met its targets (Sainsbury *et al.* 1995, Daly and Noble 1996, Roberts and Lawton 1998). Moreover, receipt of DLA does not show a clear association with severity of illness or disability as measured in specialist surveys (Daly and Noble 1996, Berthoud 2006). Nevertheless, the Disability Alliance suggest that take-up is just 40–60 per cent of those eligible, and differences in receipt among those with otherwise similar health characteristics and conditions is likely to be at least indicative of differences in take-up, particularly given what we know about the difficulties of claiming and rates of success. The self-assessment tool, intended to place the emphasis on the individual's experience, is long and very detailed. In practice few claims are successful unless assisted by professional help; and in 2004 and 2005 fewer than half of new claims resulted in an award (*Hansard* 25 Oct 2005: Column 280W). Of those that went to appeal in the third quarter of 2005, around 50 per cent resulted in the decision being reversed (DWP 2005). It has also been argued that it is particularly hard to claim for the impacts of mental health conditions (Barton 2006).

The need for ethnically disaggregated information on DLA take-up has been highlighted (Wayne 2003, House of Commons Work and Pensions Committee 2005), but the ways in which ethnicity may pattern the experience of the claiming process has not been examined in detail to date.

*Ethnicity and experiencing long-term health conditions*[2]
In addition to work that has focused on benefit access, the large sociological literature regarding the experience of long-term health conditions has an important bearing on our current research focus. Though this work has undergone a number of shifts in emphasis over the past 50 years or so (Bury *et al.* 2005, Lawton 2003), a common theme from the 1960s onwards has been to recognise that the experience of long-term health conditions is not merely medical, but rather, social. Negotiations and social interactions, particularly with family members and care givers, are now seen as central to the process, and similar health conditions have been shown to have diverse implications for different individuals (Charmaz 2000).

While much of the literature has stressed the disruption caused by long-term health conditions to individuals' social relationships (Bury 1982) and self-identities (Charmaz 2000), long-term health conditions may also be integrated into personal life-stories (Williams 1984). Studies suggest that older age, familiarity with the condition and a life context characterised by multiple socioeconomic disadvantage, may each be associated with the construction of a health condition as 'just part of life' (Pound *et al.* 1998, Sanders, Donovan and Dieppe 2002, Higginbottom 2006, Cornwell 1984). However, such accommodation can clearly be 'double-edged', allowing a reduction in the salience of symptoms but at the expense of necessary treatment and care (Bury *et al.* 1995: 8, Campbell *et al.* 2003).

Despite many commonalities across ethnic groups, there may be important ways in which ethnicity shapes the experiences of individuals with long-term health conditions. A number of studies of South Asians[3] suggest that the degree of stigma attached to long-term health conditions and the surveillance of the individual and associated carers by the family and wider community may be more intense than among the White majority, resulting in a greater desire for concealment (Molloy *et al.* 2003, Katbamna *et al.* 2000). Though far fewer studies have included UK Africans, Molloy *et al.* (2003) also reported heightened stigma and concealment among their respondents of African origin. Evidence from several studies also suggests that minority ethnic individuals with long-term health conditions have a higher propensity towards self-care or 'management' of the condition within the family (Higginbottom 2006, Katbamna *et al.* 2000). This in part reflected language barriers; but cultural dissonance between some minority individuals' and health professionals' inter-pretations of the condition and appropriate management strategies, and a consequent lack of trust and satisfaction with available services, were also factors (Higginbottom 2006, Anderson *et al.* 1989, O'Connor and Nazroo 2002, Mirza and Sheridan 2003). Such patterns should also be seen within the context of racist exclusion and structural disadvantage (Atkin and Rollings 1996, Chattoo and Ahmad 2003) in that government and voluntary agencies have a responsibility to ensure that services are accessible and appropriate to the needs of marginalised groups. Such services include access to the necessary financial support to enable continued participation in daily life.

The implications for claiming behaviour of different responses to long-term health conditions, both between individuals within groups and across ethnic groups, have not been explored. That is the contribution of this paper.

## Theoretical and methodological approach

*'Unpacking' ethnicity in health-related research*
The present paper responds to calls for health-related research to engage more critically with concepts of 'ethnicity' (Smaje 1996, Bradby 2003, Karlsen and Nazroo 2006). We recognise ethnicity not as fixed or 'essential' and linked to equally essentialised cultural practices, but as shifting, multiple and often hybrid (Gardner 2002). The importance of historical and contextual influences on ethnic identity formations and ethnic relations is acknowledged (Hall 1992, Mac an Ghaill 1999, Bhavnani and Phoenix 1994): the signifi-cance of ethnicity as a component of identity varies between individuals and collectives across time and space. Nevertheless, we agree with Ville and Guerin-Pace's assertion that identity formation remains 'deeply rooted in the organization of society' (2005: 237). There are limits to the ways in which individuals can fashion their identities. Importantly, holding a racialised identity remains a central element in the experience of minority ethnic individuals in the UK (Jenkins 1994, Modood 1988, 1998, Karlsen 2004). In addition, family, kinship and wider ethnic structures may place important constraints upon an individual's ability to negotiate their identity both directly through the use of sanctions and indirectly via the loss of rights and claims.

These theoretical insights offer the possibility of greater understanding of the ways in which ethnicity patterns the health experience of individuals and groups (Smaje 1996, Ellison 2005), urging us neither to essentialise nor to abolish ethnicity as an analytical tool. Therefore, though we acknowledge the potential dangers in taking ethnicity as a central axis of analysis and recognise that much of minority ethnic health disadvantage is linked to socioeconomic and political marginalisation (Nazroo 1997, Sheldon and Parker 1992), we nevertheless agree with Smaje's assertion that 'many insights are lost if the concept of ethnicity is simply emptied into class disadvantage' (1996: 153).

Drawing on work by Modood (2004) and Smaje (1996), who in turn are heavily influenced by Bourdieu's (1977) notion of habitus, we suggest that in seeking to understand the ways in which ethnic identity patterns health experience, we are essentially concerned with exploring: first, why and how people identify themselves and others as inside or outside particular ethnic groups in particular contexts; and secondly, the implications of such inclusion and exclusion for the (i) 'ways of being and doing' that individuals adopt, and

(ii) their access to or exclusion from resources (broadly defined). Such an approach reminds us of the need to look closely at what is implied by ethnic identity in particular situations. In the present study we therefore sought to identify (though not assume) whether, and through what processes, ethnic identity influenced access to DLA among those with a long-term health condition.

*Integrating qualitative and quantitative methodological approaches*
The present paper is unusual in integrating complementary qualitative and quantitative approaches to study long-term ill-health and benefit use across four ethnic groups. Our large-scale survey data allow an examination of the ways in which social processes are translated into differential access to resources between ethnic 'groups' at the aggregate level. This analysis is complemented by our qualitative work in which we explored in more detail processes of inclusion and exclusion, and their implications for incentives and barriers to DLA receipt.

Our qualitative data constitute a sub-set of the sample included in the quantitative dataset in three ways. First, the operationalisation of 'long-term health condition' differed slightly between the two sets of data. The broader project aim was to inform policy and programme responses to the growing numbers of individuals experiencing long-term health conditions (and associated impairment) in working-age adult life. Therefore, though we acknowledge Ahmad's (2000) observation that the distinction between 'disability' and 'chronic illness' is more blurred in reality than the academic literature and policy discourses would suggest, we nevertheless explicitly avoided using the term 'disabled'. Our sampling simply required that the health condition was on-going and that onset had occurred during adult life. In practice, our fieldwork took a very open-ended, flexible approach, though clearly identification of potential respondents required us to use some terms to indicate who we were looking for. We tended to use 'long-term illness', 'long-term health problem' and 'long-term health condition' (and their equivalents in local languages where available)[4] and, on occasion, to offer examples of conditions that might be considered as 'long-term', though no precise definitions of degree of severity or duration were employed. This approach allowed us to explore subjective interpretations of ill-health and its consequences, as well as the extent to which individuals adopted a 'disabled' self-identity.

By contrast, the Labour Force Survey (LFS) uses the following question: 'Do you have any health problems or disabilities that you expect will last for more than a year?' Clearly then the survey data includes individuals who have been experiencing their long-term health condition since childhood. It is also likely that the survey data include some individuals who regard themselves as having a 'disability' but not a 'health problem' or 'health condition'. In practice, the majority of the in-depth qualitative interview respondents had health conditions that were primarily associated with a long-term illness (see Table 1), though there were some whose condition related to accidental injury. Nonetheless, many of the experiences reported were similar across the range of conditions. In particular, those who identified themselves as having a particular illness also commonly reported associated physical impairments (such as those with heart disease who could not walk quickly), and those with injuries reported knock-on complications to physiological functioning (such as an individual whose diet was severely restricted due to internal organ damage). Many respondents experienced pain, fatigue and unpredictability of symptoms as core elements of their health condition. Clearly, then, the distinction between 'disability' and 'long-term illness' is not clear-cut and it is unlikely that the different definitions employed by the qualitative and quantitative approaches compromise their compatibility.

The second area of difference between our data sources relates to geographical spread. Whereas the LFS is a nationally representative sample, the qualitative work took place in East

Table 1  *Long-term health conditions reported by in-depth interview informants*

| | Total | Self-reported long-term health condition |
|---|---|---|
| Bangladeshi men | 5 | diabetes (1), arthritis (1), depression (2), heart disease (2), cancer (1), leg pain (1), angina (1) |
| Bangladeshi women | 8 | diabetes (3), depression (3), disc prolapse (1), kidney disease (1), back and arm pain (1), lupus (1), infertility problems (1) |
| Pakistani men | 6 | diabetes (2), arthritis (1), heart disease (1) angina (1), stroke (1), Parkinson's (1), kidney disease (1), severe back pain (1) |
| Pakistani women | 8 | diabetes (3), depression (5), heart disease (1), loss of hearing (1), lung disease (1), sight loss (1) |
| Ghanaian men | 7 | diabetes (2), arthritis (1), high blood pressure (1), partially sighted (1), kidney disease (1), stroke (1) |
| Ghanaian women | 8 | diabetes (2), depression (2), backache (1), sickle cell disease (1), arthritis (1), cancer (1), leg and foot problems (1) |
| White English men | 8 | diabetes (2), depression (4), cancer (1), muscular dystrophy (1), asthma (1), arthritis (3), leg and foot problems (1), spleen problems (1), back pain (1) |
| White English women | 7 | depression (3), anxiety (1), cancer (1), arthritis (1), loss of hearing (1), balance problems (1), mental illness (1), physical disability – wheelchair user (1) |
| Total informants | 57 | |

*Notes*:  The total number of conditions is greater than the number of informants since several informants reported multiple health conditions. Several of the family members interviewed also reported having long-term conditions.

London within four 'communities' loosely defined in geographical terms. Census data and the Index of Multiple Deprivation showed that levels of long-term health conditions were higher, and socioeconomic conditions poorer, in our study areas than nationally. Since the objective of the broader research project was to explore the links between long-term health conditions and various dimensions of poverty, we had specifically selected these study areas.

Thirdly, ethnic group membership was operationalised differently in the two datasets. Our qualitative work was driven by the desire to explore the links between long-term health conditions and poverty within and across a set of ethnic groups characterised by diverse health and socioeconomic profiles. We decided that four contrasting ethnic groups, namely Bangladeshi, Pakistani, Ghanaian and White English would provide adequate opportunity for comparative analysis. While appreciating the potentially fluid nature of both the content and boundaries of ethnic group membership, in practice the research team identified potential respondents for the four 'groups' of interest and then sought to understand emic constructions of ethnic identity as part of the research focus. This approach proved relatively unproblematic for the Bangladeshi and Pakistani individuals, who, by and large, strongly identified with these ethnic labels, and for whom there were many ethnically-based community organisations that served as points of contact. Locating Ghanaian respondents was more difficult. Though the notion of a Ghanaian 'community' was felt to be meaningful to many of our respondents, it was found to be much less visible and more geographically dispersed, and there were fewer organisations and activities that were overtly Ghanaian, though churches proved useful. Finally, seeking out suitable White English respondents was more time-consuming. Our prior experience suggested that focusing on 'White English' individuals in the area would yield a more meaningful 'group' in terms of networks of association and notions of shared ancestry and culture, rather than also including individuals identifying as Welsh, Scots or Irish. Nevertheless, potential respondents did not always readily self-identify on the basis of ethnicity, there were no community organisations that were overtly for White English people, and professionals working in the area were uncomfortable with the fact that our work was seeking to single out this group (see McClean and Campbell 2003 for similar research experiences).

Amongst our minority respondents, ethnicity (understood primarily as shared country of origin and common 'culture') was a salient part of self-identity and strong forces of inclusion operated, particularly for the Bangladeshis and Pakistanis. Shared ethnicity brought a sense of 'feeling easy' or having a shared understanding, and social ties were frequently intra-ethnic. Importantly, also, shared ethnicity entailed expectations and informal claims to support, advice, information and advocacy. Many of our minority ethnic respondents, particularly those with lower levels of education and English language competency, shared the experience of feeling alienated and excluded from 'mainstream' society and state agencies.

The LFS includes the ONS self-classification question on ethnic group, with 16 main options. In this paper we concentrate on the four groups that map most closely onto those in our qualitative sample: Bangladeshi, White British, Pakistani and Black African. Clearly Black African is a much more heterogeneous category than our Ghanaian sample (itself containing different linguistic and 'ethnic' groups). However, it is likely to include the vast majority of those who define themselves as Ghanaian and it is the closest approximation we can arrive at to our Ghanaian sample. The White British category is also somewhat broader than our White English sample, but the disparity is much smaller. It will include most of those who define themselves as White English, who numerically dominate the category, but it also includes White Scottish, White Welsh and some White Irish.

*Qualitative methods of data collection and analysis*
Our qualitative work was informed by the principles of 'critical ethnography', in that we attempted to synthesise a traditional ethnographic focus on subjective meanings and beliefs of respondents with the insights gained from a broader historical and structural analysis (Wainwright 1997). While we give a central place to the ways in which respondents describe themselves and their experiences of long-term health conditions, we nevertheless consider that such accounts require placing within an understanding of the broader social structures that facilitate and constrain the avenues open to individual actors.

Three phases of qualitative data collection were conducted between March 2004 and May 2005, as described in more detail in Salway, Platt *et al.* (2007). First, a phase of 'rapid assessment' was carried out by the research team and a group of trained community researchers. The aim of this phase was to gain a broad overview of the patterns of social, economic and cultural resources available to members of the four communities as well as an understanding of how long-term health conditions were perceived and the prominence they had in people's everyday lives. This phase also informed interview guideline development for phase two, and identification of respondents.

In phase two, in-depth interviews were conducted with (i) working-age adults reporting a long-term health condition (N = 57) and (ii) individuals living with a family member who had a long-term health condition (N = 29). Our sampling strategy was largely purposive and utilised multiple access points, with the intention of including respondents with differences in age, sex, migration, employment, health condition and degree of 'community involvement'. Interviews included history-taking methods to explore individual and household trajectories over time; they were conducted in the language of respondent's choice[5] and, subject to respondent approval, were tape-recorded, translated and transcribed. Analysis and integration of data into theory was ongoing during data collection. Researchers kept field diaries and held regular meetings and analysis workshops in which emerging findings and ideas were shared. Part-way through the second phase of data collection the information gathered so far was reviewed and some adjustments were made to the data collection tool to ensure that further detail could be gathered on issues of interest. Interview transcripts were subjected to both line-by-line coding and holistic 'narrative' analysis. The coding scheme was developed for use with the software package Nvivo through an iterative (three-stage) process involving line-by-line blind coding of a sub-sample of transcripts by three qualitative researchers. Once finalised, the coding structure was applied to the interview transcripts and, through multiple 'search-and-retrieve' actions, information from across the range of respondents was brought together for further theme building. This 'code-and-compile' approach was complemented by detailed memo writing for each respondent, using a consistent guideline in which themes running through each narrative, contextual information, and more interpretive comments (for instance regarding inconsistency between the individual with long-term ill-health's story and that of the other family member, or obvious omissions) were noted.

Thirdly, a phase of 'community feedback and consultation' was undertaken during which emerging findings were shared via a series of five informal meetings. The findings presented below draw on evidence generated during all three phases of data collection, though quotations from the second phase interviews are most commonly used to illustrate the points being made.

*Quantitative data and methods of analysis*
We used 12 pooled quarters of the quarterly LFS, from March 2002 to February 2005, to analyse DLA receipt by ethnic group among the working-age population (16–59/64 years). The LFS is a nationally representative survey covering around 60,000 respondents at each wave. Its size and its unclustered sample design makes it particularly appropriate for ethnicity analysis (Lindley *et al.* 2003). Moreover, it has a range of health questions which make it amenable to the study of long-term health conditions. In addition to the question on long-term health problems and disabilities, we made use of the question: 'Do these health problems or disabilities, when taken singly or together, substantially limit your ability to carry out normal day to day activities?' and the numbers of conditions reported, in order to approximate severity.

Each respondent is surveyed at five consecutive quarters, creating a semi-panel element to the survey. Given the amount of 'noise' typically associated with responses to questions on long-term health conditions, we exploited the semi-panel element of the survey to create a more stable measure, by requiring a positive response to the long-term health problems or disabilities question in two consecutive waves. This meant discarding the final wave observed for each individual (thus all wave five observations) and additionally making use of a 13th quarter to allow construction of the measure. In all analyses we employed sample weights, and we adjusted standard errors for repeat observations on individuals.

## Findings

*An investigation of claiming rates*
In this section we investigate variation in the receipt of DLA by ethnic group amongst individuals reporting a long-term 'health problem or disability'. As noted, lacking clear measures of eligibility, such variations can only be suggestive of differences in take-up. But

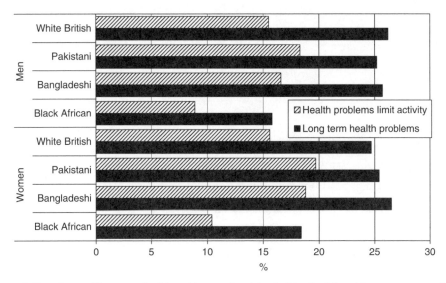

Figure 1 *Prevalence of long-term health problems and activity-limiting health problems amongst working-age adults by ethnic group and sex*
*Source*: ONS *Labour Force Survey*, March 2002–February 2005, authors' analysis, proportions are based on weighted data.

it is reasonable to assume that among those with long-term health conditions and comparable incentives to claim there would, other things being equal, be comparable patterns of receipt.

Overall, 24 per cent of working-age people reported a 'health problem or disability' that they expected to last a year or more and 15 per cent reported limitations to daily activity. Figure 1 shows the prevalence of reported long-term 'health problems and disabilities' and those that are activity-limiting by ethnic group and sex. Rates were noticeably lower among Black African men and women, while being much more similar for the other ethnic groups. Black African men and women were also much less likely to say that the health conditions were activity limiting, while Pakistani, and to a lesser extent Bangladeshi, men and women were more likely than their White British counterparts to report their condition as activity limiting. This suggests that the problems may have been more severe for these groups. Average numbers of conditions (not illustrated) were also higher for Pakistani men and women, indicating, again, greater severity.

Amongst those reporting a long-term health condition, 13 per cent of men and 12 per cent of women reported receiving DLA. This rose to 19 per cent among those reporting activity limitations (Table 2). Bangladeshis, especially men, had particularly low rates of receipt. This is surprising in the light of our discussion of income incentives, given all the evidence that Bangladeshis experience the highest rates of poverty (Platt 2002; 2003b).

Multivariate analyses were used to determine more precisely whether these ethnic group differentials reflected first, differences in the severity of the health condition and thus the probability of eligibility, and secondly, factors likely to impact on claiming and receipt. Logistic regression models were used to investigate the probability of DLA receipt among those with long-term health conditions, including proxies for severity (whether activity limiting and number of conditions) and exploring the role of a number of variables that might be expected to affect take-up. Sex and age were also controlled and a dummy for

Table 2 *Prevalence of DLA receipt amongst working-age adults with long-term health problems or disability and activity limitations by ethnic group*

| | Per cent of respondents with long-term health problems in receipt of DLA | | Per cent of respondents with activity-limiting health problems in receipt of DLA | |
|---|---|---|---|---|
| Ethnicity | men | women | men | Women |
| White British | 19.2 | 19.0 | 11.9 | 12.7 |
| Pakistani | 16.3 | 15.9 | 12.3 | 12.3 |
| Bangladeshi | 8.7 | 12.1 | 5.8 | 9.2 |
| Black African | 18.7 | 14.7 | 11.3 | 8.8 |
| All groups* | 19.2 | 19.1 | 12.8 | 12.0 |

*Source*: ONS *Labour Force Survey*, March 2002–February 2005, authors' analysis, weighted proportions.
*Notes*: * This includes those ethnic groups not quoted here.

living in inner London was included to identify any specific 'London' effects in claiming that could have differentiated our qualitative sample from the population as a whole. We examined the extent to which 'ethnic group effects' were observed once these factors had been taken into account.

In Table 3, Model 1, the probability of DLA receipt is modelled controlling for the effects of age, sex, proxies for severity and ethnicity. The coefficients for Pakistanis and Bangladeshis are negative and highly statistically significant, indicating that these groups are less likely to receive DLA than those with comparable profiles from the White British majority. This provides prima facie evidence of differentials in take-up between the groups. We then move on to look at what the intervening factors might be that contribute to differences in take-up for those with comparable levels of severity.

Given the emphasis on information needs and the difficulties of engaging with 'the system' in much of the literature, education and occupational class were included to represent a person's knowledge of and confidence in the benefits system and their perception of eligibility. Income and resources are however also associated with education and social class, which might decrease the pressure to claim. Thus, social housing tenure and benefit receipt were also included to proxy familiarity with the benefits system or local bureaucracy (for social tenants). Housing tenure was found not to contribute to the models, however, and so was excluded. Means-tested benefits were also used to indicate the economic position of the household and thus relate to the relative value of DLA. In addition, Incapacity Benefit receipt was used to indicate both knowledge of the system and acknowledgement (by self and the state) of ill-health.

As Table 3, Model 2 illustrates, introducing additional controls did not undermine the ethnic group effects. Instead they became larger in size and that for the Black African group became statistically significant, where it had not been in Model 1. Thus, for comparable levels of 'information', 'need' and 'know-how', as well as severity, all three minority groups with long-term health conditions were less likely to be in receipt of DLA than their White British counterparts. This indicates that these minority groups, both those with high levels of ill-health and those with low levels, may face specific obstacles or resistance to claiming.

Interestingly, as Model 2 illustrates, educational qualifications are negatively associated with DLA receipt. Though qualifications might potentially assist people through the claiming process and in gaining information, they are associated with a lower probability of a

Table 3 *Estimates from multivariate logistic regression indicating the effects of various characteristics on the receipt of DLA*

|  | Model 1 Coefficients (SEs) | Model 2 Coefficients (SEs) |
|---|---|---|
| *Demographic factors* | | |
| Age | −.009 [.001] | −.012 [.002] |
| Female | −.042 [.029] | −.023 [.040] |
| Living in Inner London | .198 [.079] | −.099 [.119] |
| *Health factors* | | |
| Activity-limiting health problem | 2.19 [.048] | 1.64 [.057] |
| Number of health conditions | .365 [.007] | .278 [.010] |
| *Ethnicity* | | |
| Pakistani | −.389 [.143] | −.920 [.198] |
| Bangladeshi | −.731 [.275] | −1.13 [.319] |
| Black African | −.062 [.211] | −.530 [.273] |
| *Socio-economic factors* | | |
| *Education (base = no qualifications)* | | |
| Other qualifications | | −.263 [.055] |
| Level 1 (GCSEs A-C) | | −.239 [.058] |
| Level 2 (A levels) | | −.321 [.057] |
| Higher education and above | | −.249 [.069] |
| *NSSEC (base = professional/managerial)* | | |
| Intermediate | | .162 [.064] |
| Routine & manual | | .266 [.057] |
| Never worked & long-term unemployed | | 1.36 [.077] |
| Full-time student | | .669 [.121] |
| *Other benefits* | | |
| Income Support | | .962 [.047] |
| Incapacity Benefit | | 1.23 [.043] |
| Unemployment benefits | | −.519 [.131] |
| Constant | −4.24 [.178] | −4.40 [.122] |
| Number of observations | 157,332 | 131,488 |

*Source*: ONS *Labour Force Survey*, March 2002-February 2005, authors' analysis.
*Notes*: Positive coefficients indicate that the characteristic is associated with a higher probability of DLA receipt, whilst negatively signed coefficients indicate that the chances of DLA receipt are reduced by this factor. Robust standard errors, adjusted for repeat observations on individuals and for sampling weights, are given in brackets following the coefficients. Coefficients with p-values below 0.05 have been highlighted in bold. The model also included a variable indicating calendar time which is not presented in the above table for purposes of clarity. Similarly, other ethnic groups than those which form our focus were included in the models but the results for them have not been quoted.

(successful) claim. Educational qualifications are inversely associated with severity of condition (Berthoud 2006); and they are also associated with greater assets and control over resources, and probability of remaining in work following ill-health. But it is then particularly striking to find this negative effect once we have also controlled for severity and for occupational class.

The raw data, however, indicated that this pattern, whereby education 'doesn't help' might not hold across all the ethnic groups. In particular, it was reversed for Bangladeshis and Black Africans (though not for the Pakistanis). We therefore explored the interaction between ethnic group and educational qualifications and examined predicted probabilities for different sets of characteristics. These showed that educational qualifications appeared to operate differently for the Black Africans and Bangladeshis, with higher levels of qualifications increasing their probability of being in receipt of DLA, compared both to members of the same group with lower qualifications and compared to White British with higher qualifications levels. Small cell sizes and overlapping confidence intervals made these conclusions tentative. They are, however, consistent with our qualitative findings, discussed below. For Pakistanis and White British, the pattern still clearly showed that lower qualifications were more salient for receipt of DLA than higher qualifications.

Occupational class is also significantly associated with DLA receipt, with those from lower social class backgrounds more likely to be in receipt, presumably reflecting differential need. The argument for economic incentives to claim DLA are also supported by the higher rates of receipt among those receiving Income Support (a means-tested benefit) compared to those not receiving. That this is not purely a result of familiarity with the benefits system is indicated by the fact that people receiving unemployment benefits (Job Seekers Allowance) or National Insurance credits are *less* likely to receive DLA. Incapacity Benefit increases probability of DLA receipt, which is consistent with both increased awareness of sickness-related benefits and prior experience of 'legitimated' or accepted ill-health. The causal relationship may in fact work in the opposite direction, since DLA can be used as a criterion for Incapacity Benefit receipt. But clearly, recognition at the level of one benefit is important for claiming/receipt of other sickness-related benefits, even though the relationship is not deterministic, as we discuss further below.

These results, then, indicate systematic (and unexplained) differences between ethnic groups in rates of DLA receipt. The qualitative analysis which follows explores in much more depth why these differences might arise and also how factors associated with claiming – need, information (education), know-how and legitimacy – operate across groups and take on particular meanings within them.

## Exploring the links between ethnicity, experiencing long-term ill-health and DLA

Many of our respondents had limited – or no – knowledge of DLA. Among those who had some familiarity with DLA, several respondents had thought about claiming but had not actually pursued it, others had made enquiries but taken it no further, and some had even started to complete the form and then thrown it away. We found significant commonalities across the four ethnic groups, suggesting that a complex of factors discouraged many individuals from claiming DLA. However, we also found evidence of ethnic differences in access.

### Concealing ill-health and resisting an ill (and/or disabled) identity
In common with previous research, our findings revealed that similar physical experiences (and impairments) meant different things to different people resulting in variation in the degree to which ill-health assumed prominence. Notwithstanding this variation, across all four ethnic groups, concealing the health condition, and therefore resisting an 'ill' identity, was common. Concealment took a variety of forms: withholding information, taking care with physical appearance, using euphemisms or choosing a preferred label for the condition, attending social gatherings despite feeling unwell, refusing to use aids, and direct lying. Importantly too, concealment frequently took the form of not seeking, and even refusing, help or support.

Despite this commonality, closer inspection revealed differences across the ethnic groups in the motivations and meanings attached to this concealment, as well as across the actors involved.

White English respondents tended to construct their down-playing of symptoms and concealment of the condition as a dimension of personal or, in a few cases, family character. In contrast, our minority ethnic respondents were more likely to explain their actions in terms of expected norms of behaviour for their ethnic community; thereby presenting concealment as an essential characteristic of 'our people' or 'our culture'. Among the Pakistani and Bangladeshi respondents, concealment was particularly associated with the feminine ideal of bearing distress in silence and gaining strength, maturity and high moral status through suffering (the concept of being '*sabarwali*' in Urdu). Among the Ghanaians concealment of health problems was strongly identified as a typical Ghanaian trait for both men and women (as was secrecy regarding financial matters); so much so that recruitment of suitable respondents was difficult:

I am not different, I am still Ghanaian, so I wouldn't particularly go about broadcasting my sickness you know (Ghanaian man with a long-term condition, 50–54 years).

Furthermore, while respondents from all backgrounds expressed the desire for concealment in terms of individual pride and self-reliance, our minority ethnic respondents also commonly referred to the implications of the health condition for other family members, and concerns that information would spread quickly through the community leading to gossip and negative behaviour. The notion of a 'moral community' ('moshra' in Urdu and 'shomaj' in Bengali/Sylheti) monitoring and judging behaviour of individuals and their families was important for many Bangladeshis and Pakistanis. Though Ghanaian respondents could not offer any equivalent terms in their Ghanaian languages, this concept was also meaningful to them. In this way, concealment reflected a perceived vulnerability, and several minority respondents felt pressure from family and wider community to conceal their health condition.

The extent to which a particular health condition was perceived to be a deviation from normal was also important. For all four ethnic groups, mental illnesses were problematic and the desire for concealment particularly strong. Interestingly, there was evidence of a change over time in the social consequences of revealing particular types of health condition among the Pakistani and Bangladeshi communities. With the rise in a local discourse among these groups around 'Asian diets' and 'Asian diseases', diabetes and heart disease in particular seemed less problematic and more 'normal', resulting in a reduced need for concealment. In contrast, among the Ghanaians, a community-level discourse on long-term health conditions seemed only to be emerging slowly and very recently, such that the tendency to conceal all types of health condition was very strong.

The degree to which a condition is perceived to be incompatible with valued social roles was also an important factor influencing concealment. For many, a strong desire to remain in work meant resisting revealing the extent of their health condition and identifying themselves as ill (or impaired). However, here there were important variations by gender, age and ethnicity. While Bangladeshis, Pakistanis and White English men held similar ideas regarding the inevitability of increasing age leading to reduced activity and withdrawal from the labour market, the chronological age at which this was legitimately felt to happen differed. For many Bangladeshi and Pakistani men in their forties and fifties, assuming the identity of someone with a long-term health condition did not appear to pose a serious conflict with their self-identity (though this is not to say that they did not suffer in experiencing the condition). These individuals assumed the largely economically inactive role of 'elder' ('barhe' or 'morubi'), relatively easily (see Gardner 2002). In contrast, White English men of similar ages seemed to find it more difficult to acknowledge living with a long-term health condition:

> I'd say it's pretty bad. I mean I'm only 47 and I feel as if, sort of 87 . . . It just seems I have one problem after another (White English man with long-term condition, 45–49 years).

> I feel I am a sick man, I can't do faster anything, you know, and er, . . . , but then it's also putting the things together. Like I think also I am getting old, I think that's why I'm getting weakness you know. . . . Yes, old age, you know after 40, it comes older, you know and that's it (Bangladeshi man with a long-term condition, 50–54 years).

Clearly, some willingness to recognise and to express a long-term condition is a crucial first step in the process of claiming sickness-related benefits. However, such recognition alone is insufficient to result in benefit receipt, as evidenced by the experience of Bangladeshi men, who appear to accept or adapt to ill-health comparatively successfully, but, as the quantitative analysis showed, have the lowest rates of DLA receipt. Perceived legitimacy, which we consider next, is a further necessary-but-not-sufficient criterion for pursuing a claim for benefit.

### Eligibility and legitimacy of claiming Disability Living Allowance

Across all four ethnic groups respondents expressed negative attitudes to receipt of welfare benefits, referring to notions of 'scrounging', 'losing control', 'becoming lazy' and 'feeling degraded'. Such sentiments were particularly strongly stated by our Ghanaian respondents and many expressed incomprehension of why people would continue claiming benefits for extended periods of time. Of course, much of this discussion related to the situation where claiming benefits was placed in opposition to earning one's own income. Nevertheless, this backdrop of required legitimacy (rather than eligibility per se) evidently affected people's stance towards DLA. A common theme across all four communities was that of holding off claiming until really necessary:

> Disability, actually I haven't as yet, I am able to walk about to some extent . . . and that's why I haven't applied, because I haven't become disabled as yet (Bangladeshi man with a long-term condition, 45–49 years).

> I knew there were higher levels [of DLA] but while he could still do things for himself I wasn't going to apply for it. But then once he couldn't do a lot of things for himself, I thought, well why not? (White English woman, family member, 55–59 years).

In addition, for several respondents there was the feeling that taking DLA would contribute to their being identified as 'disabled' – something to be resisted at all costs. In contrast to studies that have focused on individuals with severe impairments from early in life, we found few examples of individuals subscribing to the 'social model' of disability or of affirming their disabled identity. Respondents were often at pains to distance themselves from what they regarded as the unvarying and permanent nature of disability and its association with incapacity. This reluctance to accept a 'disabled' identity tended to deter people from taking up DLA, as we discuss below:

> They were all pushing me to do that [take DLA]. I say 'I'm getting up. I will not stay in this bed like this'. . . . They said 'You stupid, you are mad'. But I said, 'Look all that I want, I want to be on my feet'. . . . Although things were hard. But if I had compromised

me. I'd feel it was a bit of compromising. . . . Because I don't want to be accommodated into that disability thing. Funnily enough sometimes they [social workers] come here . . . they will use 'disabled'. I say 'no, no, no, no! I'm not disabled!' (Ghanaian woman with a long-term condition, 40–44 years).

People asked me to apply for it but I didn't (laughs) Why not? Because I don't want to consider myself a disabled people, that's why (Pakistani woman with a long-term condition, 35–39 years).

Notwithstanding this general aversion to claiming DLA, our qualitative findings concurred with the quantitative results in showing that the degree of financial hardship can play an important role in determining whether or not a claim for DLA is made. When faced with extreme financial difficulty, individuals tended to ignore community proscriptions against claiming benefit (as in the case of several Ghanaian women who were single parents) and actively sought out information on additional entitlements. Financial hardship thus provided a much-needed legitimacy to claiming DLA:

At that time we could not survive with the income support. I had some fights with him [husband] regarding this. I told him to get some more money somehow or other. He said he could not work. Then we consulted the doctor. He advised us to apply for disability allowance. Then we got help from this for our bills and insurance (Pakistani woman, family member, 45–49 years).

In addition, claiming DLA was felt to be more legitimate for older individuals, mirroring the differential constructions of long-term health conditions by age discussed above.

*Social networks, access to information and 'know-how' about the benefits system*
Across all the ethnic groups, many respondents expressed their feelings of ignorance and difficulties encountered in accessing information regarding the benefits system and their entitlements. Awareness and understanding of DLA seemed particularly poor; many respondents had not heard of the benefit despite having had their health condition for an extended period and, in some cases, receiving the national insurance contributions-based, sickness-related benefit Incapacity Benefit [IB]. Those that had heard of DLA often held misconceptions about eligibility criteria:

We didn't know nothing about disability allowance or anything like that, . . . I didn't know nothing about the system. [The social worker] goes 'Hasn't the income support, the social services ever interviewed you or asked your Mum about this, 'cause she's got that mental illness?', and I said 'No, I didn't know nothing'. She goes 'You've lost years and years of her disability allowance!' (Pakistani woman, family member, 30–34 years).

Over and above generally high levels of ignorance, several Bangladeshi and Pakistani respondents held misconceptions about DLA eligibility that related to an understanding of the English term 'disability' meaning only severe impairment rather than illness-related incapacity; as do the translated terms 'pongota' (Bengali/Sylheti) and 'mazoor' (Urdu) used in promotional leaflets and conversation:

No, Disability Living Allowance is a different thing. It's not for sick people. Disability is [for] those [who] are not clever enough, you know. Disability is those who can't move, or cannot speak, who [are] looked after [by] somebody else, then they get a disability allowance (Bangladeshi man with a long-term condition, 50–54 years).

A heavy reliance on personal social networks and word-of-mouth for information about benefits was evident for Pakistani, Bangladeshi and White English respondents. Many respondents mentioned friends as the ones who had initially introduced the possibility of DLA. However, despite this apparent similarity across these ethnic groups, the domination of social networks by co-ethnic ties resulted in ethnic variation in the availability of information. The Pakistani local networks stood out as being particularly well-informed about the benefit system and there was evidence of active sharing of information between Pakistani individuals:

I have helped three to four people, those who come to [name of group], they weren't getting disability, so I told them this is the way, I got them the form from the Social Service, in a legal way, like 'here, here is the department', . . . I used to take them (Pakistani man, family member, 50–54 years).

In contrast, the Bangladeshi networks were less productive and respondents less well-informed of available options. Importantly, however, many respondents in both the Pakistani and Bangladeshi groups expressed feelings of alienation and exclusion from 'mainstream' society and services, factors that reinforced their tendency to rely on 'our own people', despite the variable ability of this strategy to meet needs:

I used to feel very scared and fearful going up to the doctors . . . I had nobody to support me . . . My parents were there but they are old and don't speak English. I had no Bengali person who could support me . . . I had nobody to guide me or let me know that I had other options (Bangladeshi woman with a long-term condition, 35–39 years).

Interestingly, among the Ghanaians, a more complex picture emerged, reflecting the diverse linguistic, cultural, religious and socio-economic profile of this 'group'. Among those that were better educated and longer established, many had directly sought information on benefits from 'mainstream' services, including the Job Centre. The heightened concealment of health conditions within this community, combined with a similar sensitivity regarding the discussion of financial matters, appears to discourage exchange of information on receipt of benefits, and consequently means that social networks are unproductive on this topic. Furthermore, though the broader identity of 'Ghanaian' was clearly meaningful to individuals in certain circumstances (and was called upon in order to access certain resources, for instance 'Ghanaian' churches), it was also evident that people were included within, and excluded from, a variety of sub-networks of association and resource exchange (often based on clan heritage or 'home town' affiliation). More recent Ghanaian migrants with poorer English language skills and less confidence in dealing directly with state agencies appear to suffer as a result. Several respondents were finding it difficult to access information and could not easily tap into networks of exchange within which they were not included.

Given the complexity of the DLA claiming process, over-and-above awareness of the benefit, access to specialist support is important if a claim is to have a high chance of success. The large majority of our respondents, whether claims had been successful or not, described the process of claiming DLA as complex, time-consuming and stressful; in some cases even citing the system as a factor exacerbating the seriousness of their health condition. Many respondents, particularly those with lower levels of education or English language competency, talked about the onerous task of completing the lengthy forms.

Many also expressed the sentiments that the system does not trust people, that it is inequitable and unpredictable, and that DLA is very difficult to get:

> I got these stupid forms back asking me how far you could walk and stuff like that . . . I just couldn't be bothered to fill it in. In the end, just tore it up and threw it away. It was so stupid, bloody questions they ask you. I think they put these questions in to make it harder for you to claim anything (White English man with a long-term condition and family member, 55–59 years).

> I am a support worker and I'd say I fill in around four to five of these DLA forms a week. And you know, I never know when I send them off which ones are going to be successful (Pakistani woman, advice worker, 35–39 years, group discussion).

Our qualitative work revealed that few individuals from any of the ethnic groups had received specialist support in claiming DLA; just a small number receiving help from social workers and one from a charity. This is perhaps surprising for the Bangladeshi and Pakistani respondents, given the relatively large numbers of community-based organisations offering benefits advice and catering specifically to the needs of these individuals. The picture is less surprising for Ghanaians, since there were few support organisations for this group. Furthermore, there was evidence that where such support had been offered on an ad-hoc basis, take-up was extremely low, again reflecting the aversion to discussing financial matters and the lack of information exchange on this topic within Ghanaian networks. Interestingly, many of our White English respondents expressed feelings of being poorly supported in comparison with ethnic minority groups who were perceived to receive tailor-made services and additional support. A lack of specialist support to claims is clearly an issue affecting all ethnic groups. However, lower levels of education, poor English language competency and lack of experience with state bureaucracy is likely to make this a particularly serious problem for significant numbers among the minority groups.

A large number of respondents had had the experience of having a claim for DLA rejected, or their DLA taken away or reduced some time after their original claim. While some respondents took this in their stride, others found the process extremely stressful, receiving the rejection as a negation of their own suffering. In several cases respondents felt that mental health conditions and their associated impairments were not appropriately assessed for DLA. While some respondents had appealed, for others rejection had undermined their confidence in the legitimacy of their claim. Many could not face the stress of appealing, and for some the experience of rejection had even discouraged them from seeking other benefits and support. Again, specialist support in preparing an appeal was uncommon. It seems clear that such experiences further discourage significant numbers of individuals from pursuing their claims for DLA, even when living on extremely low incomes.

## Discussion and conclusions

Levels of DLA receipt among individuals reporting long-term health conditions are extremely low. This is partly due to the complex application procedure and the limited success of claims. Our quantitative data, however, revealed that Bangladeshi, Pakistani and Black African individuals have significantly lower levels of receipt than White British people who are comparable in terms of health status and socioeconomic characteristics.

Both our quantitative and qualitative data supported the indication that financial hardship encourages some people to seek out additional benefits (including DLA). However, significant obstacles deterred many individuals living on low incomes from pursuing claims for DLA despite potential eligibility and clear evidence of hardship. Factors we identified included: a reluctance to assume a 'disabled' identity; concerns about the legitimacy of claiming; very limited knowledge of the benefit and lack of specialist support to claiming; a perception that the benefits system is complex and stressful, and negative experiences of prior claiming. We also found evidence that while these factors were common across the four groups, they took particular expressions or were particularly salient for the different ethnic groups. Ethnic identity was found to be linked both to certain ways of 'being and doing' and patterns of resource access that had a bearing on DLA take-up.

Our findings suggest that 'being' Ghanaian places particular constraints upon the revealing of health conditions and the assumption of a 'disabled' identity. Similar, but less stringent, constraints were evident for Bangladeshis and Pakistanis. In all three ethnic minority communities, overtly assuming a 'disabled' identity carried the potential for greater social costs than among the White English and this clearly encouraged concealment and discouraged the uptake of DLA. However, the fluid and contingent nature of such 'ways of being and doing' was also clearly evident among the Bangladeshi and Pakistani groups in the increasing acceptability of acknowledging diabetes and heart disease (so-called 'Asian diseases') particularly among older men. Furthermore, the importance of structural factors, including migration histories and settlement patterns, in shaping opportunities and constraints to individual action must also be recognised. Importantly, for many Ghanaians, strong trans-national family links meant pressures to earn money and establish resources 'back home', and being precariously positioned with respect to employment, state welfare and even medical care all encouraged ignoring and/or concealing health conditions and a focus on income generation.

Consistent with previous qualitative studies, the role of information seemed to be important in our qualitative sample. Again this was true across the groups, but ethnicity patterned access to networks and the levels of resource they provided. While being 'Pakistani' and 'Bangladeshi' did appear to have meaning in relation to networks of information access in our current context, 'Ghanaian' was less useful, and the White English did not identify an ethnic 'community', beyond immediate kin, as an obvious source of advice and information. The effectiveness of networks also varied, with the Pakistani-based community resources providing apparently much more direct and pertinent advice and support in benefit claiming than those for the other groups, despite the apparent proliferation of Bangladeshi community organisations. Such effective networks may, of course, be specific to our sample, since our quantitative data indicated that all the minority groups were significantly less likely to receive DLA than their White British counterparts. On the other hand, the lack of sources of information and support for less-well educated Ghanaians and Bangladeshis, is consistent with the finding from the quantitative data that educational qualifications are more significant for DLA receipt for these two groups.

Being categorised as a member of a particular ethnic group (even if this ascription conflicts with your own) by significant actors outside your ethnic group, particularly those in powerful positions, has implications for one's relationship with 'mainstream' institutions. Our qualitative data did not allow us to draw any firm conclusions regarding the impact of racial exclusion on the processes involved in making a successful claim for DLA. Indeed, some respondents from all groups talked about feeling degraded by DWP staff and that their claims had been unfairly dismissed. The construction of discourses of legitimacy in relation to state is likely to impact across groups, particularly among those who, as our sample did, share high levels of deprivation. However, our qualitative data did confirm the high levels of alienation and exclusion from 'White' society and mainstream services felt by many ethnic minority individuals. These feelings seemed particularly strong among more recent migrants, those whose English was poor and those with lower levels of education, though they were evident across all types of respondent.

The recent Green Paper on welfare reform emphasised restriction of ineligible claiming of sickness benefit (DWP 2006b). However, it had little to say about non-take-up, or the low take-up of DLA, in particular. Our results indicate low levels of DLA receipt even among those to whom it would offer greatest value – those on low incomes and those who feel they have a strong case for an award. The results also indicate that there may be systematic differences in take-up between ethnic groups. A more balanced focus at the policy level in relation to supporting take-up by those with apparent entitlement would be welcomed. The means to achieve greater parity across ethnic groups also begs sustained policy attention.

## Acknowledgements

We are grateful to ONS for the use of the *Labour Force Survey* and to the Data Archive for providing access to the data. They bear no responsibility, however, for the use made of them here and the interpretation put upon them. Crown copyright material is reproduced with the permission of the Controller of HMSO and the Queen's Printer for Scotland. We also acknowledge with thanks the hard work of our team of Community Researchers, our partner organisation, Social Action for Health, and the generosity of all the study participants. The Joseph Rowntree Foundation funded the larger project from which this paper is derived.

## Notes

1   UK national surveys have employed a range of similar, though not identical, questions to ascertain levels of long-term health conditions. We describe below the measures used in the present analysis. The terms 'long-term', 'chronic' and 'long-standing' are commonly used interchangeably in the UK research and policy literature, and only in some circumstances is a time period explicitly stated. These terms indicating an enduring nature are variously combined with 'health condition', 'health problem', 'illness', 'illness or disability' and 'illness, impairment or disability'. In the present paper we opt for the term 'long-term health condition' and we describe our rationale and operational definitions.

2   Limited space precludes a comprehensive review of the literature on ethnicity and experiencing long-term health conditions. Instead we highlight existing evidence that has a bearing on our present research focus.

3   Though the usefulness of the aggregate term 'South Asians' is questionable, it has often been used in research papers to refer to samples of respondents with origins in the Indian sub-continent, primarily India, Pakistan and Bangladesh.

4   Among Bengali/Sylheti speakers the term 'chirourughi' was often used as the appropriate translation, though the term literally means 'permanent illness'. Among the Urdu/Punjabi speakers we found no equivalent term but instead used the expression 'lambe arse ki bimari', *i.e.* 'illness of long duration'. Among the Ghanaian community we found the term 'chronic' to be preferred over 'long-term', since the latter was felt to be more stigmatising.

5   The research team included fluent speakers of Bengali, Sylheti, Urdu, Punjabi, Hindi, Twi and Ga. Over half of the interviews with Pakistanis and Bangladeshis were conducted in languages other than English, though among the Ghanaians only two respondents chose not to be

interviewed in English. In a small number of interviews it was felt that the respondent had chosen English but would have been better able to express him/herself in another language. Translations into English were carried out by research team members and other experienced translators with whom we were in close contact. The focus was on retaining conceptual consistency and in many cases we opted for the transliteration of significant words and phrases so as not to lose meaning (Atkin and Chattoo 2006).

# References

Ahmad, W.I.U. (2000) Introduction. In Ahmad, W.I.U. (ed.) *Ethnicity, Disability and Chronic Illness.* Buckingham: Open University Press.

Anderton, J.M., Elfert, H. and Lai, M. (1989) Ideology in the clinical context: chronic illness, ethnicity and the discourse on normalisation, *Sociology of Health and Illness*, 11, 3, 253–78.

Atkin, K. and Rollings, J. (1996) Looking after their own? Family caregiving among South Asian and Afro-Caribbean communities. In Ahmad, W.I.U. and Atkin, K. (eds) *Race and Community Care*. Buckingham: Oxford University Press.

Atkin, K. and Chattoo, S. (2006) Approaches to conducting qualitative research in ethnically diverse populations. In Nazroo, J. (ed.) *Health and Social Research in Multiethnic Societies*. London: Routledge.

Barnard, H. and Pettigrew, N. (2003) *Delivering Benefits and Services for Black and Minority Ethnic Older People*. Leeds: Corporate Document Services.

Barton, A. (2006) *What the Doctor Ordered? CAB Evidence on Medical Assessments for Incapacity and Disability Benefits*. London: Citizens Advice Bureau.

Berthoud, R. (2006) *The Employment Rates of Disabled People*. Research Report of Department for Work and Pensions, Paper 298. London: Her Majesty's Stationery Office.

Bhavnani, K. and Phoenix, A. (1994) Shifting identities shifting racisms: an introduction. In Bhavnani K. and Phoenix, A. (eds) *Shifting Identities Shifting Racisms: a Feminism and Psychology Reader*. London: Sage.

Bloch, A. (1993) *Access to Benefits: the Information Needs of Minority Ethnic Groups*. London: Policy Studies Institute.

Bloch, A. (1997) Ethnic inequality and social security. In Walker, A. and Walker, C. (eds) *Britain Divided: the Growth of Social Exclusion in the 1980s and 1990s*. London: Child Poverty Action Group.

Bourdieu, P. (1977) *Outline of a Theory of Practice*. Cambridge: Cambridge University Press.

Bradby, H. (2003) Describing ethnicity in health research, *Ethnicity and Health*, 8, 5–13.

Bury, M. (1982) Chronic illness as disruption, *Sociology of Health and Illness*, 4, 2, 167–82.

Bury, M., Newbould, J. and Taylor, D. (2005) *A Rapid Review of the Current State of Knowledge Regarding Lay-led Self-management of Chronic Illness*. London: National Institute for Health and Clinical Excellence.

Campbell, R., Pound, P., Pope, C., Britten, N., Pill, R., Morgan, M. and Donovan, J. (2003) Evaluating meta-ethnography: a synthesis of qualitative research on lay experiences of diabetes and diabetes care, *Social Science and Medicine*, 56, 671–84.

Charmaz, K. (2000) Experiencing chronic illness. In Albrecht, G.L., Fizpatrick, R. and Scrimshaw, S.C. (eds) *Handbook of Social Studies in Health and Medicine*. London: Sage.

Chattoo, S. and Ahmad, W. (2003) The meaning of cancer: illness, biography and social identity. In Kelleher, D. and Cahill, G. (eds) *Identity and Health*. London: Routledge.

Cornwell, J. (1984) *Hard earned Lives – Accounts of Health and Illness from East London*. London: Tavistock.

Craig, P. (1991) Cash and benefits: a review of research on take-up of income related benefits, *Journal of Social Policy*, 10, 537–66.

Craig, G. (2004) Citizenship, exclusion and older people, *Journal of Social Policy* 33, 95–114.

Daly, M. and Noble, M. (1996) The reach of disability benefits: an examination of the Disability Living Allowance, *Journal of Social Welfare and Family Law*, 18, 37–51.

Department for Work and Pensions [DWP] (2005) *Quarterly Appeal Tribunal Statistics: September 2005*. London: DWP. Available at: http://www.dwp.gov.uk/asd/asd1/appeals/Appeals_Sep05.asp

Department for Work and Pensions [DWP] (2006a) *Income Related Benefits: Estimates of Take-up in 2003/2004*. London: Department for Work and Pensions.

Department for Work and Pensions [DWP] (2006b) *A New Deal for Welfare: Empowering People to Work*. London: The Stationery Office.

Ellison, G.T.H. (2005) 'Population profiling' and public health risk: when and how should we use race/ethnicity? *Critical Public Health*, 15, 65–74.

Erens, B., Primatesta, P. and Prior, G. (2001) *The Health Survey for England. The Health of Minority Ethnic Groups 1999*. London: The Stationery Office.

Falkingham, F. (1986) *Take-up of Benefits: a Literature Review*. Nottingham: Benefits Research Unit, University of Nottingham.

Fry, V. and Stark, G. (1993) *The Take-up of Means-tested Benefits 1984–90*. London: Institute for Fiscal Studies.

Gardner, K. (2002) *Age, Narrative and Migration: the Life Course and Life Histories Amongst Bengali Elders in London*. Oxford: Berg.

Gordon, P. and Newnham, A. (1985) *Passport to Benefits? Racism in Social Security*. London: Child Poverty Action Group/Runnymede Trust.

Hall, S. (1992) The question of cultural identity. In Hall, S., Held, D. and McGrew, T. (eds) *Modernity and its Futures*. Cambridge: Polity Press.

Higginbottom, G.M.A. (2006) 'Pressure of life': ethnicity as a mediating factor in mid-life and older peoples experience of high blood pressure, *Sociology of Health and Illness* 28, 5, 583–610.

House of Commons Work and Pensions Committee (2005) *Delivery of Services to Ethnic Minority Clients*, 6 April 2005. London: House of Commons Paper No. 268.

Jenkins, R. (1994) Rethinking ethnicity: identity, categorization and power, *Ethnic and Racial Studies*, 17, 197–223.

Joint Surveys Group (2004) *Health Survey for England 2003: Summary of Key Findings*, London: Department of Health.

Karlsen, S. (2004) Black like Beckham? Moving beyond definitions of ethnicity based on skin colour and ancestry, *Ethnicity and Health*, 9, 107–38.

Karlsen, S. and Nazroo, J. (2006) Defining and measuring ethnicity and race. In Nazroo, J. (ed.) *Health and Social Research in Multiethnic Societies*. London: Routledge.

Katbamna, S., Bhakta, P. and Parker, G. (2000) Perceptions of disability and care-giving relationships in South Asian communities. In Ahmad, W.I.U. (ed.) *Ethnicity, Disability and Chronic Illness*. Buckingham: Open University Press.

Law, I., Hylton, C., Karmani, A. and Deacon, A. (1994) *Racial Equality and Social Security Service Delivery: a Study of the Perceptions and Experiences of Black Minority Ethnic People Eligible for Benefit in Leeds*. Leeds: University of Leeds.

Lawton, J. (2003) Lay experience of health and illness: past research and future agendas, *Sociology of Health and Illness*, 25, Silver Anniversary Issue 23–40.

Lindley, J., Dale, A. and Dex, S. (2003) *Ethnic Differences in Women's Demographic and Family Characteristics and Employment Profile 1992–2002*, Discussion Paper. Manchester: Cathie Marsh Centre for Census and Survey Research.

Mac an Ghaill, M. (1999) Introduction. In Mac an Ghaill, M. (ed.) *Contemporary Racisms and Ethnicities. Social and Cultural Transformations*. Buckingham: Oxford University Press.

McClean, C.A. and Campbell, C.M. (2003) Locating research informants in a multi-ethnic community: ethnic identities, social networks and recruitment methods, *Ethnicity and Health*, 8, 41–62.

Mirza, H. and Sheridan, A. (2003) *Multiple Identity and Access to Health: the Experience of Black and Minority Ethnic Women*. Manchester: Equal Opportunities Commission.

Modood, T. (1988) 'Black', racial equality and Asian identity, *New Community*, 14, 397–404.

Modood, T. (1998) Anti-essentialism, multiculturalism and the 'recognition' of religious groups, *The Journal of Political Philosophy*, 6, 378–99.

Modood, T. (2004) Capitals, ethnic identity and education, *Cultural Trends*, 13, 87–105.

Molloy, D., Knight, T. and Woodfield, K. (2003) *Diversity in disability: exploring the interactions between disability, ethnicity, age, gender and sexuality*. Department for Work and Pensions Research Report no. 188. London: The Stationery Office.

National Association of Citizens Advice Bureaux [NACAB] (1991) *Barriers to Benefit: Black Claimants and Social Security*. London: National Association of Citizens Advice Bureaux.

National Association of Citizens Advice Bureaux [NACAB] (1996) Failing the test, *Benefits*, April/May 1996, 19–20.

Nazroo, J. (1997) *The Health of Britain's Ethnic Minorities: Fourth National Survey of Ethnic minorities*. London: Policy Studies Institute.

O'Connor, W. and Nazroo, J. (ed.) (2002) *Ethnic Differences in the Context and Experience of Psychiatric Illness: a Qualitative Study (EDCEPI)*. London: Department of Health.

Platt, L. (2002) *Parallel Lives? Poverty among Ethnic Minority Groups in Britain*. London: Child Poverty Action Group.

Platt, L. (2003a) Social security in a multi-ethnic society. In Millar, J. (ed.) *Understanding Social Security: Issues for Policy and Practice*. Bristol: The Policy Press.

Platt, L. (2003b) *Newham Household Panel Survey: Poverty and Deprivation in Newham*. A report prepared by Institute for Social and Economic Research, University of Essex, for the London Borough of Newham. London: London Borough of Newham.

Pound, P., Gompertz, P. and Ebrahim, S. (1998) Illness in the context of older age: the case of stroke, *Sociology of Health and Illness*, 20, 4, 489–506.

Pudney, S., Hancock, R. and Sutherland, H. (2004) *Simulating the Reform of Means-Tested Benefits with Endogenous Take-Up and Claim Costs*. Working Paper of Institute for Social and Economic Research, paper 2004-04. Colchester: University of Essex.

Roberts, K. and Lawton, D. (1998) *Reaching its Target? Disability Living Allowance for Children*, Social Policy Report No. 9. York: Social Policy Research Unit, University of York.

Salway, S., Platt, L., Chowbey, P., Harriss, K. and Bayliss, E. (2007) *Long-term Ill-health, Poverty and Ethnicity*. Bristol: The Policy Press and York: The Joseph Rowntree Foundation.

Sanders, C., Donovan, J. and Dieppe, P. (2002) The significance and consequences of having painful and disabled joints in older age: co-existing accounts of normal and disrupted biographies, *Sociology of Health and Illness*, 24, 2, 227–53.

Sainsbury, R., Hirst, M. and Lawton, D. (1995) *Evaluation of Disability Living Allowance and Attendance Allowance*, Department for Work and Pensions Research Report No. 41. Leeds: Corporate Document Services.

Scharf, T., Phillipson, C., Smith, A.E. and Kingston, P. (2002) *Growing Older in Socially Deprived Areas: Social Exclusion in Later Life*. London: Help the Aged.

Sheldon, T.A. and Parker, H. (1992) Race and ethnicity in health research, *Journal of Public Health Medicine*, 14, 104–10.

Smaje, C. (1996) The ethnic patterning of health: new directions for theory and research, *Sociology of Health and Illness*, 18, 2, 139–71.

Smith, A. and Twomey, B. (2002) Labour market experiences of people with disabilities, *Labour Market Trends*, August 2002, 415–27.

Smith, N., Middleton, S., Ashton-Brooks, K., Cox, L. and Dobson, B. with Reith, L. (2004) *Disabled People's Costs of Living: More than you would think*. York: Joseph Rowntree Foundation.

Ville, I. and Guerin-Pace, F. (2005) Identity in question: the development of a survey in France, *Population-E*, 60, 231–58.

Wainwright, D. (1997) Can sociological research be qualitative, critical *and* valid?, *The Qualitative Report*, 3, 2, http://www.nova.edu/ssss/QR/QR3-2/wain.html

Wayne, N. (2003) *Out of Sight: Race Inequality in the Benefits System*. London: Disability Alliance.

Williams, G. (1984) The genesis of chronic illness: narrative construction, *Sociology of Health and Illness*, 6, 2, 175–200.

# 8

# Interpreted consultations as 'business as usual'? An analysis of organisational routines in general practices
# Trisha Greenhalgh, Christopher Voisey and Nadia Robb

## Background

Large-scale immigration to the UK, especially in recent years, has meant that language barriers between patients and health professionals are now commonplace in some areas (Baker and Eversley 2000, Salt 2005). Such barriers, even when an interpreter is present (but especially if one is not) distort communication and may undermine physician-patient trust (Angelelli 2005, Green *et al.* 2005, Greenhalgh *et al.* 2006, Robb and Greenhalgh 2006). They account for failure of vulnerable groups to access the services they need (why seek help when you will not understand or be understood?) as well as for a rising proportion of medical errors such as administering medicines to which the patient is allergic, giving inappropriate vaccinations to children, and dismissing early symptoms of cancer as 'non-specific complaints'. (Angelelli 2005, Chief Medical Officer 2001, Green *et al.* 2005, Greenhalgh *et al.* 2006, NHS Executive London Regional Office 2004). The UK National Health Service (NHS) has expressed its commitment to providing an equitable service defined by need, including providing a professional interpreter to any patient if needed (Department of Health 2004).

This study, jointly funded by a local Primary Care Trust (PCT) and Primary Care Research Network, was set up to address a perceived organisational problem in the NHS locally. Policymakers were concerned that the NHS interpreting service was inefficient (*e.g.* it was not easy to incorporate the booking of hourly-paid interpreters in a range of languages into the busy and time-constrained routines of GP surgeries). There was wide variation in practice (some GP surgeries made very high use of the NHS interpreting service but an estimated 50% did not use it at all), and anecdotal stories abounded of limited English speaking patients receiving suboptimal (and possibly dangerous) care because of communication difficulties. Use of professional interpreting services was said to be particularly low in single-handed practices.

Our empirical work (described below) produced rich data and our initial analysis of this dataset produced a Habermasian analysis of communication within the interpreted clinical consultation (Greenhalgh *et al.* 2006) and a study of the role of the interpreter in the mediation of trust between clinicians and patients (Robb and Greenhalgh 2006) – papers which align with recent sociological work on the varying and conflicting roles of the interpreter in the clinical consultation (Angelelli 2005, Green *et al.* 2005, Jalbert 1998, Leanza 2005). In a further analysis reported here, we sought to address the wider organisational questions relevant to the NHS locally – that is:

a. Why are current NHS interpreting services [perceived as] inefficient?
b. Why is there such variation in the use of the interpreting service between general practices, with some not using the service at all?

These questions must be placed in the context of a rising proportion of consultations that take place across a language barrier. An estimated five per cent to 25 per cent of primary care consultations in inner London either involve an interpreter or are compromised for the lack of one (Haringey and Islington Primary Care Trusts, personal communication). This is especially true for refugees and asylum seekers, many of whom have complex, serious and stigmatising conditions such as HIV or mental health problems (Robb and Greenhalgh 2006). It is a statutory requirement for both primary and secondary care organisations to provide interpreters whenever needed (Department of Health 2004). Yet, with up to 340 languages spoken at home in London alone (Baker and Eversley 2000), and with the languages needed in any area changing rapidly as new populations migrate (Salt 2005), the mismatch between ideal and actual practice is wide and (in many places) getting worse.

The provision of a professional interpreting service for clinical consultations can be conceptualised as a complex service innovation, defined as 'a novel set of behaviours, routines and ways of working, which are directed at improving health outcomes, administrative efficiency, cost-effectiveness, or the user experience, and which are implemented by means of planned and coordinated action' (Greenhalgh *et al.* 2004). The assimilation of a complex innovation in an organisation is usually a stop-start process, progressing via a series of triggers and shocks and usually incurring set-backs and obstacles that must be overcome before the innovation can be said to be 'business as usual' (Van de Ven *et al.* 1999).

This framing of interpreted consultations as organisational innovation begs the question of what it means for an innovation to be 'routinised'. A routine can be defined as 'a repetitive, recognizable pattern of interdependent actions, involving multiple actors' (Feldman and Pentland 2003). In a recent systematic review, Becker (2004) suggested that the routine may be the most fruitful unit of analysis when studying organisational change, and set out its defining characteristics (see Box 1). The term 'routine' can refer to both the idealised, abstracted understanding of the action to take in a particular circumstance ('ostensive' aspects) and also to specific performances in specific times and places ('performative' aspects).

Box 1: *Organisational routines: key characteristics (Becker 2004)*

- Routines are recurrent, collective, interactive behaviour patterns
- Routines are specific (they have a history, a local context and a particular set of relations) – hence, there is no such thing as universal best practice
- Routines co-ordinate (they work by enhancing interaction among participants)
- Routines have two main purposes – cognitive (knowledge of what to do) and governance (control)
- Routines, by allowing actors to make many decisions at a subconscious level, conserve cognitive power for non-routine activities
- Routines store and pass on knowledge (especially tacit knowledge)
- The knowledge for executing routines may be distributed (everyone has similar knowledge) or dispersed (everyone knows something different; overlaps are small)
- Routines reduce uncertainty, and hence reduce the complexity of individual decisions
- Routines confer stability while containing the seeds of change (through the individual's response to feedback from previous iterations)
- Routines change in a path-dependent manner (i.e. depending on what has gone before)
- Routines are triggered by actor related factors (e.g. aspiration levels) and by external cues

Two theoretical controversies are relevant to the study of how complex innovations are routinised in healthcare organisations. The first is between 'routines as the preservation of past practice' and 'routines as embodying scope for change'. Much of the traditional literature on routines has emphasised the former, and linked routines with the maintenance of stability and even organisational inertia. But more recent work has emphasised that routines are sustained and evolve through the agency and choice of individual actors, especially in response to failure or in a turbulent or threatening external environment (Feldman and Pentland 2003, Howard-Grenville 2005). This is an example of Giddens's structuration theory, which, briefly stated, holds that structures – defined as enacted sets of rules and resources that inform ongoing action – shape human actions and identity, which in turn reaffirm or modify structures (Giddens 1986).

Routines can be thought of as an 'organisational grammar', offering a repertoire of choices that could be made in particular circumstances, but the final decision of what to do in any *actual* circumstance must be made judiciously by the actor (Pentland 1995). It is here, in the tension between ostensive and performative aspects of the routine, that the scope for incremental change lies (Feldman and Pentland 2003, Orlikowski 2000). The second controversy is the role of individual agency in the enactment of routines. This can be framed as 'routines as unconscious choices' ('mindlessness') versus 'routines as effortful accomplishments'. In periods of stability, many organisational routines are followed at a subconscious level, but sustained change requires effort. And there is much more to human agency than whether an action is 'mindless' or 'mindful'. As Feldman has put it, 'Routines are performed by people who think and feel and care. Their reactions are situated in institutional, organisational and personal contexts. Their actions are motivated by will and intention. All of these forces influence the enactment of organisational routines and create in them a tremendous potential for change' (Feldman 2000: 614). A person who faithfully enacts (or modifies, or resists) a routine in a particular situation is influenced by a host of factors including knowledge, confidence, experience (especially the outcome of previous enactments of the routine), values, expectations, access to resources, and orientation (*e.g.* to past habits, problem-in-hand, or future possibilities) (Howard-Grenville 2005).

If routines, by virtue of being structured and enacted by human agents, contain the scope for their own refinement and evolution, it follows that they are heavily susceptible to human resistance and failure. If an innovation is introduced into an organisation, but does not become routinised, this may have a number of explanations. First, the people on whom the routine depends may not know what needs to be done or may lack the competence to do it – a particular challenge with technology-dependent routines (Gavetti 2005, Orlikowski 2000, Tripsas and Gavetti 2000). Secondly, they may know what needs to be done but choose not to do it because it does not fit with their identity, values, or goals (Pratt, Rockmann and Kaufmann 2006, Rao, Monin and Durand 2003). Thirdly, they may fail to interact effectively with other actors to achieve the necessary collaboration for executing the routine – because they lack social skills or organisational power, and/or because of clashes of professional culture (Barley 1986). Fourthly, there may be a variety of organisational level problems (*e.g.* the routine is under-resourced or poorly co-ordinated; the technology is inadequate; the new routine conflicts with other more established or critical routines; key actors lack the necessary autonomy, and so on (Howard-Grenville 2005)). Fifthly, there may be institutional constraints or drivers such as NHS regulations and policies (Scott 2001). Finally, all the above are susceptible to wider environmental forces (demographic, economic, political, legal and so on) (Figure 1 summarises these multiple levels of influence).

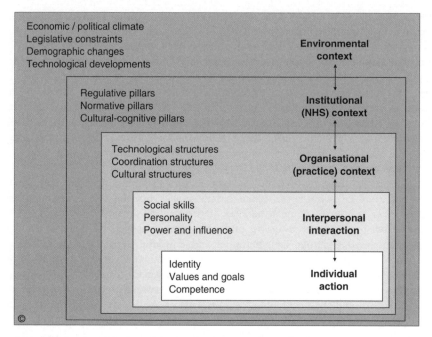

Figure 1 *A multi-level model of routinisation for interpreted consultations*

Taking account of the literature on routinisation, our research questions might be amended to read:

a. In general practices where the provision of professional interpreters has been successfully routinised, to what can this success be attributed (and what influences the choice of face-to-face, video and telephone interpreting)?
b. In practices where routinisation of professional interpreting services has not occurred (or been abandoned), what have been the main reasons for this?
c. What insights can be drawn that might inform organisational support towards the policy goal of supporting effective communication with limited English speakers?

## Participants and methods

The overall aim of the research was to identify and explore ways to improve communication across a language barrier in primary healthcare. Details of NHS ethical approval and institutional consents are available from the authors.

### Sampling

The study was undertaken in a part of London where Black and Minority Ethnic (BME) groups comprised approximately 40 per cent of the population. Participants and recruitment methods have been described in detail elsewhere (Greenhalgh *et al.* 2006). In summary, 83 participants (18 service users, 17 professional and nine family member interpreters, 13 GPs, 15 primary care nurses, eight receptionists and three practice managers) were interviewed in 69 individual interviews and two focus groups. We used a theoretical sampling frame for

GPs to obtain maximum variety in language spoken, age, gender, length of time in UK, deprivation score, and size of practice. GPs were identified from PCT lists and approached by telephone; other practice staff were recruited by 'snowballing' from an index GP. Professional interpreters were recruited via the local NHS interpreting service. We recruited five service users through the NHS interpreting service; these were interviewed by NR through an independent interpreter (interviews U1 through U5). We recruited four additional service users through the informal community contacts of a Bengali social scientist; he interviewed them in their own homes in their own language (U6 through U9). Nine service users, recruited through a Turkish language health advocacy organisation, were interviewed in a focus group by two Turkish advocates that we had briefly trained in focus group techniques, with NR present as observer. Family member interpreters were recruited through GP colleagues and via the social networks of the research team; four were interviewed individually and five (by their own preference) joined a focus group.

*The interview*
We asked service users, health service staff, and interpreters to 'describe a consultation in primary care that involved an interpreter'. Thus we sought to collect our data in narrative form (*i.e.* as an account from the narrator's perspective of how events and actions unfolded over time (Greenhalgh *et al.* 2005)). We used standard narrative prompts aimed at obtaining a complete and coherent story, such as 'tell me more about that'; 'what happened next?' and 'can you think a way that this story might have ended differently?' We sought examples of consultations which, in the perception of the interviewee, had gone well and also those that had not gone well. Interview guides used for different participants are available from the authors.

*Processing and analysis of data*
All interviews were audio-taped, transcribed and annotated with contemporaneous field notes. Interviews in a language other than English were translated by an independent translator. Two researchers read all transcripts and coded responses independently. We applied Muller's (1999) method of narrative analysis which took the story as a whole, rather than segments of text, as its main unit of analysis. This enabled us to highlight, in addition to the themes covered in each account, the wider organisational and environmental context in which a particular consultation took place, emplotment techniques (the narrator's use of metaphors, imagery and rhetorical devices to imply causality and agency), and the patterns or inconsistencies that emerged from multiple stories about comparable events (Greenhalgh *et al.* 2005). The interview schedule and analysis framework was modified substantially through progressive focussing as the fieldwork unfolded (Glaser and Strauss 1967). For this paper, we focused on the organisational dimension of interpreting services. We used a grounded theory approach to move from descriptive categories to preliminary theoretical categories and thence to higher-order theoretical constructs (Table 1).

**Main findings**

Approximately one in three people approached in all subgroups consented to be interviewed, reflecting the sensitivity of the research topic. GPs who did not use the interpreting service were less likely to consent to interview; these were mainly but not exclusively from single-handed practices. Despite this response bias, our sample of 19 practices included eight single-handed or husband-and-wife teams. Full details of practice characteristics are

Table 1  *Overview of data structure*

| First-order (descriptive) codes | Theoretical category | Higher-order theories |
|---|---|---|
| Accounts of what it's like to work in a practice<br>Individuals' descriptions of what they do and why | (a) Organisational type (culture, ethos and values of general practice, identity of staff) | |
| Stories of how an interpreter is booked (or of frustrations when trying to book one)<br>Stories (usually indirect) of individuals and practices that did not use the professional interpreting service | (b) Nature of the routine for ensuring the presence of professional interpreters in consultations | (1)<br>Multi-level model of routinisation for interpreted consultations<br>- Individual<br>- Interpersonal |
| Stories of the unpredictable nature of illness and healthcare need<br>Stories of 'inappropriate' patient expectations and behaviour<br>Stories of administrative tensions between the practice and interpreting service<br>Stories of inefficiency and inadequate capacity in the interpreting service | (c) Difficulties and constraints in routinising professional interpreting services within general practice | - Organisational<br>- Institutional<br>- Environmental |
| Stories of multilingual practice staff using their skills as needed<br>Stories of family member interpreters being encouraged to attend with patients and welcomed by practice staff<br>Stories of 'ad hoc' solutions to interpreting need (*e.g.* soliciting bilingual patients from waiting room)<br>Stories of formal alternatives for meeting interpreting need (*e.g.* video interpreting) | (d) Alternative routines for meeting interpreting need outside the standard interpreting service | (2)<br>Hypotheses about why single-handed GPs are low users of the NHS interpreting service |
| Stories of efforts by practice staff to make the system for booking and using professional interpreters more efficient<br>Stories of efforts by practice staff to make family member interpreting more efficient<br>Stories of practice staff 'dragging their feet' over interpreter booking | (e) Role of individuals in refining, shaping and resisting routines | |

available from the authors, and we discuss the limitations of the sample in the Discussion. It should be noted that only one GP whose practice made no use of the professional interpreting service consented to an interview and allowed his staff to be interviewed. Hence we could not fully document the GP or practice perspective on whole-scale rejection of this service (which occurred in an estimated 45 per cent of all practices in the area studied).

The data structure is shown in Table 1. Our first reading of the data produced a number of descriptive codes which we subsequently linked to five theoretical categories: (a) an organisational taxonomy of general practices; (b) the nature of routines for organising professional interpreters in consultations; (c) difficulties and constraints in establishing these routines; (d) the presence of alternative routines (such as multilingual staff or family member interpreting); and (e) the role of individuals (practice staff, interpreters, and service users) in refining, shaping and resisting routines. From these categories, and incorporating insights from the literature, we developed two higher-order interpretations: (1) a multi-level model to explain the routinisation (or non-routinisation) of the use of professional interpreting services in general practices; and (2) a hypothesis to explain why some traditional practices make very limited use of this service. Below, we present the five theoretical categories and then discuss our more abstracted interpretation of the data.

*Organisation of general practices: 'traditional' and 'contemporary'*
An early theme that emerged from our data was that some practices (single-handed or husband-and-wife and operating from an owner-occupied converted house) were run as a traditional 'family business', while others (typically multi-partner and based in a purpose-built health centre) were run in a more contemporary fashion with a wide range of employed and attached staff. Whilst few practices could be classified categorically as one or other of these, all could be matched to a greater or lesser extent with one of the organisational 'ideal types' shown in Table 2. This taxonomy accords closely with one developed independently by others (Green 1996). To map our participating practices against these ideal types, we supplemented our qualitative analysis by publicly available data on type and ownership of premises, year established, list size, number of full-time and part-time partners, diversity of clinics offered, and languages spoken by doctors.

Table 2 *'Traditional' and 'contemporary' general practices*

|  | The traditional general practice | The contemporary general practice |
| --- | --- | --- |
| Practice | Single handed or family unit; list size 2,000–4,000 Offers basic ('GMS') services provided by a few core staff | Multi-partner; list size 4,000–9,000 Offers multiple extra clinics and add-on services provided by a wide range of staff and contractors |
| Premises | Converted house GP usually owner occupier | Purpose built health centre Owned collaboratively or leased from private funder |
| History | Often established in 1960s or early 1970s following expansion of NHS services with 1964 GP Contract | Usually established in late 1970s or 80s, perhaps through merging of several single handed practices |
| GP's identity | Family doctor = 'respected pillar of the community', committed to job for life | Member of staff in an efficient and caring organisation, committed as per contract |
| GP's link to practice | Often lives on site or locally and takes active part in local events *e.g.* campaigns, festivals | Often commutes from another area and has no link to the community other than via the list |

Table 2 *Continued*

|  | *The traditional general practice* | *The contemporary general practice* |
|---|---|---|
| Practice structure and ethos | Family business with roles and responsibilities defined loosely and informally. Appointment and status influenced by kinship *e.g.* senior partner is usually the oldest. Admin staff may include doctor's own relatives. Few formal systems; may not have differentiated management roles (GP or spouse may undertake these). Everyone is expected to 'muck in'. Often on call 24 hours for own patients. | Bureaucratic organisation in which roles and responsibilities are formal, differentiated and explicit and multiple systems and procedures are in place. GP's status influenced most by qualifications and other external measures of merit. There is often equity of status and parity of pay between all GPs, many of whom work part time and have outside interests. Out of hours care usually contracted out or shared in a co-operative. |
| Values and virtues | Loyalty, thrift, continuity, interpersonal relationships, friendliness, integrity, self sufficiency. | The 'Maxwell six': effectiveness, acceptability, efficiency, accessibility, equity and relevance. |
| External links | Few and based around GP's social networks. | Many and based around collaborative work practices. |
| Strategy | Develop and maintain good GP-patient/family relationships<br>Provide a good basic service to the sick<br>Support and care for the family who have chosen you as their GP<br>Don't waste money | Provide comprehensive, up-to-date, evidence-based care for all (including proactive, preventive care)<br>Pay special attention to poor, disempowered, and socially excluded patients, whose health problems are often linked to social disadvantage<br>Draw on as many additional services as needed to extend the care package offered to patients |
| Environmental stress<br>• Low<br><br>⇓<br><br>• High | Broad, undifferentiated clinical agenda dealt with by generalist GP<br>GP may pursue a specialism out of personal interest<br><br><br><br><br>Restriction of remit *e.g.*<br>• Limit services to 'core business' (GMS)<br>• Limit agenda to biomedical<br>• Refer complex cases to secondary care<br>• Discourage resource-intensive patients (complex, demanding, needy, or geographically mobile) from registering | Economies of scale compared to single handed practice<br>Professional support and stimulation<br>Weakly developed and voluntary division of labour based on interests of GPs<br><br>Efficiency measures *e.g.*<br>• Limit agenda to biomedical<br>• Strongly developed and enforced division of labour, incorporating 'hierarchy of appropriateness' (see text)<br>• Categorisation and triage of patients according to tasks needed to 'process' them<br>• Extension of opening hours (*e.g.* evening assistants) to make maximum use of space<br>• Creative use of technology |

Staff from traditional practices generally described their organisation as friendly, caring, and well liked by the patients; they emphasised a personal atmosphere and continuity of care. In these practices, the personality and commitment of the doctor – who typically worked full time and put in long hours – was often highlighted by staff, and organisational values were personalised in terms of what Dr X believes or stands for:

We definitely have a nice atmosphere, there's a nice rapport with our patients (Practice manager, PM2, traditional practice).

Staff from contemporary practices talked more about efficiency, accessibility, and equity. They rarely attributed views to particular doctors but emphasised 'corporate' values and principles such as evidence-based care and a commitment to redressing inequalities and supporting the vulnerable:

OK, X---- [local estate] as you know is a community and the community encompasses what I will call an ethnic mix. We have people from Somalia, Romania, Turkey, Kosovo, Kurdish and African and Afro-Caribbean descent OK. Because of the sheets of people that we have interpreting service is very, very important to this practice and from inception of this Health Centre (Receptionist, R5, contemporary practice).

GPs from more traditionally oriented practices typically described themselves as committed to the practice and working hard for the patient population. They accepted (and usually expected) senior status in the practice. Many were disinterested in activities that went beyond what they saw as the core business of traditional general practice – *i.e.* treating the sick as and when they presented:

. . . the point is I don't have an appointment system, I don't understand how anybody can be sick by appointment. So that's why we keep the door open here, so what am I going to do with ring and wait for two weeks for an interpreter? Usually they can make themselves understood as they bring somebody with them (Male GP, G7, traditional practice).

Most of these single-handed GPs were first generation Asian immigrants; a high proportion of their established patient list were people of the same minority ethnic origin. They had been serving their own community since before the official interpreting service had been set up. Meeting the needs of minority ethnic patients was thus integral to their identity rather than a special interest that they had to develop and declare.

GPs in more contemporary practices, on the other hand, typically presented themselves as part of a multi-disciplinary team without a formal figurehead or senior partner. They took pride in being up-to-date and evidence-based, and most had a side interest beyond General Medical Services (such as teaching, research or a clinical assistant post at a local hospital). These GPs, though less likely to be from an ethnic minority, were more likely to declare an interest in ethnic health or reducing inequalities:

I mean I enjoy the cultural differences, that's why I'm a GP in London (Female GP, G9, contemporary practice).

Receptionists and managers in traditional practices embodied the 'family' culture and presented an identity that was approachable, empathetic, and informal (they talked, for example, of spotting patients who looked upset and taking them aside for a cup of tea).

Those in contemporary practices generally presented themselves in a more impersonal manner, with an emphasis on professionalism, efficiency, and risk management (especially maintaining order and safety in the waiting room).

Because of the marked differences in the approach to interpreted consultations taken by staff in practices that were either strongly traditional or strongly contemporary, we tried to classify all stories told by service users and interpreters according to the type of practice the story related to, though this was not possible if the participant did not remember key details.

*Routines for organising professional interpreters*
All but one practice (a traditional single-handed GP, discussed below) had established some sort of routine for providing professional interpreters for clinical consultations. This routine comprised four key steps, the first of which was to ascertain which language the patient spoke and ensure that this information was recorded (preferably by inserting a pop-up prompt on the patient's electronic record). This was usually the receptionist's role:

> We have a book downstairs with different languages and different phrases, so we ask them, 'What language do you speak?' [. . .] we show them that and they pick out their language, so there's basic questions on that and we go from there (Receptionist R5, contemporary practice).

Secondly, there was the booking of an interpreter to link in with a future consultation, either as a follow-up from a previous consultation (typically mediated by the interpreter in attendance for that consultation) or through a new contact by the patient (in person, by phone, or via a relative). Responsibility for the booking step varied considerably between practices. Sometimes it was done by receptionists using a faxed booking form; sometimes the clinician could book by phone:

> Where I was trained before I remember we could use the telephone to contact the people if you wanted somebody to translate and we had all the numbers down there with the languages and everything next to the phone (Community nurse C3, speaking of contemporary practice).

This booking step within the practice triggered a further routine in the interpreting service – getting hold of an interpreter (typically by mobile phone), ensuring his or her availability, and confirming back with the practice. The third step in the general practice's routine, on the day of the appointment, was linking the interpreter to the correct clinician and patient – something that required key administrative data to be exchanged:

> We enter the GP surgery, then we introduce ourself to the receptionist. And we give the name of the patient. And sometimes they ask which doctor. And sometimes we don't have it. The PCT sends it to us, we don't have the name of the doctor. This sometimes makes problem because some of the receptionists they are not familiar with the system. [ . . . ] And they keep asking me 'What is the date of birth?' 'I'm sorry I don't know the date of birth' (Female Farsi speaking interpreter, I12).

Finally, after the consultation, a staff member (clinician or administrator) completed the paperwork so that the interpreter could get paid.

For patients presenting as 'emergencies', receptionists used judgement to decide whether to squeeze them in on a booked clinic list or send them away, and clinicians either muddled through with no interpreter or opted to use an expensive commercial telephone interpreting service:

> I mean some people . . . you sort of judge the situation. If someone's got a bit of English you know you do maybe try and work round it as much as possible. But if it is a struggle then you know you reach for Language Line. We do normally have a card up. I don't know where this one's gone today. And it's got the number on, it's got our code, so it's actually very easy. I mean you just phone the number, they usually answer immediately and then you just say you know 'I need an interpreter in so and so language' and give our code (Female GP, G10, contemporary practice).

There was considerable variation between practices in how well-developed this whole routine was. In general (but by no means universally), contemporary practices had stronger routines, and where these existed, staff described them with confidence and evident satisfaction. Where routines were weakly developed, both interpreters and service users expressed frustration and confusion:

> The other thing that they can actually improve, when they say 'interpreter booked', on the computer, when they actually put it in front of the patient, that means that that should mean something, that I shouldn't actually go and remind them a hundred times 'excuse me, isn't there – did you talk to the doctors – excuse me' (Female Farsi speaking interpreter, I2).

*Difficulties and constraints in routinising professional interpreting services*
Staff in both traditional and contemporary practices described a number of constraints to the successful routinisation of professional interpreting services. The first of these was the high (and rising) demand for the service. Our field work was undertaken in London at a time (2003–2005) of rapid and profound demographic changes, including an influx of some 300,000 migrants from former Eastern European countries in the six months following their accession to the European Union, plus large asylum seeker populations arriving from Iraq, Afghanistan, and central Africa (Salt 2005). Many newly registered patients had complex and challenging problems (*e.g.* one interpreter estimated that over 90% of her female clients from a war-torn African country had been raped). Particularly high-maintenance for practices were the numerous families who had been placed in temporary housing and who were likely to be moved on shortly after the labour-intensive processing stage (registration, new patient medicals, catch-up immunisations and so on). Linked to these demographic changes was a growing diversity of language need (one GP documented 27 different languages spoken by attenders at his practice in the space of a fortnight), and a mismatch between the languages provided by the interpreting service and those needed by the most recent immigrants:

> Recently, in the last couple of years, they have a lot of people [immigrated] from China mainland itself, but those are mainly Mandarin, and I don't do Mandarin (Female Cantonese speaking interpreter, I4).

The second constraint was the nature of clinical need, much of which was seen as being inherently unpredictable:

> If we get a new birth, baby's day 10 and the new birth [home visit] needs to be done in the next two or three days, it can be difficult to get interpreters (Practice nurse, P11, contemporary practice).

Another perceived constraint was patient expectations and behaviour. Many limited English speakers failed to attend follow-up appointments booked weeks in advance, perhaps because they did not have a cultural tradition of going to the doctor when they had no symptoms:

> Interviewer: Why didn't you ask in advance [for an appointment]?
> Participant: Didn't need to. When I needed the doctor, I would go then, say it then (Male Sylheti speaking service user, U6, registered with traditional practice).

Conversely, such patients often attended as 'emergencies' for non-urgent problems. For this reason, some practices had given up booking appointments in advance altogether and operated a 'turn up and wait' system for seeing the doctor. Another frequently expressed difficulty was the expectation of many patients for a referral, perhaps based on past experience of primary healthcare as a 'transit zone' to definitive healthcare in their country of origin (Greenhalgh, Robb, and Scambler 2006), and (implicitly) a lack of awareness that the NHS has limited resources that must be distributed according to clinical need:

> . . . and they [Somalian patients] always want a referral. Referral, referral. And the GPs, they have to try their best to be fairest (Female Somali speaking interpreter, I15).

Staff in many general practices perceived serious inefficiencies and inadequate capacity in the interpreting service. They described non-availability ('they don't do Somalian', 'they close at 4'), failure to confirm provisional bookings, late cancellations, and interpreters turning up speaking a different language from the one that had been booked. Likewise, interpreters and interpreting service managers often highlighted organisational inefficiencies in the general practices, most often attributed to lack of time and the limited capability and autonomy of administrative staff:

> Only problem I've found with all the GP surgeries, they don't – they don't want to take the – they just say: 'We don't have time to book interpreters', there is only a phone call. But the receptionists are really actually tied up, and they must be assisted some way, I mean or given some freedom where the interpreters have the leeway if they've got your own patients, if they're struggling with bookings (Female Gujarati speaking interpreter, I6).

Participants were frustrated by the lack of alignment between the interpreter booking system and the practice appointments system. As described above, the former requires the receptionist to send a request and wait for confirmation of date and time, by which time the patient has gone home and may be difficult to communicate with by phone:

> . . . and the fax comes back one day before the appointment that we cannot provide you an interpreter (Male GP, G12, traditional practice).

Interpreters sometimes embodied the confusion when the relevant information had not been exchanged between interpreting service and general practice (see quote from interpreter I12 earlier). A particular problem was that GP surgeries are typically only booked about three weeks ahead; for a later follow-up, patients are asked to phone back in a few weeks' time – something that raises major practical difficulties for limited English speakers:

> Participant: We were going to do a follow-up appointment and she [receptionist] said, 'No, you can't, you have to phone [later]', I said, 'We can't phone because the patient

doesn't know how to talk, to make an appointment talk in English and make an appointment', I said, 'No, no, no', and I said, 'Please, you know, For my sake, I am here, we'll try to do it' and . . and she said 'No, we're not, you have to phone'. So I had to give the. . . .

Interviewer: What, they wouldn't allow you to make an appointment . . . ?

Participant: A follow-up appointment. . . .

Interviewer: Then and there?

Participant: That's right, because I think it was something – I think, actually, the doctor was away on holiday or something he was going, and they couldn't make an appointment in a month's time (Female Albanian speaking interpreter, I3).

One of the most commonly cited problems was the inflexibility of the interpreting service, which (at the time of this study) restricted its services to office hours:

I had a case where I was working with the learning disabilities team and we used to visit a mother who had two children who – two children completely disabled, even physically sort of, and mentally – so they had feeding problem, the lot, and the OTs [occupational therapists], the physio[therapist] and the social worker, they wanted to assess because mother is very old now and she's not able to – they wanted to help mum to provide the services. And the feeding time for these two, well mum used to feed – they're about 40-year-old gentleman now – was 6.30 in the evening, so they wanted to observe how mum feeds them – and they [interpreting service line manager] refused. And I've, I had been an interpreter for a long time with them and they said: 'No, we cannot provide for that time because it's out of our office hours' (Female Gujarati speaking interpreter, I6).

The role of individuals in overcoming (and in some cases exacerbating and perpetuating) these problems is discussed below.

*Alternative routines: ad hoc interpreting or other service models*
A striking feature of many traditional practices was the number of languages spoken by clinicians and other practice staff. It was not uncommon for an Asian GP to advertise three minority languages spoken fluently. Such practices often also employed bilingual staff and used these for interpreting on an ad hoc basis:

Participant: Right. Well we are a very multiethnic practice because our doctors are Indian, then we have a Somali doctor who works part time. Then we've got [other staff] Irish, Nigerian, British, one Indian too. So you know, then we've got Bangladeshi as well. So you know we've got all sorts of different things. So that way I suppose many people from small groups come to us, because if they don't have an interpreter then one of us translates for them.

Interviewer: Oh right.

Participant:  Okay? Because the doctors also speak some . . . I think it's um . . . oh crumbs . . . some Nigerian language or something like that, cos they used to work in Kenya.

Interviewer: Oh right.

Participant: Yeah I don't know what it's called.

Interviewer: But an African language.

Participant: Yeah they speak some African language too, and they speak about four or five Indian languages. And then we have the little girl who's a Bangladeshi, she can

translate for the Bangladeshi patients. And then . . .
Interviewer: Who is she?
Participant: She's our receptionist (Practice Manager, PM3, traditional (husband and wife) practice).

It is apparently seen as the norm for staff in this practice not only to be bilingual or multilingual but to offer this skill as needed for ad hoc interpreting. Note that the official NHS interpreting service is not mentioned and that the practice appears to have responded to an influx of a new minority ethnic group by employing a bilingual doctor on a sessional basis.

Some practices, particularly (but not exclusively) traditional ones, routinely asked patients to bring a family member or friend to interpret. We also heard stories of practices in which it was normal for selected patients to be brought in as unpaid interpreters and even for bilingual patients to be solicited ad hoc from the waiting room:

If they're Asian a lot of the time Mrs X--- [doctor's wife] is here, so she will help us. With others, we have got one lady who's a patient, Turkish lady, and she very kindly says like 'Phone me up if you get stuck', if someone just walks in. [ . . . ] If there's someone in the waiting room that speaks that language then yeah they will help out (Receptionist, R2, traditional practice).

Whereas staff in contemporary practices tended to perceive family member interpreters as 'second best', many staff in traditional practices preferred family members to professional interpreters and found they fitted in better with existing routines and ways of working. A common statement from staff was 'Dr X finds the official interpreting service frustrating; he prefers the patient to bring a relative'. Clinicians in such practices consistently justified this approach on the grounds that it 'works better'. They often believed that they were offering their patients a *better* service because multilingualism was seen as better than a triadic conversation, and ad hoc interpreting by on-site staff was seen as more reliable than hiring external interpreters and better aligned with practice opening hours.

In a few cases, the standard model for providing professional interpreters had been tried and deemed to have failed, so had been abandoned in favour of a different model. The following GP, an enthusiast for interpreting services who had put a lot of effort into securing a regular Turkish-speaking interpreter for a particular afternoon every week, describes how the system had unexpectedly generated more problems than it had solved:

But the sessions themselves were incredibly unpleasant and stressful because for me, and I daresay for the patients, and probably for the interpreter – because the interpreter would arrive at say two o'clock. Every Turkish patient who'd been turned away or asked to book for the previous week or two were sitting in the waiting area expecting to be seen during this special time. They invariably have of course accumulated absolutely every problem under the sun because time passes and people bring everything when there's a limited amount of opportunity. And at four o'clock the interpreter leaves – leaves through a waiting room full of angry Turkish-speaking patients, understandably angry, because the service is over (Male GP, G3, contemporary practice).

A receptionist from this practice gave a different version of the same narrative, describing a violent physical assault from one frustrated Turkish patient. The practice subsequently abandoned the booked interpreter surgery in favour of remote video-interpreting – an expensive option that was justified mainly on safety grounds.

In another example of a radical solution to the conventional service, a single-handed Asian (Tamil) GP had become frustrated that his Tamil patients persistently brought him social problems (such as housing or immigration issues) and expected him to sort these out within the biomedical consultation. After unsuccessful attempts to divert such patients to social workers and the Citizens Advice Bureau, he developed an idea to train one of his own Asian patients in a 'customised' link worker role (part healthcare assistant, part health promotion officer and part community worker). He expressed frustration that the PCT would not pick up the funding of this post.

*The role of individuals in refining, shaping and resisting routines*
We heard numerous examples of practice staff using their initiative in an attempt to develop and refine routines – and also examples of the potential wrecking power of staff who sought to resist a particular routine. Receptionists had developed 'tricks of the trade' for identifying what language a patient spoke, getting the interpreting service booking clerks to pick the phone up rather than take an answering machine message, and using interpreters in the most time-efficient way:

> The girls are very good, they try and group book. So what happens is the interpreter might be running between all the rooms for about three hours. Even with the other surgery [which shares the same health centre] to try and make their time most useful (Female GP, G9, contemporary practice).

Interpreters, too, described numerous 'workarounds' that they had developed to overcome glitches in the system. For example, some (though not all) routinely gave their private phone number to patients and provided an unpaid booking service for GP appointments. This was a highly effective solution to the problem of limited English speakers being unable to 'call back later' – but it explicitly contravened their professional code of practice and in some cases contributed to high levels of perceived job stress.

Patients, to some extent, also had some agency in shaping routines. In the following excerpt, a patient, despite being conventionally 'disempowered' and speaking no English, successfully cadges a lift to hospital in the interpreter's car:

> I said I thought it would probably be best . . . that she had an x-ray. And then he [husband] just told the interpreter, 'You, you, take me to the x-ray, you drive me there', and was really quite aggressive and rather a little bit I thought – but I had a chat with the interpreter and said, 'What do you feel about that?', because I said, 'In actual fact it's going to be very useful when this lady's assessed in the x-ray department, there is actually somebody can tell her to get in the right position, so I can see it may not necessarily be your job or role to provide a transport service, but I can see that it would be useful to have a continuation of interpreter to help when she gets to the hospital'. And the other thing is that she'd come regularly, so they'd come with this same interpreter on a number of times. I've looked after this family for probably about 18 months now and they've mainly come almost exclusively, 90 per cent of the consultations, with this particular interpreter (Male GP, G2, contemporary practice).

This patient's success should be measured not merely in that he got his lift to hospital, but in that his GP subsequently mused on how efficient this action had been in terms of achieving continuity of care for a frail patient across the primary-secondary care interface. It is not inconceivable that the use of interpreter as taxi and chaperone as well as translator could now become part of a more mainstream routine when patients with complex needs are referred for hospital investigations by this GP.

Interpreters told numerous stories of resistance by practice staff to implementing the interpreter booking routine:

> Sometimes I've come across when I have seen the patient and they've had follow up and I say 'My name is so and so'. Because sometimes patients say 'Can we have you?' because it's easier for them, the patient. It's easier for me and the doctor as well. 'Can we have you for a follow up?' And I write it down in my diary and everything and you know they [general practice] can't be bothered. You phone them up it's like, 'Oh. I thought you were just going to come along' It's like 'No, you know the procedure, you have done it before'. 'I am not allowed to come to appointments, although I've kept myself free . . .' 'You have to give me . . . and then I have to get a code and reference number. Without them I can't' (Female Bengali speaking interpreter, I16).

The interpreter in the next quote described attending with a patient who had been 'allocated' to a GP surgery (*i.e.* compulsorily assigned by the PCT because no GP in the area would take the patient on). The receptionist appears to believe (incorrectly) that the practice would be charged for the interpreter and is therefore not prepared to book her for any future appointment:

> So it started when I came, they were allocated GPs and we just came in, the receptionist almost, you know: 'No, no, no, no', and she's so . . . [ . . . ] But, you know, the practice nurse and the health visitor, they both asked: 'Can we book you?' So – and when we went back to the receptionists, 'I told you already that: No, no, no, no, we haven't got funds', and something else (Female Romanian speaking interpreter, I7, speaking of a traditional practice).

As well as the motivation of staff (and the evident wrecking power of even very junior staff in this particular routine), interpersonal relationships between different staff groups also appeared to be critical to the successful routinisation of interpreting services. Both receptionists and interpreters often spoke positively of one another, especially when their relationships were longstanding, and of creative efforts to improve services for limited English speakers that appeared to have arisen from this positive relationship:

> X--- [interpreter] in particular is extremely helpful. She was aware of – in the toilet, we had notices up, you know, not to put nappies down the toilet, and this sort of thing. And she offered to do them in a variety of languages for us, which was a great help. And she done 'em very nicely, much better than our scrappy notices. And we found them very helpful. Always. Not a problem (Receptionist, R6, contemporary practice).

But examples of interpersonal tensions (especially lack of respect for one another's role and implicit status wars) were also common:

> Participant: Some of them [interpreters] can be a bit rude. Mainly I've found a couple of gentlemen, Turkish gentlemen are quite rude.
> Interviewer: Uhuh.
> Participant: I've actually requested not to have somebody actually in the surgery no more.

Interviewer: To you or to the patient, or both?

Participant: To us. To us, just the way they speak to us (Receptionist, R4, traditional practice).

......

I also notice generally speaking that the lower the grade of the professional, the health professional, the more suspicious they are [of hours claimed]. If you are dealing with a professor he'll say 'You put the time whenever you want', because he appreciates you (Male Arabic speaking interpreter, I17).

## Interpretation

### *A multi-level model of routinisation for interpreted consultations*

Figure 1 shows the model of routinisation derived from both the wider literature (Becker 2004, Edmondson *et al.* 2001, Feldman and Pentland 2003, Howard-Grenville 2005, Orlikowski 2000) and our empirical data. The five levels – individual, interpersonal, organisational, institutional, and environmental – interact dynamically and reciprocally with one another such that, for example, individual identity shapes interpersonal interaction, the outcome of which feeds back to influence identity.

At the individual level, the perceptions, values and goals of the actors involved in the routine are extremely important, and these are strongly linked to both organisational and individual identity. The most fundamental aspect of identity appears to be the extent to which the individual (whether GP, nurse, receptionist or manager) is him- or herself multilingual and using more than one language in daily living. Where this is the case, a patient's need for interpretation is likely to prompt a solution from the 'lifeworld' of the individual making the decision (*i.e.* the patient would be offered a multilingual staff member or ad hoc interpreter, or invited to bring a family member) (Scambler and Britten 2001). But where the individual is monolingual, this need is more likely to prompt a solution from the 'system' – that is, a paid professional interpreter. The second dimension of individual identity is how that individual constructs and enacts their organisational role (the GP as 'family doctor' or 'member of efficient multi-disciplinary team', or the receptionist as providing 'tea and sympathy' or a 'well-managed service'). As Table 2 suggests, these two dimensions of identity are often aligned, the one reinforcing the other.

The GP (perhaps unsurprisingly in this hierarchical organisation) has a powerful influence over the routinisation of interpreting. Especially in single-handed practices, decisions about how and to what extent a routine develops are individualised to the GP ('Dr X does/ does not use professional interpreters'; end of story). As has been observed previously, 'different actors are more or less able to use a routine flexibly, and more or less able to influence whether a new kind of performance will be taken up as part of an ongoing routine' (Howard-Grenville 2005: 619). But our data also suggest some degree of agency for reception staff in enacting the interpreting routine. This may reflect a differential status gradient amongst staff in different physical areas within the organisation (reception staff holding low status in the clinical areas but relatively high status and autonomy in the waiting room). As one receptionist put it, 'we are the front line. To get to the doctor they've got to get past us'.

An interesting aspect of this particular routine is that the interpreter, whilst professionally qualified and trusted with confidential information, is remarkably powerless to influence the routines in most practices, as the earlier quote from interpreter I6 shows. Interpreters are independent contractors sent by an external organisation, whose official status in the practice waiting room is no higher than that of the patient. Some (though by no means all) receptionists seemed to assign them to the category of 'intruder'.

At the interpersonal level, our data show that a successful routine depends on a level of collaborative interaction between staff that is sometimes but not always achieved. Friendship and reciprocity, built through repeated encounters over time, can oil the wheels of routines that cross professional and organisational boundaries. Conversely, lack of respect and disputes over one another's role and status will block both the implementation of the routine and its successful evolution over time.

At the organisational level, our data strongly support the findings of previous researchers that routines are almost never performed in a vacuum, but overlap with other routines (Becker 2004). Booking the interpreter must link with booking an appointment for the patient to see the GP. The interpreting service must process requests from practices, contact the interpreter to confirm availability, and send confirmation to the practice. With a typical PCT offering around 70 different languages and dialects through peripatetic interpreters who are contacted via a mobile phone (which must be switched off in the GP surgery), the sheer administrative complexity of this task should not be underestimated. Overlapping routines are especially hard to align if (as in this case) they occur at different speeds or frequencies (Becker 2004) or cross organisational boundaries (Gittell *et al.* forthcoming).

At an institutional level, the NHS rests on three pillars: (a) regulative pillars (formal rules, regulations and policies (Department of Health 2003, 2004), implemented via Executive Letters, Service Level Agreements and so on, and assured through clinical governance mechanisms); (b) normative pillars (professional standards and expectations, implemented through training and assured through certification, accreditation and appraisal/revalidation); and (c) cultural-cognitive pillars (constitutive schemata based on cultural understanding of 'what goes on around here', implemented through cognitive schemata and assured by common beliefs and shared logics of action) (Scott 2001). In terms of each of these pillars, routines can be thought of respectively as rules and protocols, roles and standards, and 'knowing the ropes'. Our data suggest that the introduction of new policies in primary care – such as the requirement to provide interpreting services – may challenge longstanding normative values and belief systems about what a good health service is and how best to deliver it. This is especially true in primary care – partly because GP surgeries, like the corner shop, are by their nature isolated, organisationally idiosyncratic, and difficult to regulate; and also because the GP's role in the NHS has always been ambiguous, resting as it has (until recently at least) on a fiercely defended independent contractor status (Lewis 1997).

In contrast to studies of routines in many commercial companies (where the main impetus for changing routines is the agency of forward-looking individuals within the organisation (Edmondson *et al.* 2001, Feldman and Pentland 2003, Howard-Grenville 2005)), we found that the most powerful influence on interpreter booking routines was changes in the external environment. The profound demographic changes occurring in the few months prior to our empirical work served as a classic 'organisational shock' to general practices (Van de Ven, Polley, Garud *et al.* 1999). New immigrants often brought multiple physical, mental and emotional problems; they were not familiar with the values of the NHS or expected patient behaviour, and a small minority were aggressive or violent (something that would be particularly unacceptable in a practice with a 'family' ethos). In practices where GPs had served a relatively stable and compliant population for 20 years or more, the influx of recent immigrants was perceived as draining time and energy away from its 'established customers'. The response to this shock is discussed in the next section.

*Explaining the 'we don't do interpreters' response*
There are several possible explanations for the weak or absent routines for booking professional interpreters which we documented in some practices. One is a simple size effect. Damanpour (1992) has shown in a meta-analysis that large organisations are significantly more innovative than smaller ones, probably because of a more sophisticated division of labour and greater slack resources, and research in UK general practice confirms that there is less formal organisation and less internal specialisation in single-handed practices (Campbell, Ramsay, and Green 2001, van den Hombergh, Engels, and Grol 2006). Without wishing to dismiss this explanation, and acknowledging that we were unable to access the most resistant practices in this study, we believe our data are also consistent with an explanation based on the ideal types of general practices shown in Table 2.

Faced with the 'organisational shock' caused by a turbulent external environment (see previous section), a policy of offering an open door and a welcoming interpreter to limited English speakers seeking to register was seen by some as potentially 'opening the floodgates' to large numbers of high-maintenance patients. The bottom row of Table 2 shows two possible responses as a practice moves from a period of low to high environmental stress. The traditional single-handed GP generally responds by restricting his or her remit – by discontinuing all services except core General Medical Services, increasing referrals to secondary care, and – crucially for this study – discouraging resource-intensive patients from registering in the first place.

Conversely, the contemporary general practice responds to the same shock by introducing efficiency measures such as extending and enforcing the inter-professional division of labour, most notably by employing nurses and healthcare assistants to take on some of the GPs' work; triaging patients to the cheapest professional who can complete the tasks needed to 'process' them; increasing throughput (*e.g.* by extending opening hours); and making creative use of technology (such as the shift from face-to-face to video interpreting previously described by respondent G3). Table 2 suggests that in times of organisational stress, the resource-intensive patient (including the limited English speaker) is more vulnerable in the traditional practice than in the contemporary one, since the former might refuse even to register the patient, whereas the latter is likely to accept them but will 'manage' their complaints more efficiently.

**Discussion**

To our knowledge, this study is the first to analyse interpreted consultations as a complex innovation using the organisational routine as the focal unit. As an interdisciplinary team, our different perspectives (general practice and health services research, organisational sociology, and medical sociology) led each of us to focus on different areas and notice different patterns in the data, leading to a richer understanding of the phenomena under investigation than any of us would have produced alone. The study explicitly redresses a recognised imbalance in the sociology of health and illness – the absence of a rigorous approach to the organisational dimension (Davies 2003). We have combined three background literatures – on the diffusion of innovation in healthcare (Greenhalgh, Robert, Macfarlane, Bate, and Kyriakidou 2004), organisational routines (Becker 2004, Feldman and Pentland 2003), and the changing nature of work and professional identity in general practice (Charles-Jones *et al.* 2003, Jones and Green 2006), along with our empirical findings, to produce an integrative model for the organisational aspects of interpreted consultations that takes the routine as its focal unit (Figure 1).

Previous work on organisational routines has been developed almost exclusively in the USA, based on empirical work in the commercial sector or large private hospitals, where the routine being studied has been either commercially crucial (*e.g.* microchip development (Howard-Grenville 2005)) or a complex medical investigation or procedure (Barley and Tolbert 1997, Edmondson *et al.* 2001, Kellogg 2005), and where the agents involved were senior professionals with a high degree of expertise and autonomy. Our own focus was much more mundane – the implementation by reception staff of a routine in general practice that is not directly (though it may be indirectly) life saving for patients. Our study thus makes a unique contribution to the literature by considering medical routines that depend heavily on people who are not highly trained and who lack autonomy and organisational power.

Two concepts are important to understanding the organisational dimension of routines: embeddedness and resourcing. A routine can be central to the workings of the organisation (*e.g.* booking appointments for patients to see the GPs) or it can be marginal (*e.g.* ordering the coffee supply). To become central, a routine must be embedded in three types of organisational structure – technological (*e.g.* whether the pop-up computer alert 'interpreter needed' is in use), cultural (*e.g.* social hierarchies, norms and values, especially whether the routine aligns with staff understanding of the practice's mission and their expectations for one another's behaviour – as in the first quote from respondent R5), and co-ordination/control (*i.e.* structures that achieve the interdependence of multiple actors and multiple routines – for example, the extent to which a receptionist responsible for booking a GP appointment also has the knowledge and autonomy to book the interpreter) (Howard-Grenville 2005). Even when practices are positive about the use of professional interpreters, and especially when they are lukewarm or negative, the booking routine may be only weakly embedded in technological and co-ordination/control structures. As one interpreter put it, '*They are very unorganised – very, very unorganised, and I hate it*'.

Shifting a routine from 'marginal' to 'central' requires not only the introduction of an appropriate technological and co-ordination infrastructure but also a shift in cultural structures such as organisational values and goals (what is our 'core business' and why?) and the identity of individual staff (what is my role and purpose here?). As Sewell, cited in Howard-Grenville (2005), has observed, the multiple structures operating within an organisation may 'operate in harmony or may have conflicting claims and empowerments' – as in the interpreter who is pulled in one direction by her professional body (which exhorts staff not to give out their private phone numbers to clients) and in another by her identity as an advocate (which drives her to develop a 'kinship' bond and use informal as well as formal means to improve the client's experience within the system). Greater recognition of the inherent ambiguities in the interpreter role, and a package of training and support that addresses these tensions, is likely to reduce some of the current dissonance and perhaps improve interpersonal relationships with practice staff (Robb and Greenhalgh 2006).

It is a truism that routines must be adequately resourced. In organisational theory; the term 'resources' includes not only traditional allocative resources (money, knowledge, technical expertise), but also authoritative resources (command over things and people), and relational resources (such as trust, respect for skills and expertise, and complementarity). Difficulty in routinising the provision of professional interpreters arises because those most closely involved lack all three kinds of resources. 'Allocating resources for interpreting' is not as simple as assigning a budget at PCT level for paying sessional interpreters. Rather, relational resources must be addressed – for example by those with power and influence (the GPs and senior interpreting service manager) taking proactive initiative to help build relationships between those who lack these resources. In this way, alignment between the cultural and co-ordination structures within which current routines are (more or less) embedded will increase.

One hypothesis that should be explored more fully is that communication with limited English speakers may occur through a very different routine if both the clinicians and relevant administrative staff are multilingual and the practice population drawn from a small number of minority ethnic communities. In both mainland Europe and the old Commonwealth, it is the norm rather than the exception for people to be multilingual and use different languages in different social situations (for example, at work/school and at home). In relation to multilingual general practices, there has never been a systematic study of what languages are spoken and to what level of proficiency, nor has there been a systematic study of the extent to which GPs' language proficiency matches the languages actually needed, so it seems premature to problematise the single-handed GP for providing a 'substandard' service to the limited English speaker.

There are some important limitations of our study design (based on 69 one-shot interviews and two focus groups). To fully understand the processes by which routines are introduced and evolve (or fail to evolve) in organisations requires longitudinal data and, ideally, a multi-method approach in which ethnographic observations are combined with interviews and documentary analysis (Barley and Tolbert 1997, Edmondson *et al.* 2001, Feldman and Pentland 2003, Howard-Grenville 2005). For this reason, our findings should be seen as a preliminary analysis of how the organisational, institutional and environmental contexts shape the actions and interactions that make the interpreted consultation possible, and how successive enactments of the routine in turn shape the organisational structures. We strongly recommend further empirical work, with a longitudinal dimension, to test and refine the structurational model presented here, and explore the mutually reinforcing relationships shown in Figure 1.

In conclusion, the current NHS policy of seeking to offer a professional interpreter to all patients who need it poses huge organisational challenges for general practices, especially in the context of rapid expansion in (and increasing heterogeneity of) language need. The development by general practices of strong and efficient routines for providing an effective interpreting service to primary care patients, whether through physically present professional interpreters, remote interpreters or multilingual staff, will go some way towards addressing this challenge. The well-described dangers of attempting to provide clinical care in the absence of an interpreter (see **Background**) suggest that the routinisation of this aspect of the service should be a clinical as well as an administrative priority. There is a potentially fruitful research agenda linking the organisational dimension of interpreting services with studies of clinical care and outcomes.

The theoretical and empirical approach described in this paper, based on structuration theory, is widely used in organisational science (see in particular the work of Orlikowski and Perlow *et al.* on reference list) but has rarely been applied in mainstream health-services research on innovation, which in our opinion has been compromised by weak theory and an over-emphasis on experimental methods (Greenhalgh *et al.* 2004). The effective study of the important and fascinating field of health service innovation demands the use of concepts and theories that do justice to its complexity. A central tenet of structuration theory is that structuration takes place simultaneously across multiple levels (Perlow *et al.* 2004). For this reason we believe that it has much to offer researchers of service innovation, change and transformation and that the approach described in this paper could, with appropriate modification, have much wider applications.

## References

Angelelli, C. (2005) *Medical Interpreting and Cross-cultural Communication.* Cambridge: Cambridge University Press.

152 Trisha Greenhalgh, Christopher Voisey and Nadia Robb

Baker, P. and Eversley, J. (2000) *Multilingual Capital. The Languages of London's Schoolchildren and their Relevance to Economic, Social and Educational Policies.* London: Battlebridge Publications.

Barley, S. (1986) Technology as an occasion for structuring: evidence from observations of CT scanners and the social order of radiology departments, *Administrative Science Quarterly*, 31, 78–108.

Barley, S.R. and Tolbert, P.S. (1997) Institutionalization and structuration: studying the links between action and institution, *Organization Studies*, 18, 93–117.

Becker, M.C. (2004) Organizational routines: a review of the literature, *Industrial and Corporate Change*, 13, 643–77.

Campbell, J.L., Ramsay, J. and Green, J. (2001) Practice size: impact on consultation length, workload, and patient assessment of care, *British Journal of General Practice*, 51, 644–50.

Charles-Jones, H., Latimer, J. and May, C. (2003) Transforming general practice: the redistribution of medical work in primary care, *Sociology of Health and Illness*, 25, 1, 71–92.

Chief Medical Officer (2001) *An Organisation with a Memory.* London: Department of Health.

Damanpour, F. (1992) Organizational size and innovation, *Organization Studies*, 13, 3, 375–402.

Davies, C. (2003) Some of our concepts are missing: reflections on the absence of a sociology of organisations in Sociology of Health and Illness, *Sociology of Health and Illness*, 25, 3, 172–90.

Department of Health (2003) *Review of Service Delivery Models for Translation and Interpretation.* London: Department of Health.

Department of Health (2004) *Guidance on Developing Local Communication Support Services and Strategies.* London: Department of Health.

Edmondson, A.C., Bohmer, R.M. and Pisano, G.P. (2001) Disrupted routines: team learning and new technology implementation in hospitals, *Administrative Science Quarterly*, 46, 685–716.

Feldman, M.S. (2000) Organizational routines as a source of continuous change, *Organization Science*, 11, 611–29.

Feldman, M.S. and Pentland, B.T. (2003) Reconceptualizing organizational routines as a source of flexibility and change, *Administrative Science Quarterly*, 48, 94–118.

Gavetti, G. (2005) Cognition and hierarchy: rethinking the microfoundations of capabilities' development, *Organization Science*, 16, 599–617.

Giddens, A. (1986) *The Constitution of Society.* Berkeley: University of California Press.

Gittell, J., Weiss, L. and Wimbush, J. (forthcoming) Linking coordination networks and organizational design to improve the coordination of work, *Academy of Management Journal*, in press.

Glaser, B.G. and Strauss, A.L. (1967) The constant comparative method of qualitative analysis. In Glaser, B.G. and Strauss, A.L. (eds) *The Discovery of Grounded Theory.* Chicago: Adline.

Green, A.R., Ngo-Metzger, Q., Legedza, A.T., Massagli, M.P., Phillips, R.S. and Iezzoni, L.I. (2005) Interpreter services, language concordance, and health care quality. Experiences of Asian Americans with limited English proficiency, *Journal of General and Internal Medicine*, 20, 11, 1050–6.

Green, J. (1996) Time and space revisited: the creation of community in single-handed British general practice, *Health and Place*, 2, 85–94.

Greenhalgh, T., Robert, G., Macfarlane, F., Bate, P. and Kyriakidou, O. (2004) Diffusion of innovations in service organisations: systematic literature review and recommendations for future research, *Millbank Quarterly*, 82, 581–629.

Greenhalgh, T., Russell, J. and Swinglehurst, D. (2005) Narrative methods in quality improvement research, *Quality and Safety in Health Care*, 14, 6, 443–9.

Greenhalgh, T., Robb, N. and Scambler, G. (2006) Communicative and strategic action in interpreted consultations in primary health care: a Habermasian perspective, *Social Science and Medicine*, 63, 1170–87.

Howard-Grenville, J.A. (2005) The persistence of flexible organizational routines: the role of agency and organizational context, *Organization Science*, 16, 618–36.

Jalbert, M. (1998) Travailler avec un interprete en consultation psychiatrique, *P.R.I.S.M.E.*, 8, 3, 94–111.

Jones, L. and Green, J. (2006) Shifting discourses of professionalism: a case study of general practitioners in the United Kingdom, *Sociology of Health and Illness*, 28, 7, 927–50.

Kellogg, K.C. (2005) *Challenging Operations: Changing Interactions, Identities, and Institutions in a Surgical Teaching Hospital. (unpublished Ph.D.)* Cambridge, MA: Massachusetts Institute of Technology.

Leanza, Y. (2005) Roles of community interpreters in pediatrics as seen by interpreters, physicians and researchers, *Interpreting*, 7, 2, 167–92.

Lewis, J. (1997) Primary care–opportunities and threats. The changing meaning of the GP contract, *British Medical Journal*, 314, 895–8.

Muller, J. (1999) Narrative approaches to qualitative research in primary care. In Crabtree, B.F. and Miller, L. (eds) *Doing Qualitative Research*. London: Sage.

NHS Executive London Regional Office. Survey of Language Support Services (2004) Ref Type: Unpublished Work.

Orlikowski, W.J. (2000) Using technology and constituting structures: a practice lens for studying technology in organizations, *Organization Science*, 11, 4, 404–28.

Pentland, B.T. (1995) Grammatical models of organizational processes, *Organization Science*, 6, 5, 541–56.

Perlow, L.A., Gittell, J.H. and Katz, N. (2004) Contextualizing patterns of work group interaction: toward a nested theory of structuration, *Organization Science*, 15, 5, 520–36.

Pratt, M.G., Rockmann, K.W. and Kaufmann, J.B. (2006) Constructing professional identity: the role of work and identity learning cycles in the customization of identity among medical residents, *Academy of Management Journal*, 49, 235–62.

Rao, H., Monin, P. and Durand, R. (2003) Institutional change in Toque Ville: nouvelle cuisine as an identity movement in French gastronomy, *American Journal of Sociology*, 108, 4, 795–843.

Robb, N. and Greenhalgh, T. (2006) 'You have to cover up the words of the doctor': the mediation of trust in interpreted consultations in primary care, *Journal of Healthcare Organisation and Management*, 20, 5, 434–55.

Salt, J. (2005) *Current Trends in International Migration in Europe*. Strasbourg: Council of Europe (CDM 2005/2).

Scambler, G. and Britten, N. (2001) System, lifeworld, and doctor-patient interaction. In Scambler, G. (ed.) *Habermas, Critical Theory and Health*. London: Routledge.

Scott, W.R. (2001) *Institutions and Organizations*. Thousand Oaks, CA: Sage.

Tripsas, M. and Gavetti, G. (2000) Capabilities, cognition, and inertia: evidence from digital imaging, *Strategic Management Journal*, 21, 1147–61.

Van de Ven, A.H., Polley, D.E., Garud, R. and Venkataraman, S. (1999) *The Innovation Journey*. Oxford: Oxford University Press.

van den Hombergh, P., Engels, Y. and Grol, R. (2006) Saying 'goodbye' to single-handed practices; what do patients and staff lose or gain? *Family Practice*, 22, 20–7.

# Index